Whakataka te hau ki te uru
Whakataka te hau ki te tonga

Kia mākinakina ki uta
Kia mātaratara ki tai

Kia hī ake ana te atākura
He tio, he huka, he hauhu

Tihei Mauriora

Stand ready for the westerly wind
Be prepared for the southern wind

It will be icy cold inland and
icy cold on shore

May the dawn rise red-tipped on ice,
on snow, on frost

A new day dawns.

GO FISH

AL BROWN

RANDOM HOUSE
NEW ZEALAND

A RANDOM HOUSE BOOK

Published by Random House New Zealand

18 Poland Road, Glenfield, Auckland, New Zealand

For more information about our titles go to www.randomhouse.co.nz

Random House New Zealand is part of the Random House Group

New York London Sydney Auckland Delhi Johannesburg

A catalogue record for this book is available from the National Library of New Zealand

First published 2009

© 2009 text Al Brown; photographs Kieran Scott unless indicated otherwise;

illustrations and poster courtesy of George Clement, Clement & Associates;

Matau 1769 (page 32), Te Papa Tongarewa

The moral rights of the author have been asserted

ISBN 978 1 86979 176 6

Design: Ocean Design Group Limited

Printed in China by Everbest Printing Co Ltd

To Liz,
Thank you for your unwavering support,
in all my endeavours, and for letting
me wash my fishing rods in the shower!

Contents

The Recipes 38

Crustaceans 40

Shellfish 74

Fin Fish 138

Go To Recipes 300

Introduction

IT'S FAIR TO SAY THAT BESIDES MY PATIENT AND OFTEN LONG-SUFFERING FAMILY, MY TWO GREATEST LOVES ARE FISHING AND COOKING. WHILE I HAVE MADE A CAREER OUT OF COOKING, MY RECREATIONAL RELEASE HAS ALWAYS BEEN FISHING. HOWEVER, THERE HAVE BEEN NUMEROUS TIMES WHEN I'VE WISHED IT HAD BEEN THE OTHER WAY AROUND.

It has always intrigued me how we covet the lives of other people and their work. The sight of a crayfish boat heading out of the harbour, a trawler unloading its catch or a charter fisherman gearing up for another trip with a bunch of enthusiastic amateurs always evokes the same dream — that is, tossing in my tea towel and making a living off the briny somehow.

I grew up on a farm inland. However, ever since I can remember I have had a strong desire to be close to the sea. Wellington has been my home now for well over half my life. Whether when renting in my early student days or over the countless moves ever since, the style of house and practical things such as kitchen layout, access or commute always had little bearing. If I could get a decent view of the ocean, all those pragmatic issues seemed to pale into insignificance. After quite a few shifts, we now live 50 metres or so from the shore, and boy does it feel good!

For me each day starts with the same ritual — drawing the curtains and gazing out to sea, often for just a split second or, if I'm lucky, for a minute or two. I find it's like checking on a friend — it's the enigma and the character of the sea that I find so addictive. I delight in all its moods and find its beauty often intoxicating. It has healing qualities and a turbulent stormy sea gives me as much pleasure as a calm soft sunrise over a flat ocean.

I've always wanted *Go Fish* to be more than a seafood book containing a bunch of recipes. I'm as passionate a New Zealander as you will find anywhere and I believe we're lucky to live in one of the most beautiful parts of the world. As we are all well aware, there are not too many countries left where you are still able on most days to go out and 'catch a feed'! I'm not a 'greenie' or serious conservationist, but what is plain to me is that the fishery, the coastline and the waters that surround New Zealand are so very precious and special to us all. *Go Fish* celebrates what we have. I hope it educates, challenges and even provokes a little, but most of all I trust it gets people thinking, talking and appreciating what we are so fortunate to call our own.

To catch a fish and then cook it, as simple as it may sound, brings me more gratification than almost anything else. I enjoy all parts of the day, but undoubtedly find the most rewarding aspect of the process is sitting down and sharing the catch around a table with friends and loved ones. Cooking seafood is really only about a couple of things to me: it must be fresh and, second, never cooked in an over-complicated fashion. This book represents my style and the way I like to cook, with the passing on of recipes, tips and techniques. It is, I hope, straightforward to understand, unpretentious and full of delicious things to eat.

Go the fish!

My Love of Fishing

MY FATHER WAS A MODESTLY KEEN HUNTER AND FISHERMAN — NOT OBSESSED BY ANY MEANS, BUT HE NEVERTHELESS ENJOYED THE OUTDOORS. I BELIEVE IT WAS THE SOCIAL ASPECT AND CAMARADERIE THAT DREW HIM IN, RATHER THAN A DESIRE TO BE A PURIST IN ANY SUCH DISCIPLINE.

Dad introduced me, from an early age, to all his outdoor experiences. Some of my earliest and strongest memories are of times such as the opening weekends of duck shooting, or watching Dad and his mates disappear out over the horizon in an old Seagull-powered wooden dinghy, or donning wetsuits and dive gear and swimming off the reef to catch a feed of crays. I can still remember the frustrations and overwhelming disappointment of not being old enough, strong enough or grown-up enough to join 'the men' in their many pursuits.

Each time they began to get prepared, I was well aware of the pending adventure they were embarking on. The smell of gun oil, leather belts filled with ammunition, rods and reels, hooks and lures, pointers and retrievers, early-morning breakfasts were all high-octane stuff for a kid longing to grow up.

For a three-year-old, it was a sensory overload and while I felt part of it all, standing in the doorway waving goodbye (actually, more like stamping my foot and screaming), enduring those agonisingly slow hours waiting for their return was tough.

On seeing the lights of the Land Rover cross the cattle stop, or the dinghy chugging back into view and sliding up the beach, I'd sprint from wherever I was, bursting with excitement to see how they had got on. Their prey was like loot or jewels to me. I would carefully lay each duck down, making sure all their feathers were in place, or line the fish up from small to large, in order of species, all the while listening with intent as the hunters recalled the day's events with laughter, sledging and stories. For me, any introduction to hunting, fishing or gathering was completely addictive.

My first fishing experience took place when I was, I guess, about four years old. I grew up on our family farm called Waihi, in hill country in the heart of the Wairarapa. We had what we always called 'the river', the Whangaehu, running through the length of the property. It wasn't really a river, but more like a slow-running, willow-lined creek, punctuated with a good number of dark, deep pools and overhanging riverbanks, which concealed numerous eels.

Eeling gear was pretty low-tech — an old thread handline wrapped around a piece of kindling, a wingnut or similar for a sinker, and a single hook attached. For bait, it was usually a hunk of raw mutton cut from the 'dog tucker' hanging in the killing shed. Burley for eeling back then was whatever was available: sheep guts, a dead possum off the road, or an old roast bone from the kitchen safe. I would walk the river, looking for a 'sign' — a swirl of mud, a

dark shape showing itself ever so slightly from deep under the bank, or a deep fishy-looking pool with plenty of cover from the numerous willows lining the banks.

It was always a similar ritual. Once I had settled on a likely spot, I would find a good willow branch, whittle a point on one end and push it into the bank. Using bailing twine, I would tie the burley on one end and the other end to the branch. Then, with my pocket knife, I would cut a perfectly square piece of raw mutton and carefully thread it through the hook, leaving plenty of barb showing, before edging slowly towards the water.

Once positioned, I would unwind enough string, then get the old round and round dump cast going like an underhand lasso, let it fly and watch it disappear into the depths. From there it was

a matter of finding a spot on the most comfortable-looking tuft of grass close enough to the pending action. My eyes would then be transfixed on where the string entered the water, looking for the slightest movement.

For me, eeling was all about the anticipation and the catch. It was an adventure I never tired of, walking the river, rain or shine, equally happy alone or with a mate. We never ate the eels, as Mum wouldn't have had a clue where to start. Generally, once I had pulled them up the bank, some weighing up to eight pounds or more, I would dislodge the hook and they would slither back down through the grass and disappear into the depths.

However, there was a two-week period every year when I would go eeling at any spare moment I had. We had the 'main shear'

on the farm's calendar, which usually coincided with the school holidays a couple of weeks before Christmas. The gang would stay on the property in our old shearers' quarters. Shearing gangs' diets basically revolved around one main protein: lamb or mutton. Back then all farmers would provide as much meat as was necessary to keep these incredibly hard-working teams fed and energised. Lamb chops for breakfast, cold mutton sandwiches for lunch or smoko, and roast hogget for dinner.

The chance of a change in diet for a week or two was always appreciated and there was always a good number of Maori in attendance, who liked their eels. So I would catch them and for payment they would give me chocolate and large bottles of Coke and Fanta. You can imagine who thought they were getting the best

With Dad's help, I managed to land that kahawai and at that exact exhilarating moment, flooded with adrenalin and elation, I was hooked on fishing for life.

deal! Life couldn't get any better, eeling all day and building a stash of delicious fizz and candy bars.

I would enjoy eeling for many years and it taught me the fundamentals of fishing from a very early age. The thrill of the moment when I felt the weight come on the line with my first eel and with every fish ever since — that split millisecond when you realise you've hooked up — is why, like many people, I fish.

From the slow meandering muddy creek, the next adventure involving a hook was trolling in the dinghy with my father between Kapiti Island and the mainland, catching my first kahawai. I can still remember that day as if it were just yesterday. What's etched in my mind is the absolute astonishment that came over me as I battled this iconic and wonderful fighting fish. It was a combination of thrill and fear — the excitement as the kahawai

cavorted and leapt out of the water, and the fear of not having the strength to wind the fish in or, more to the point, the real possibility of the fish pulling the rod out of my grip. With Dad's help, I managed to land that kahawai and at that exact exhilarating moment, flooded with adrenalin and elation, I was hooked on fishing for life.

I simply enjoy all facets of catching fish. Whether fishing with my young daughters for sprats off the wharf with handlines, dragging a net with mates at low tide for flounder, or snorkelling for paua by myself on the south coast — all give me equal pleasure.

People fish for all manner of reasons. Many earn a living from the sea; others fish through necessity, supplementing the grocery bill to help make ends meet. For me, without question, fishing and gathering is my favourite pastime. I would rate

myself as an average angler, somewhere in the middle of the pack. But, as for all those who fish, the learning curve has no end and, simply put, the more time you get out on the briny, the more you read, listen and observe, the more fish you will catch.

There are aspects of fishing and gathering that bond all who partake. Whether trolling in a million-dollar game-fishing boat for marlin, or sitting in a 20-buck deck chair with your surfcaster poised nearby in its rod holder, it's being outdoors among the elements, it's the anticipation, the solitude or the companionship, a chance to think or switch off. And of course, for me, the two greatest things about fishing are that unprecedented rush that washes over you in that moment when the weight comes on the line and you're hooked up; and the chance to prepare and cook something so delicious and wonderfully fresh.

My First Memories of Living Next to the Sea

AS A KID, I GREW UP HAVING EXTRAORDINARY SUMMER HOLIDAYS WITH MY FAMILY — MUM, DAD AND SISTERS, ROSEMARY AND VICKY. WE WERE SITUATED TWO ROWS BACK FROM THE DESIRABLE WATERFRONT REAL ESTATE AND ONE ROW ACROSS FROM THE ABLUTIONS BLOCK AT THE CASTLEPOINT CAMPING GROUND.

Our caravan was a bit of a classic. Built of plywood and two-toned green and blue, it was known to all by the dubious title 'The Pie Cart'. As someone who had understood the culinary value and taste qualities of a pie from a very early age, I was proud of the humble nickname bestowed upon our caravan with the striped awning.

They were heady days for a kid from the farm. I still vividly remember Mum and Dad tossing my sisters and me overboard in our lifejackets from the dinghy, 100 metres offshore beyond the breakers. I still don't understand quite what that was all about but, looking back, it was somewhat liberating — a shock no question, but for me it was one of my first real connections with the ocean. A rite of passage and an understanding of respect.

Remembering those bulky lifejackets, weren't they something? We all looked like little Michelin men or five doughnuts shuffling about in a 14-foot tinny. Still, it was brilliant. We were out on the briny!

The memories of those holidays are ingrained in my mind for ever and this is how those first 14 days of every January played out . . .

I would wake up in the awning at first light on one of those really 'comfortable' wire camp stretchers in my cotton sleeping bag with the Hawaiian surf print. Dad would walk out, probably belching and scratching some part of his anatomy, while flicking on his Jandles and lighting his first cigarette of the day. It was a short stumble to the tinny, which he would lean on and look out towards the bay. At this stage all my focus would be firmly fixed on his face and demeanour. A slight wince and the mumbling of words to the effect of 'it's lookin' dirty, son' was as deflating as a tenth attempt at serving a successful soufflé. Whereas, 'Son, when you get the milk out of the chilly bin for a brew, pull out a couple of bags of bait,' was a different story altogether, creating an immediate burst of excitement of unprecedented proportions.

The next hour would go super-slow. First, a bowl of Honey Puffs (our holiday treat) and a couple of pieces of slightly charred white toast off the four-sided gas toaster rack. Then I'd break down the camp stretcher and make the campsite tidy and organised, and, more than likely, I'd be on drying breakfast dishes over at the communal kitchen. It was a painfully slow process for a kid absolutely nuts about going fishing with his father.

With a bit of luck, the camping ground tractor would be available for a tow and launching. Dad would stand in the tinny as I ran around gathering handlines, rods, fishing tackle and oars, and then strain to help lift the crayfish pot up to him. Strategically, he would load the gear in the boat as Mum would wander over, wishing us well and stuffing a warm homespun jersey under the bow in case the wind got up. A Thermos, a plastic bottle of Quench, some cold mutton sandwiches and, hopefully, a couple of slices of ginger crunch floating around in the cake tin and we'd be all set.

I would sit up in the back of the boat as the tractor towed us the short ride along the waterfront from the camping ground to the sheltered beach and the lee of the lighthouse where we would launch.

As a kid, it gave me the feeling that, like in the movies, you were riding a tank going to war for the first time, waving at all the people you passed, beaming from ear to ear, as the tractor towed you to the 'front line': the foreshore.

It was always a little bit of an ordeal for Dad to get the Seagull started. It seemed to take him three or four pulls of the old piece of rope with the knot in the end to purge a puff of smoke out of her rusty exhaust. He would always say, as he clambered in and opened the throttle, 'Seagulls, son, are the most reliable outboards ever made!'

We would anchor, drift or, if we saw some birds working in the distance, throw out a spinner and troll for kahawai.

I can never recall coming home empty-handed. It was pretty simple stuff, using the original Kiwi 'fish finder' — lining up a couple of points in the distance as markers, say the large pine tree next to the church with the red-roofed wool shed on the horizon. Dad fished with a rod and I had my trusty old coil of green nylon handline. Typically, our catch would contain one or two kahawai, a good chance of a gurnard, with blue cod or a tarakihi being realistic possibilities.

Two or three hours would pass very quickly, even with conversation at a bare minimum (Dad was no chatterbox), or on occasion we would experience a tough day's fishing. We would put any fish we had caught in a heavy wet hemp sack that seemed to do the trick of keeping the fish in pretty good nick.

Returning to the camping ground was almost as exciting as the fishing, as now you had the spoils to show as many people as possible. I would wait patiently next to the fish and every time I saw some people walking towards us on their way to the beach I would pull the largest specimen out of the sack right on cue. If my timing was spot on I'd get to spend the next couple of minutes recalling the morning's adventure, showing them what hook we used, explaining what bait works best and basically having a good old-fashioned brag! We would clean the fish up on the outside gutting bench, complete with sink. The fillets would then be placed between frozen slicker pads in the old steel chilly bin.

The rest of the day was as typical as it probably is today, with rounders on the beach, sliding down the sand dunes, five cents a day to walk to the shop to get a lolly mixture (you could get an aniseed wheel back then for two cents), rockpooling at low tide for a feed of paua and numerous swims in the surf with our polystyrene surfboards.

The barbecue, a cut-down old 44-gallon drum, would be lit as the sun started to slowly drop behind the hills. Those still summer evenings from about 5pm onwards in camping grounds were golden, with the smell of food cooking, small gatherings of campers dotted about, the ladies sipping their gin and tonics out of plastic mugs while preparing 'tea' and the men consuming large chilled brown bottles of beer while tinkering away on some piece of equipment.

The entertainment each afternoon and evening was watching the new campers arrive and struggle to back their caravans into position as everyone looked on, with the odd family argument and loss of patience while they attempted to put up tents.

As the sun disappeared the babies were put down to bed and the kids would be playing Last Card, while the slightly awkward teenagers hung out, trying to be cool, next to the communal kitchen.

With the approach of darkness, the noise would start to dissipate, replaced by the hiss of Tilly lanterns being lit and the sounds of zips being drawn, as one and all hunkered down for the night after a day filled with fresh air, salt spray and sunshine.

I now treasure those priceless memories and continue this unique Kiwi tradition with my own family. To me, camping grounds and holidays by the sea are part of the fabric that makes New Zealand a place like no other. It saddens me every time I see another camping ground being sold to developers, only to be replaced by modern homes for the few wealthy who can afford that sort of real estate. Camping grounds provide an affordable place for all New Zealanders to share and celebrate, for a couple of weeks a year, all that is special about where we live.

Like historic buildings and places, camping grounds should have a covenant placed on them and the owners of these sites should be subsidised by our government. I have believed for a long time now that if we lose these exceptional spots it will have the effect of ripping the soul out of New Zealand.

How I Cook

I CAN HONESTLY SAY THAT MY PHILOSOPHY ON COOKING HASN'T CHANGED SINCE I BEGAN MY CAREER MORE THAN 20 YEARS AGO. IT'S ALWAYS BEEN ABOUT THE SIMPLICITY OF DELIVERING TASTE WITHOUT OVERWORKING OR, FOR THAT MATTER, OVERHANDLING THE FOOD YOU ARE COOKING.

I have always loved ingredients in their purest and freshest form, and eating perfect examples of produce at their absolute prime, be it a sun-warmed freshly picked tomato, a perfectly ripe greengage plum, or a beautifully marbled piece of cooked beef, seasoned with only salt and a grind of fresh pepper, can take me back to particular moments in my life. For me, good food has always been about the freshness of produce, looking after it and getting it from the source to the plate with as few hands touching it as possible.

Since 1996, our restaurant Logan Brown has always had that same mindset regarding the ingredients we serve. For co-owner Steve Logan and me, it has always been about the food having integrity, cooking and seasoning correctly, and being generous. We used the term 'eat well' as a benchmark. I would always have it in mind before putting a new dish on the menu. Do the flavours work well together? Are all the components in harmony? Is there good contrast of textures? If I could tick all these boxes, the dish would always pass the 'eat well' test. Presentation is also important, but has always been last on the list. Flavour comes first!

Logan Brown is in its thirteenth year of business, as I write. We have a great reputation and what we can be proud of, among other things, is serving food that always 'ate well'. If you look at the restaurants that have been around for a decade or more, you will find that most have the same culinary gene. They have become legendary through serving perfectly cooked, simple, classic food, consistently year after year. These kitchens cook with 'heart' not 'ego'.

For me, cooking has never been about reinventing the wheel. It is a way of respecting, celebrating and paying tribute to the great cooks and chefs of the world who have created timeless, classic dishes from their respective cuisines. Sure, I've embraced some trends along the way and as a chef your food must evolve and you must be constantly stimulated and passionate to be successful. However, I've always been more interested in learning the classic preparations and cooking techniques of the various cuisines of the world than trying desperately to come up with totally original dishes or recipes. This is not to say that my way is the only way — far from it. And how boring the world would be if we all cooked the same way.

I respect the new breed of chefs out there, pushing the boundaries of cooking. However, I am convinced that, like nouvelle cuisine of the 1980s, the molecular gastronomy that is all the rage at present will have a speedy demise once everyone has tried it a couple of times. There are most definitely some brilliant exponents of this science-lab style of cooking, but in my experience they are few and far between. What we have now is a whole bunch of new chefs trying to emulate this trend and failing miserably. Try as I might, I just don't get it! I find most of this food overhandled, tortured and completely soulless — small, miserable portions of foams, spheres and smears. Deconstructed food that ends up cold, alone and lifeless, $200 designer plates — pieces of art, no question, but I eat with my mouth, not my eyes. As I have said to many a young chef over the years, if what's most important to you is presentation and arranging pretty products on a plate, I think you may have the wrong job — there's a florist hiring down the road!

I think what all chefs have in common and what ultimately drives us is an overwhelming desire to give and to please. The hard work, long hours, burns and cuts, failures and stress all seem to dissipate in a millisecond when you receive a compliment on the taste of what you have just created. You may have spent hours, or even days, on getting a dish just right, but that one 'Hey, the snapper I ate tonight was outstanding' is all that is needed to keep you going.

It may seem ridiculous that just five or six words paying tribute to your skills is what will make you turn around tomorrow to work another 14-hour day, your

sixth or seventh in a row. But genuine positive feedback is kind of like feeding our 'compliment addiction'. It may only be a passing comment like 'Had a great night at your gaff last month — the food and service were terrific'. This is like a little 'ego cookie', a small and satisfying snack that doesn't weigh you down. A full-blown five-star review in a well-respected publication has you feeding in the smorgasbord trough of 'all you can eat' accolades for a day or two. Too many of these and one's ego can become extremely large, bordering on obese!

On the other side of the coin, negative feedback or criticism can come in many forms and undoubtedly the worst, for me, is when guests or friends who have just eaten a meal you have lovingly slaved over say absolutely nothing! That sort of silence can send the likes of me into a downward spiral of depression, anxiety, sleepless nights and lack of appetite. Well, actually, not lack of appetite — that's never really happened to me — but you get the picture.

The most important word for me that cooking evokes is 'share'. This word has a lot to do with why I cook. Over my entire cooking career, I have never considered not giving out a recipe to anyone who asked. The sharing of recipes is like a culinary chain letter, passing on something great and meaningful that so much pleasure can be derived from. And it's how food evolves and gets better and better. The thought of a recipe being passed on from hundreds or maybe thousands of cooks, then being

shared and enjoyed by people gives me immense pleasure.

Over the years I have had the satisfaction of working with many young kitchen hands and cooks in restaurants all over the world. To teach and share your knowledge of food and cooking with budding chefs and watch them move up through the kitchen, gaining confidence as they begin to understand the fundamentals of cooking, is extraordinarily gratifying. Many have gone on to become well-known and respected chefs.

What gives me the most delight is eating in their restaurants and, even though they now have their own unique style, still seeing a lot of the same components, flavour combinations and sometimes exact replication of dishes you taught them years earlier. That to me is the ultimate compliment and fills me with a huge sense of pride. Likewise, the many chefs and cooks who taught me and shared their knowledge of cooking and technique can recognise their cooking DNA in my dishes.

Being secretive about recipes denotes miserable insecurities and highlights a mean streak of selfishness.

The sheer joy gleaned from sitting around a table with loved ones, sharing food, wine, conversation and laughter is without a doubt my most enjoyable pastime of all.

I am often asked what is the most favourite thing or meal I have ever eaten. As odd a question as it is, it always relates to where I am and who I am with. All the greatest and most memorable meals I have eaten have all been with great friends. Some of those meals have been in some pretty amazing restaurants; others in camping grounds. The occasions are widely varied — it may have just been with Steve (Logan) in a tapas bar in Barcelona consuming lumps of fresh foie gras, or with my wife Lizzie and the girls, hunkered down under the awning next to the campervan when it's pouring with rain, cooking fresh kahawai and chips over a gas hob with a couple of other families up the East Cape.

Brilliant memories all of them, and somehow the food always seems to have risen into another stratosphere of flavour, taste and enjoyment. Food doesn't need to be flash to be tasty. On the contrary, the simplest of combinations, flavours and cooking methods can offer up the greatest culinary experiences.

The recipes in this book are all very approachable. I love straightforward, uncomplicated food where the emphasis is on using first-class ingredients, cooking them correctly and serving generous portions that 'eat well'.

I have written this book on my laptop, sitting on a Bentwood chair at our kitchen table in our very old 'new' house that we purchased recently in Lyall Bay, Wellington. The kitchen is at least 50 years old, with a tiny Formica bench, lots of small cupboards and drawers that stick all the time, no dishwasher, an old meat safe as a pantry and, the crowning glory, an ancient Atlas Milford electric range.

At the beginning I was completely overawed by the thought of trying to produce a book, creating and testing all the recipes in this humble kitchen. However, the more I considered it, the more it made sense. Sometimes I think too many cookbooks are produced in high-tech commercial kitchens with the latest culinary gadgets where the chef is surrounded by a photographer, a food stylist, someone on lighting and any number of other hangers-on. Every component is strategically placed, down to a see-through wafer, precariously balanced on top of a perfectly symmetrical quenelle, with not a single grind of pepper out of place. It can take half a day to get the perfect shot! Those cookbooks are destined to become what we describe in the industry as 'food porn', with beautiful pictures of food that you salivate over as you turn page after page, but which you will probably never attempt to reproduce.

Not for me. I want this book to be used, to have notes written on the recipes, oil stains, dog-eared pages . . . the lot. I have tried my darnedest to keep things as simple as possible. Cooking seafood to me is about cooking it correctly, showing off its natural and individual attributes. I can't think of any fresh seafood that can't be cooked and served with just a squeeze of lemon juice, a pinch of salt and a grind of fresh pepper. A lot of the time, adding as little as possible to the cooking process is the key to delicious seafood.

Most recipes will have different components that make up each dish. I urge you to mix and match these components — many will work equally well with different varieties and species.

A lot of the motivation behind producing this book is my desire for people to think differently about the bounty of seafood that surrounds our shores and I have deliberately developed recipes that involve less commonly eaten species. If you are an angler, next time you catch a species that in the past you have thrown back because it wasn't a snapper, for example, I encourage you to keep it. I guarantee you will enjoy it. It's also about getting away from just eating loads of pearly white boneless fillets. Yes, I love eating these, however, I believe we throw far too much of our catch away. As you'll see in the following recipes, there is a lot more eating in one fish than just the fillets.

We also seem to have this absolute fear of bones. In my lifetime, I am yet to read a headline 'Man Dies After Swallowing Fish with Bones'! Sure, if the fillet is meant to be boneless, coming across one can be slightly irritating. However, as the rest of the world can attest, fish cooked whole and complete with all their bones present make for wonderful eating. It most certainly slows down the eating process, which I celebrate, as the longer we sit around a table eating, the better! It's also better for your digestion, the presentation is more natural and, most importantly, the fish will always be more succulent and flavourful.

So embrace our other friends from the ocean. Go eat a herring!

Handling Fresh Fish

THE BEST-TASTING FISH YOU WILL EVER EAT WILL BE FISH THAT YOU HAVE CAUGHT AND LOVINGLY HANDLED YOURSELF, FROM THE HOOK TO THE FORK.

Reputable fishmongers are your next port of call — clean, well-organised outfits that handle the iced-down fillets of fish gently and correctly, and give you advice on other interesting species on offer you may be unfamiliar with. Fresh fish, when handled and stored in the correct manner, can last perfectly well for days. On the other hand, fish that hasn't been treated with respect every step of the way from the moment it's caught will result in inferior eating. Just walk into your local supermarket to realise this fact. The fish sold as 'fresh' through these outlets is a crime. It's no wonder so many people are put off eating fish for life after eating that bought from many supermarkets. To add insult to injury, check out the exorbitant prices you have to pay for stale old brown fillets of 'fresh' fish! The fact is that anyone licensed to sell fish is able to put the word 'fresh' in front of any product that hasn't been frozen. Work that one out!

Looking to the future, I'm a believer that all seafood sold should be able to be traced to the source — where it was caught and when it was landed. Fish retailers should have to pass a certificate on the knowledge of species, how to handle the product correctly and even basic points on how to cook. I urge you to bypass these stale fish sections of ill repute. Seek out the good guys who love their product and love what they do.

The following important points are those I practise when catching, handling, storing and buying fresh fish.

- Always use a clean saltwater-soaked rag when removing the hook from a fish. It's easier to handle and if you decide to put it back, it helps protect its microprotective layer (basically, its slime) and scales, reducing the chance of fatality.

- Iki-jime the fish immediately upon removing the hook. This is the process of spiking the brain of the fish with a sharp nail-like point. It kills the fish instantly and significantly decreases spoilage if combined with rapid icing down. Believe me, this small step makes a huge difference in the eating quality of the fish, as it drains the blood out and away from the fillets.

- Once iki'd, the fish should be placed in a slurry of ice immediately to bring down the temperature as fast as possible. The optimum slurry is made of four parts freshwater ice with one part clean saltwater.

- After the fish has been in the ice slurry and is chilled through, the best way to store them is described as the 'soldier' method where the fish are lined up top and tail, belly down and then covered with ice.

- When carrying a fish, never let it bend. This tends to split the fillets, especially in species like snapper. Always support the middle of the fish when you lay it down on a flat surface. The same goes for handling individual fillets.

- It's imperative to use a sharp knife. No excuses. Not negotiable!

- When filleting a fish, dry it down with an old clean rag, tea towel or similar. This keeps the fish from slipping about and makes filleting easier and more effective, rendering a higher yield.

- When removing the skin from a fresh fillet, take the knife and position it through the flesh at the tail end of the fillet, with the blade lying ever so slightly angled on the skin. Keep the

HOW TO: | Fillet a Fish

1. Make an incision angled from the belly up to behind the head.

2. Run the knife down the back of the fish, lifting the fillet away as you cut.

3. Continue down through the belly, keeping the blade running along the bone.

4. Trim the edge, removing the bottom fin off the belly of the fillet.

knife firm and steady. Grip the small tab of skin tightly at the end of the fillet, then pull and wiggle the skin backwards under the stationary knife. The knife effectively stays in one position. Keep your filleting knife wet as you skin the fillets. It acts like a lubricant, making the job easier and more effective.

- If the fillets are bloody or dirty with scales and so on, rinse quickly in saltwater and pat dry with a clean towel. Again, keep the fillets lying flat at all times.

- Fresh fish fillets are best stored at 0°C. It's often said that fresh fish loses a day's shelf life for every hour left at room temperature. The method I use for storing fillets is to place them in a perforated self-draining pan, then cover them with plastic wrap or place in a plastic bag and top with ice. I then put this in the fridge over a container to catch the water as the ice melts. Each day I replace the ice. It's important that the fillets do not come in direct contact with the ice or water.

- Storing fish whole on the bone extends the shelf life of the fish. To store whole, the fish should be scaled, gutted and have the gills removed. Store as above.

- When purchasing fresh fillets ask where they came from, when the fish was caught, and ask your fishmonger to put some on a piece of paper for you to have a closer inspection, especially for the sniff test! The fillets should be firm, glossy and translucent in appearance. When purchasing whole fish, look for clear, shiny eyes and bright red gills. Remember you are paying top dollar for these precious products and you should only accept super-fresh fish that has been handled correctly all the way from the moment it was caught.

- It pays to have a small chiller bag to transport your fresh fish in, preferably with a slicker pad or similar to keep the contents cold. It's imperative to get it into the fridge as soon as possible.

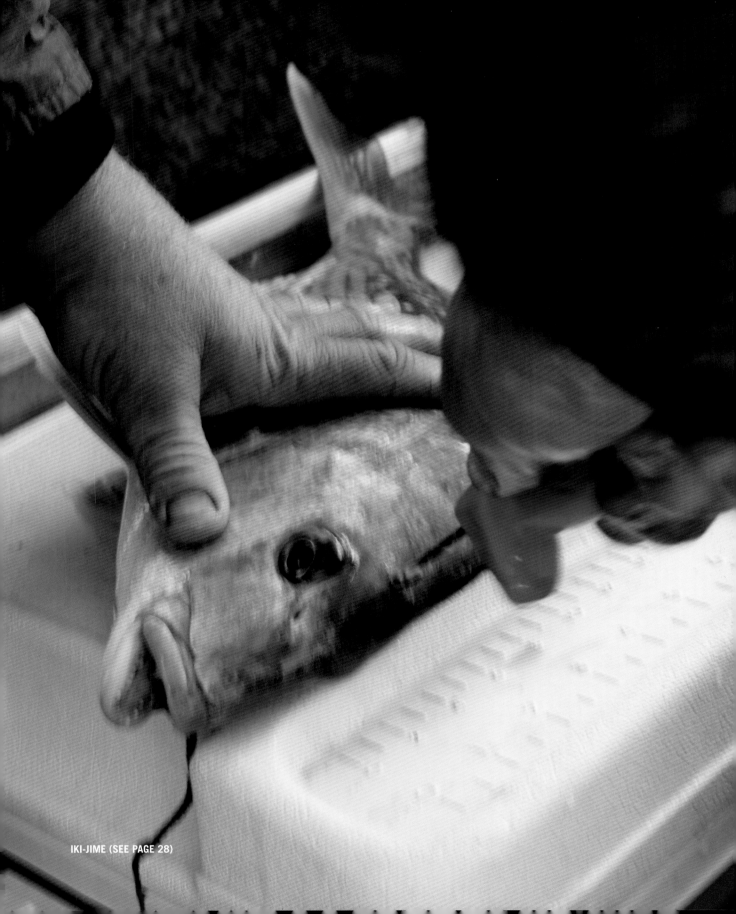
IKI-JIME (SEE PAGE 28)

Kaimoana

I LOVE FISHING AND COOKING FRESH SEAFOOD. IT HAS ALWAYS BEEN A PART OF MY LIFE – ITS PART OF OUR KIWI DNA.

Fishing has always been important to the people of Aotearoa or New Zealand. Its significance is highlighted in the story of the first catch of this country by Maui, who according to the legend fished up the North Island of Aotearoa.

Maui was the last born in his family, so his rank was low but he compensated for this by being far more resourceful and imaginative than his older brothers. One day Maui smuggled himself aboard his brothers' canoe in Hawaiki, the traditional homeland of the Māori people. The brothers were annoyed by his trickery and wanted to return to shore, but they were so far from land when he was found that they decided to continue their fishing expedition as planned.

After the brothers had filled the canoe with their catch, Maui produced his own hook, the barb of which was made from a fragment of his grandmother's jawbone. The other brothers refused him bait so Maui struck his own nose and smeared the hook with his blood. He lowered the line and almost immediately hooked a fish of unimaginable size. The only way he could haul it up was by reciting a karakia, or chant, to make heavy weights become light.

When the mighty fish had been brought to the surface, Maui left the canoe to find a tohunga (priest) to make offerings to the gods and perform the appropriate rituals and thank them for such a magnificent catch. He warned his brothers not to touch the great creature until this was complete. The brothers, however, ignored him and left the canoe and commenced scaling the fish and hacking bits off it. The mighty fish raised its fins and withered in agony. As the sun rose the flesh became solid underfoot, its surface rough and mountainous, because of the brothers' mutilation. It remained that way and the name given to it was Te Ika-a-Maui, the fish of Maui, and what we know today as the North Island of New Zealand.

This story appeals to me for so many reasons. The area around Young Nick's Head is called Te Matau-a-Maui or the hook of Maui, which is said to remain there to this day — a tangible connection to the ocean and the origins of this country.

Māori do not make a distinction between the sea and land. The sea, its fishing grounds and fish should be as important to everyone as the land. Fishing is an important recreational activity and export product. However, we can't look at the sea as only being a major source of food — it has huge cultural value as well.

Seafood, or kaimoana, was a major source of protein, fats, vitamins and minerals for Māori. And kaimoana remains a hugely important way of showing hospitality (manaakitanga) and generosity at tribal gatherings. The food provided for guests is a great status symbol in Māori culture and kaimoana rates very highly. If Māori cannot access kaimoana this has a major impact on their mana, or status. Naturally the importance of a clean environment has a direct bearing on the ability of all fishers, including Māori, to harvest from culturally important fisheries.

Māori were very knowledgeable and skilled fishers. Lines were made from flax fibre and sinkers from stones. Hooks were exquisitely and skilfully carved from wood, bone, stone and shell. They even developed an ingenious piece of fishing gear called a gorge that was used instead of a hook. It was a straight piece of bone, sharpened at each end and attached in the middle. When a bite was detected the line was pulled and the gorge turned sideways and lodged itself in the unsuspecting fish's throat.

Iwi (tribes) and their hapu (subtribes) were and still are kaitiaki or guardians of their marine resources. Systems to regulate when and how fishing could occur were developed. Early Māori understood a great deal about the life cycles of different fish. A fishing calendar was developed to work out when certain fish should be caught, what techniques to use and whether it should be caught during the day or night. The fishing

calendar was used as a tool for sustainable fishing at certain times of the lunar month.

And this knowledge of fishing continues today. The remarkable, and under-acknowledged, aspect of Māori customary and recreational fishing is that there are families who are fishing the same areas they have fished for the past 200 or more years. Over this time an overwhelming abundance of local knowledge has been built up around their local fishery, often within several key families. This information, and indeed the knowledge of recreational fishers, is presently undervalued and underutilised.

In the past a great variety of nets and fish traps were made, also from flax fibre or vines. Their design depended on the type of fish targeted and where the nets or traps were used (varying according to the depth, type of bottom and so on). Some nets were very long and needed the entire community to set them and haul them ashore. Different whanau owned different sections of the net. Spears were also used to catch some fish, such as eels and flounder, and still are today. Many shellfish where gathered by hand, including paua, kina, rock lobster and octopus.

The traditional Māori fishing operations were very well organised. Different tribes had their own fishing areas and tribal boundaries were marked by landmarks and stakes. Fishing was a community activity. Tasks involved everything from observing the movement of schools of fish, making gear, to catching and processing the fish. The catch, once it was processed, was given as a koha to members of the tribe for all to enjoy. The idea of giving a koha, or gift, is all about reciprocity and is an important custom, which continues today. Often when Māori gather kaimoana more ends up on the tables of others than on the fisher's table. Isn't this what enjoying this fantastic ocean is all about — others not ourselves?

While a lot of the kaimoana was consumed fresh, it was important to avoid waste by preserving it. Traditional methods for preserving kaimoana are smoking, drying, salting and fermenting. Most of these methods are still used today — just maybe not to the same degree as 100 years ago.

A number of rules have been developed to ensure that the resources of the ocean are not depleted.

- Karakia (prayers or chants) or waiata (songs or hymns) are offered to Tangaroa (the guardian or god of the sea) before fishing.
- If someone drowns, a rahui or fishing ban is put in place and no one may fish there until Tangaroa returns the dead or until the rahui is lifted.
- The first fish taken is returned to the sea with a karakia to invite an abundance of fish and ensure sustainability.
- Body wastes infringe tapu and none must enter the sea from the beach . . .
- In some places kaimoana cannot be eaten on the beach; it must be taken home and prepared for eating there.
- Large canoes, eel weirs and nets are protected by tapu.
- Nets and lines must not drag on the seabed, because this could damage the fishing ground. On shore, sacks and baskets must be lifted and never dragged over shellfish beds.
- Dislodged rocks should always be returned to their exact position.
- Only certain fish could be taken at certain times and places.
- If a feeler of a rock lobster (koura) is snapped off, the feeler must be removed from the water before any more koura can be taken; otherwise other life forms would be disrupted.
- Rahui, or total bans, on fishing were applied at certain times for various reasons, such as to protect fishing grounds under pressure and to give species of fish, shellfish and seaweed a chance to spawn or multiply.
- The amount of bait, length of line and so on were carefully controlled so that only the right amount of fish of the right species was caught.
- Māori also have strong beliefs about protecting fisheries from pollution. For example, it is forbidden to gut fish in the open sea or throw small fish, excess bait, food or rubbish into the water. Waste like this is seen as attracting predators and polluting sensitive habitats.

Māori have continued their affinity with fishing and now account for 100 per cent of customary fishing, 30 per cent of commercial fishing and 40 per cent of recreational fishing. I heard a saying that Māori were fishing in Aotearoa a thousand years ago and will be fishing in another thousand years. I imagine by observing the conservation (or kaitiaki) practices above we might all get there.

The Recipes

Ahead of you are dozens of recipes covering all manner of New Zealand fish and shellfish species. I have covered many of our favourite 'usual suspects'. However, I encourage you to expand your seafood horizons by embracing a few of the more uncommon but equally delicious varieties of fish that share our waters.

   Please don't think that all the recipes are set in stone. Many of the components that make up a certain dish, such as a sauce or vegetable side, will work equally well with another species of fish. I urge you to have fun and don't take your cooking too seriously.

Experiment a little and don't get too hung up on following the recipes exactly — use them as a guideline and add a few of your own twists and turns on the way. Make notes in the book as you go, not just for yourself but for other people to read too.

Recipes are for sharing and to be enjoyed by as many people as possible. I take immense pleasure in seeing recipes I have used and passed on, change and evolve as they become personalised to the new caretaker's taste. So enjoy them, adapt them and keep them moving!

Crustaceans

Crustaceans

We do not have a huge number of crustaceans in and around our New Zealand waters. Though hardly a scientist, I'm picking this is mainly because our seas are particularly cold and not that conducive to certain species of shrimp and prawns that seem to make their homes in the warmer waters.

However, our shortfall in variety is certainly made up for in what many renowned chefs regard as the finest in taste and quality.

Our rock lobster (crayfish), and scampi are prized throughout the world for their natural sweetness and wonderful texture. We also have many delicious eating crabs, some commercially available and others gathered by recreational divers and those who set pots.

When purchasing crayfish and crabs, both should preferably be alive or just freshly cooked and chilled. Crabs shed their shells many times before reaching maturity, so be wary of pale shells that feel light or hollow, as these crabs will have recently shed and therefore have less meat which will be of inferior quality. Both crabs and crayfish should be drowned in fresh water or put in the freezer for 30 minutes before being placed in boiling water to cook. This prevents the legs falling off and from rendering the meat tough. Finally, make sure you have a good pair of kitchen shears to help extract the sweetest meat, which is located in the head and legs of the crayfish.

Incidentally, once removed, that equates to nearly a third of the weight of flesh contained within. Don't waste a morsel!

For lovers of seafood, the sight of crayfish, scampi or crab is always considered a treat. Simply delicious served in most any style, hot or cold, crustaceans are always very rich. So eating them occasionally will normally suffice as my 'fix' for a week or two . . .

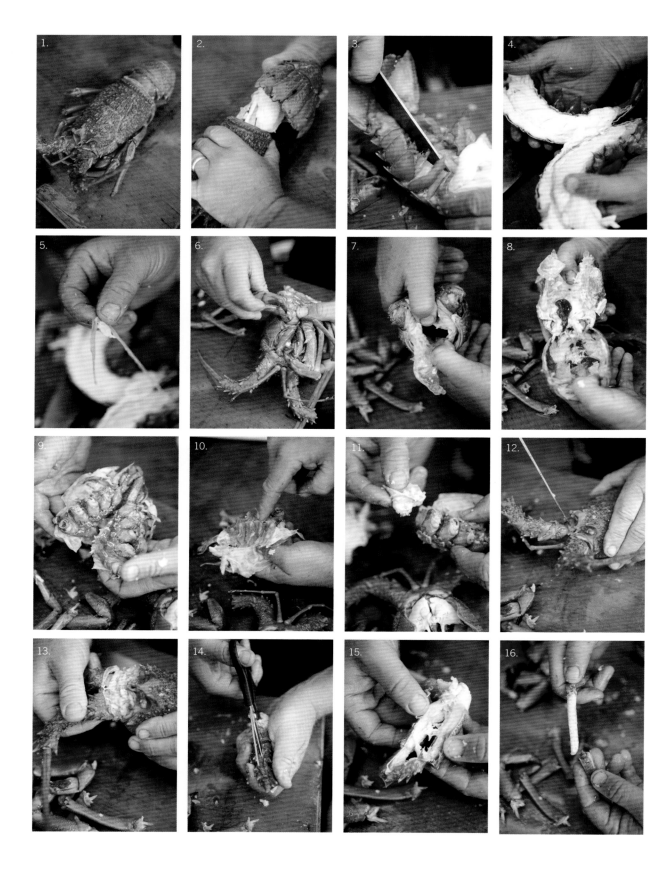

HOW TO: | Deal to a Cooked Crayfish

1. A whole crayfish.

2. Hold the body with one hand and twist the tail with the other.

3. Slice lengthwise through the underside of the crayfish tail.

4. Splitting the tail.

5. Remove the excretion tube.

6. Break off the legs from where they are attached to the body.

7. Place each thumb inside the body cavity.

8. Split the under cavity from the top shell by pulling apart.

9. With your hands, snap the under cavity in two.

10. Remove the feather-like filters from both pieces of the under cavity and discard.

11. Access the cooked flesh from the leg joints by crushing the shell with your fingers.

12. Make a slice where both feelers connect to the head of the crayfish.

13. Snap the feelers off.

14. With sturdy sharp scissors, cut down the centre of each feeler.

15. Remove the cooked flesh from the feelers.

16. Snap the legs at each joint and carefully pull out the cooked flesh.

Step 1: Lime and Horseradish Butter
250g butter, diced
juice and minced zest of 3 limes
½ cup horseradish sauce
¼ cup finely minced parsley

Step 2: To Cook and Serve
6 live crayfish
cooking oil for brushing
sea salt and freshly ground black pepper
lime wedges to serve

Chargrilled Crayfish with Lime & Horseradish Butter

Serves 6 or 12 (depending on how greedy you are)

I generally enjoy crayfish the most when it is cooked and then served chilled in one form or another as I find it a little rich when served hot. In saying that, serving it straight from the barbecue, as in this recipe, is my favourite way to eat it. If you can cook it over charcoal or even just on your grill grates to get a little char or burnt action happening, then even better. The lime zest and juice, along with the kick of the horseradish, really help cut through a lot of the richness. It's quite a sight seeing half a dozen whole crayfish cooking in this manner. In fact, as I write this, my salivary glands are working overtime at just the thought of it all!

Step 1: Lime and Horseradish Butter
Place the butter in a bowl and leave at room temperature for 30 minutes to soften. Once soft, add the remaining ingredients. With clean hands, work all the ingredients together until fully combined. Place in a clean container and refrigerate until required.

Step 2: To Cook and Serve
Heat the chargrill or barbecue to high heat.

Drown the crayfish in fresh water. With a solid sharp knife, split the crayfish down the centre from the head to the tail. Remove the obvious guts from the head cavity and the excretion tube that runs down through the tail.

Brush the flesh side with cooking oil and season with liberal amounts of sea salt and pepper.

Place on the heat, flesh side down. Let it cook for at least 2–3 minutes without turning so they get some good char flavour and caramelisation. Depending on the size of the crayfish, cook for about the same amount of time on both sides. You can tell the crays are cooked in two ways. First, the whole shell has turned from purple and red to a bright orange. Second, the flesh of the tail comes away easily from the shell.

Once cooked, brush the crayfish with excessive amounts of the lime and horseradish butter. Serve with lime wedges and a pile of paper towels!

Never buy dead uncooked crayfish. In fact, that goes for all crustaceans as, once dead, they deteriorate extremely quickly and you've got a good chance of getting a 'sore tummy'.

Step 1: Smoked Tomatoes
400g tomatoes (preferably vine-
    ripened)
brown sugar
sea salt

**Step 2: Smoked Tomato
    Vinaigrette**
2 teaspoons freshly ground cumin
    seeds
1 teaspoon sweet smoked
    Spanish paprika
3 tablespoons sherry vinegar
1 tablespoon sugar
1½ tablespoons tomato paste
½ cup canola oil
salt and freshly ground black
    pepper

Step 3: Orzo Pasta
1 tablespoon cooking oil
½ teaspoons salt
1½ cups orzo pasta (or another
    small dried pasta)
¼ cup olive oil

Step 4: To Assemble and Serve
1 avocado (ripe but firm), cut into
    medium dice
⅓ cup thinly sliced shallots (halve
    first then slice)
½ bag mizuna or rocket, roughly
    torn
½ cup fresh basil leaves, sliced
    into strips
¼ cup finely chopped chives
1 x 500g crayfish, cooked, meat
    removed (yields about 250g),
    and chopped
sea salt and freshly ground black
    pepper
lime wedges to serve

Crayfish & Orzo Pasta Salad with Smoked Tomato Vinaigrette

Serves 6 as an entrée or light lunch

Any fresh kaimoana you are given is truly an offering appreciated more than most. But a whole crayfish — well, that raises gift-giving into another stratosphere. Crayfish cooked then chilled, with every morsel painstakingly extracted from even the smallest cavity with the precision of a microsurgeon, is a scenario most Kiwis can definitely appreciate. Then comes the decision of how this treasure from the depths is to be devoured. I can clearly recall, as a child, my parents suggesting on more than one occasion, as they passed out the legs of a cooked crayfish to the kids, that we probably wouldn't like the taste of the tail! Of all the hundreds of platters of food that I have passed around over the years, a simple dish of chilled crayfish, humbly adorned with no more than a squeeze of lemon juice and dollop of mayonnaise, will always cause the biggest stir. It can turn the most well-mannered individual into something that resembles a hungry child in a high chair recklessly stuffing food into their gob. So the dilemma faced when given just one 'bug' is always a toughie. Hide it from everyone and simply consume the whole thing yourself in the shade behind the water tank out the back of the bach, then bury the evidence? Yes, guilty as charged on more than one occasion. Or there's the less selfish and more bounteous approach of finding a dish that stretches this delicacy for a few more to enjoy. The following recipe does just that. I have used just one 500g cooked crayfish to produce a delicious salad that would make a terrific lunch or a great start to an evening meal. The smoked tomato vinaigrette works very well with the slightly sweet flesh of the cray.

It's illegal to spear or lasso rock lobster (crayfish).

Step 1: Smoked Tomatoes
Bring a saucepan of water to the boil. Score the tomatoes by making a little cross incision at the base and carefully cutting out the small core at the top. Fill a bowl with cold water and add a few ice cubes. Once the water in the saucepan has

reached the boil, drop in the tomatoes. Remove after 20 seconds or so and plunge immediately into the ice-cold water. Leave for a minute then peel off and discard the skins.

Now slice the tomatoes in half horizontally. Place on the smoker rack and liberally sprinkle with brown sugar and sea salt.

Toss a handful of wood chips into the smoker, light the heat source and, once smoking, place the tomatoes in for 10 minutes. Remove from the rack with care, as they will be very delicate without their skins, but will have absorbed a good deal of the smoke flavour.

Step 2: Smoked Tomato Vinaigrette

Purée the tomatoes with a wand blender or similar. Pass through a fine sieve into a bowl, discarding the seeds. Add the cumin, paprika, vinegar, sugar and tomato paste. Whisk until combined. Drizzle in the canola oil as you continue to whisk. Taste and season with salt and pepper if needed. Refrigerate until required.

Step 3: Orzo Pasta

Fill a large saucepan with water to halfway, add the oil and a good teaspoon or 2 of salt. Place on the heat and bring to the boil. Once boiling, add the pasta and cook until al dente (check after 10 minutes).

Remove from the heat and strain through a sieve, then spread out on a tray. Pour the olive oil over and mix in to prevent the pasta from sticking. Leave to cool, then refrigerate until required.

Step 4: To Assemble and Serve

Place the orzo in a large bowl and add the avocado, shallots, mizuna or rocket, basil, chives and the crayfish meat. Gently fold together with a wooden spoon.

Add ½ cup of the tomato vinaigrette. Mix through and taste. If you feel it needs more, go ahead and add a little more, but you don't want to overpower the crayfish with too much smoked flavour. Season with sea salt and black pepper.

Serve onto chilled plates if you can be bothered — it's a nice touch. Give each serving a grind of black pepper and add a wedge of lime. Serve now!

CRAYFISH & ORZO PASTA SALAD WITH SMOKED TOMATO VINAIGRETTE

Step 1: Crayfish Stock
2 litres of crayfish stock (see recipe on page 309)

Step 2: Crayfish Soup Base
cooking oil for frying
150g rindless bacon, cut into small dice
2 cups finely diced onion
1 cup finely diced fennel bulb
1 cup finely diced celery
2 tablespoons finely chopped fresh tarragon
pinch of saffron, soaked in ¼ cup warm water
2 litres crayfish stock
3 cups kumara, cut into 1cm dice

Step 3: To Cook and Serve
30 scampi tails, peeled, de-veined, halved and diced (or substitute other seafood)
300ml cream
¼ cup finely chopped fresh chives
¼ cup finely chopped fresh parsley

Scampi & Crayfish Soup with Kumara & Saffron

Serves 10

This soup is decadent and rich, and would make a wonderful and elegant start to a special meal. There's definitely a bit of work involved, especially with making the crayfish stock, but this can be made weeks ahead and frozen if you like. Once the stock is made it's pretty basic, and on the day you serve it, it's pretty much a heat-and-eat situation. If you can't get scampi, by all means use another shellfish or some fresh fish fillets cooked in it just before serving.

Step 1: Crayfish Stock
Make crayfish stock from the recipe on page 309.

Step 2: Crayfish Soup Base
Place a little oil in a large saucepan on high heat. Once hot, add the bacon. Cook until caramelised then add the onion, fennel, celery and tarragon.

Reduce the heat and sweat the vegetables and bacon for 30 minutes or so until soft. Stir in the saffron and its soaking liquid, then add the crayfish stock.

Bring up to a rolling boil then lower the heat to a simmer. Cook for 20 minutes then add the kumara. Cook for another 10 minutes then remove from the heat and set aside to cool. Store in the fridge until ready to serve.

Step 3: To Cook and Serve
Place the soup base in a large saucepan and slowly bring to the boil. Add the scampi and the cream. Cook for 1 minute, then remove from the heat.

Ladle out into warm bowls, then add a pinch each of chives and parsley. Serve, sit down and enjoy!

When cooking with saffron, remember a little goes a long way. We have a good number of people in New Zealand producing this wonderful spice, so hunt out theirs, as a lot of the imported saffron is quite inferior, old and without the pungent and exotic flavour saffron is famous for. When cooking with saffron, place the few strands you are using in a dry pan and place on the heat for a minute or so to toast it. Next, crumble the saffron between your fingers into the soaking water, then use accordingly.

**Step 1: Highlander Condensed
   Milk Mayonnaise**
1 tin Highlander Sweetened
   Condensed Milk
½ cup canola oil
2 egg yolks
½ cup malt vinegar

2 teaspoons dry mustard powder
pinch of cayenne pepper
1 teaspoon salt

Step 2: Crayfish Rolls
2–3 chilled cooked crayfish, all
   the meat removed from the
   tails, legs and head cavity
1 large iceberg lettuce
12 white hot dog rolls, split
   halfway through lengthwise

6–8 medium tomatoes, sliced
   into rounds
juice of 2 lemons
sea salt and freshly ground black
   pepper

Crayfish Roll with Highlander Condensed Milk Mayonnaise, Iceberg Lettuce & Tomato

Makes 12

I doubt I'll pick up any culinary awards for this recipe, but it's one of my favourite ways of eating crayfish and, with every mouthful, it transports me back to my childhood holidays at the Castlepoint camping ground. I grew up with just two sauces: Wattie's Tomato Sauce and Highlander Condensed Milk mayonnaise — both Kiwi classics and justifiably so. Why do they get served and how come they work with so many foods? Simple. They have saltiness, sweetness, acidity and heat, which, as components for a sauce, make them work with practically anything.

The other important ingredient here is the bread roll — fresh processed hot dog rolls are the only way to go! Try them, you'll love them.

Step 1: Highlander Condensed Milk Mayonnaise
Place the condensed milk in a bowl. Add the remaining ingredients and whisk together until blended. Taste and adjust the seasoning accordingly. Place in the fridge to cool and thicken.

Step 2: Crayfish Rolls
Chop the crayfish meat into smallish chunks and place in a bowl. Fold in enough of the mayonnaise just to coat.

Peel off the lettuce leaves and rip them in half. Open up the split rolls and add 1 or 2 pieces of lettuce to line the inside, then add 3 slices of tomato to each.

Divide the crayfish between each roll and stuff into the lettuce- and tomato-lined cavity. Add a squeeze of lemon juice over each, a pinch of sea salt and a grind of black pepper.

The condensed milk industry was established in Europe in 1897. Our famous Highlander Condensed Milk was first produced in 1901.

HOW TO: | Prepare, Cook and Extract Crab Meat

1. Paddle crab.

2. From the back of the crab, grip the top shell and bottom cavity.

3. Holding the bottom cavity with one thumb, pull the shell up, over and off.

4. Remove the feather-like gills and discard.

5. Grip the eye socket frames with thumb and forefinger.

6. Remove by pulling away.

7. Turn the crab over and remove the tail flap.

8. Split the body down the centre with a sharp knife.

9. Chop off the outside last joints of the crab legs.

10. Drop the crab halves in boiling salted water for 2–4 minutes, depending on their size.

11. Once removed, take to the crab with a rolling pin.

12. Roll over the body and legs both ways to extract the crab meat.

13. Crack open the claws.

14. Use a small knife to extract the meat from the cracked claws.

Step 1: Tartare Sauce
1 cup Al's mayonnaise (see recipe on page 302)
2 tablespoons finely chopped capers
2 tablespoons finely chopped red onion
¼ cup finely chopped gherkins
¼ cup finely chopped green capsicum
2 tablespoons finely chopped parsley
½ tablespoon finely chopped tarragon*
2 tablespoons wholegrain mustard
sea salt and freshly ground black pepper

Step 2: Crab Cakes
canola oil for frying
¼ cup finely diced celery
½ cup finely diced green capsicum
1 cup finely diced onion
½ tablespoon minced garlic
500g crab meat
⅓ cup Al's mayonnaise (see recipe on page 302)
1 teaspoon lemon juice
½–¾ cup breadcrumbs, plus extra to coat the cakes
salt and freshly ground black pepper to taste

Step 3: To Cook and Serve
cooking oil
6 lemon wedges to serve

Crab Cakes with Tartare Sauce

Serves 6 as an entrée (12 crab cakes)

Crab cakes have featured numerous times on the menu at Logan Brown since opening in 1996. I'm convinced they are a favourite with our loyal customers because they enjoy the subtle sweetness of the crab, with all the tricky work of extracting the delicate flesh from the shell done for them. We have always sourced our fresh crab meat from the nearby Kapiti Coast where our friends Matt Whittaker and Narina McBeath of Waikanae Crab fame have been fishing for paddle crab for many years.

The secret to a great crab cake is to have a generous amount of crab, with just enough other ingredients to add a little flavour and barely enough binding component to hold the cakes together when cooking. Tartare sauce has always been my condiment of choice with these, adding just the right amount of acidity along with the creaminess of mayonnaise.

Step 1: Tartare Sauce

Place the mayonnaise in a mixing bowl. Add the remaining ingredients, except the salt and pepper then, with a wooden spoon, stir together to combine. Taste and season with salt and black pepper. Pour into a suitable container and refrigerate until required.

* If fresh tarragon isn't available, try basil or just add more parsley.

Step 2: Crab Cakes

Add a little oil to a saucepan and, over low heat, sweat the celery, capsicum, onion and garlic for at least 30 minutes, stirring occasionally. Once the vegetables are soft, remove and cool to room temperature.

In a medium mixing bowl, place the cooked vegetables, crab meat, mayonnaise and lemon juice. Mix to combine. Add the breadcrumbs and stir through to firm up the mixture. Taste and season accordingly. Divide the mixture into 12 then, with your hands, mould into cakes and lightly cover with the extra breadcrumbs.

Step 3: To Cook and Serve

Preheat the oven to 120°C. Place a little cooking oil in a sauté pan on medium heat. Cook the crab cakes for a minute or so on each side until golden. Remove from the pan, place on an oven tray and put in the oven for 3–5 minutes to heat through the centres.

To serve, place a couple of crab cakes in the centre of each plate, add a dollop of tartare sauce and a wedge of lemon on the side. Serve.

Paddle crabs are widely distributed on most sandy beaches throughout New Zealand. You don't need a boat or expensive equipment to target this wonderful delicacy. A collapsible crab pot at the cost of $30 or $40, a fish head or a chicken frame for bait and you're away.

Step 1: Flour Tortillas
1 cup milk
3 tablespoons vegetable oil
2½ cups flour, plus a little extra for kneading
2 teaspoons baking powder
1½ teaspoons salt

Step 2: Tomatillo and Avocado Salsa
1½ cups diced tomatillos (or substitute ripe tomatoes)
½ avocado, cut into small dice
½ cup peeled, seeded and diced roasted red capsicum
3 tablespoons finely diced red onion
1 teaspoon finely diced fresh chilli
¼ cup roughly chopped fresh coriander

1 teaspoon ground toasted cumin seeds
3 tablespoons canola oil
1½ tablespoons lemon juice
1 teaspoon sugar
sea salt and freshly ground black pepper

Step 3: Lime Zest Sour Cream
150g sour cream
finely grated zest of 2 small limes

Step 4: Crab Quesadillas
400g grated cheese
300g crab meat
1 cup fresh sweetcorn, cooked and cut off the cob
1 cup peeled, seeded and diced roasted red capsicum
½ cup finely diced red onion
½ bunch fresh coriander
6 lime wedges to serve

Crab Quesadillas with Tomatillo & Avocado Salsa & Lime Zest Sour Cream

Makes 12

Quesadillas are a favourite of mine, served as a snack, starter or light meal. Really, they are just a Mexican toasted sandwich made simply by sandwiching various ingredients (always including cheese) between two flour tortillas and cooking them on a griddle top or in a skillet until crisp on the outside and oozing deliciousness on the inside. They are a great way to stretch a small amount of kaimoana. The ingredients you use are limited only by your imagination or by what's in the fridge. Combinations I have used in the past include smoked kahawai with tomato relish, leftover seafood paella and Christmas turkey and cranberry — all bound together with plenty of grated cheese. It's also a great way to use up all the bits and pieces from the crayfish bodies and legs after gorging yourself on the tails. If you don't have time to make your own tortillas, use store bought.

Step 1: Flour Tortillas

Pour the milk and oil into a small saucepan and warm slightly.

Mix the dry ingredients in a bowl. Once the milk and oil are warm, pour into the dry ingredients and mix together with your hands to form a dough.

Knead the dough for 2–3 minutes, then cover with plastic wrap and allow to rest for 15 minutes.

Divide the dough into 12 balls. On a clean, lightly floured work surface, use a rolling pin to roll out the tortillas as thinly as possible.

Place a dry skillet on medium-low heat. Once hot, cook the tortillas for 20–30 seconds on each side. Remove, place on a plate and continue until you have a stack of 12 tortillas. Cool to room temperature, then cover until required.

Step 2: Tomatillo and Avocado Salsa

Combine all the ingredients except the salt and pepper in a bowl and mix together. Season with the sea salt and fresh black pepper to taste. Refrigerate until required.

Step 3: Lime Zest Sour Cream
Place the ingredients in a bowl and mix together. Refrigerate until needed.

Step 4: Crab Quesadillas
Preheat the oven to low (100°C).

Lay out 6 flour tortillas on a clean bench. Sprinkle evenly over each the cheese followed by the crab meat, sweetcorn, red capsicum, red onion and fresh coriander. Sprinkle a little more cheese over, then top each with another flour tortilla.

Cook the quesadillas one at a time. Carefully place in a dry skillet or sauté pan on medium-low heat and cook for 1–2 minutes until crisp on the bottom and the cheese has begun to melt, sticking the ingredients together. Using your widest 'flipper' or fish slice, carefully flip the quesadilla onto its other side and cook until crisp. Remove and keep warm in the oven. Repeat with the remaining quesadillas.

To serve, cut the quesadillas into quarters and arrange on warm plates with a heaped spoonful of tomatillo and avocado salsa and a dollop of the lime zest sour cream. Serve with a cold cerveza and a wedge of lime.

Tomatillo is a green fruit that grows inside a husk and is related to the tomato. They are becoming more and more available in New Zealand at good farmers' markets and specialised produce stores. Look for them from mid to late summer. They have a slightly tart, apple-like flavour and are terrific cooked or served raw in salsas and salads. They are used extensively in Mexican cuisine.

Step 1: White Bean Purée
¼ cup olive oil
½ cup minced shallots
1½ tablespoons minced garlic
2 x 400g tins cannellini beans, drained and rinsed
½ cup chicken stock (see recipe on page 319)
½ cup cream
1 tablespoon lemon juice
sea salt and freshly ground black pepper

Step 2: Crisp Chilli Breadcrumbs
60g butter
1 tablespoon finely grated lemon zest
1 teaspoon freshly ground cumin
½ teaspoon sweet smoked Spanish paprika
1 teaspoon Tabasco Chipotle Pepper Sauce
2 pinches of dried chilli flakes
1 cup panko crumbs or coarse homemade breadcrumbs
sea salt and freshly ground black pepper

Step 3: To Cook and Serve
2 handfuls rocket (if large rip into smallish pieces)
vinaigrette (see recipe on page 315)
600g scampi tails, removed from their shells and de-veined
sea salt and freshly ground black pepper
cooking oil for frying
lemon wedges to serve

Seared Scampi Tails with White Bean Purée, Rocket & Crisp Chilli Breadcrumbs

Serves 6 as an entrée

To me, New Zealand scampi is the Rolls-Royce of all crustaceans to come out of our surrounding oceans. It's a relative newcomer to this country, with quota only being established in the past 15 years or so. A great deal of this valuable seafood is being exported. However, we are now beginning to see scampi become more available in our larger cities' premium fish markets and delis, and gracing the tables of high-end restaurants. Scampi are caught all around New Zealand at depths of 200–750 metres using specialised deep-water trawls and are all immediately frozen at sea. They fetch a premium price and are graded upon size. The most economic way to buy this delicacy is to purchase the tails only, unless of course you are looking for the whole 'presentation deal'. However, be warned: you will be paying for looks only, as the head and long extended claws contain little or no edible flesh.

This is a terrific dish, with lots of flavours and textures going on. If scampi are lean on the ground, by all means substitute other crustaceans, shellfish or fish fillets. The crisp chilli breadcrumbs are a great garnish and give a nice texture and kick to any dish.

Step 1: White Bean Purée

In a medium saucepan place the olive oil, shallots and garlic. Place on low heat and sweat for 30 minutes before adding the beans, stock, cream and lemon juice. Turn up the heat a little and cook for 10 minutes, stirring occasionally, until the liquid has reduced by half.

Remove from the heat and pour half the mixture into a liquidiser or food processor (pour the rest into a mixing bowl). Process until the purée is silky smooth, then add this to the rest of the bean mixture. Taste and season accordingly with sea salt and black pepper. Refrigerate until required.

Step 2: Crisp Chilli Breadcrumbs

Preheat the oven to 150°C.

Place a medium saucepan on medium heat. Add the butter and, once melted, add the lemon zest, cumin, paprika, Tabasco Chipotle Pepper Sauce and chilli flakes. Stir to combine then add the breadcrumbs, salt and pepper, and mix together with a wooden spoon.

Remove from the heat, place on an oven tray and put in the oven. Cook for 5 minutes or so until the breadcrumbs are golden and crisp. Cool on the tray then place in an airtight container.

Step 3: To Cook and Serve

Reheat the bean purée in the microwave or in a small saucepan over low heat, stirring occasionally.

Dress the rocket with a little vinaigrette.

Heat a skillet or sauté pan to high heat. Season the scampi with sea salt and black pepper. Add a little cooking oil to the pan and sauté the scampi in a couple of batches over high heat for no more than 45 seconds on each side. Remove and keep warm while you cook the second batch.

To serve, divide the purée out onto 6 warm plates. Add a little rocket on each serving then top with the sautéed scampi. Sprinkle the crisp chilli breadcrumbs over and garnish with a wedge of lemon. Serve now!

The easiest way to remove the tail shell off scampi is to take some small scissors and cut two incisions — one along the length of the top of the tail and then turn over and make an incision the length of the underside of the tail. The shell will pull away from the flesh with ease. Remember to remove the 'excretion tube', which runs just under the skin on the top of the tail, before cooking, just like with shrimp.

Step 1: Caramelised Nuoc Cham Dressing
1 x nuoc cham dipping sauce (see recipe on page 314)
½ cup sugar
2 tablespoons water

Step 2: Thai-Style Peanut Salad
250g mung bean sprouts
250g snow peas, very finely sliced
150g carrots, peeled
250g cucumber, peeled
75g red onion, very finely sliced
2 tablespoons grated or finely chopped fresh lemongrass
⅓ cup roughly chopped fresh mint leaves
⅓ cup roughly chopped fresh basil leaves
¾ cup coriander leaves (left whole)
2½ cups freshly roasted unsalted peanuts, finely ground

Step 3: To Cook and Serve
600g peeled scampi tails, excretion tube removed
sea salt and freshly ground black pepper
cooking oil
1 cup roasted unsalted peanuts, roughly chopped
lime wedges to serve

Seared Scampi with Thai-Style Peanut Salad & Caramelised Nuoc Cham Dressing

Serves 6 lunch or brunch

This is my wife Lizzie's favourite salad. She adores good Thai and Vietnamese food and this dish ticks all the boxes — fresh, sharp flavours and great crunchy textures with that slightly sour, salty and sweet combination going on. Scampi works a treat, and crayfish or crab would be my next port of call. There's a fair bit of preparation in this recipe, but it's all fairly simple and much of it you could prepare over a couple of days, then bring it all together and finish it off just before serving. You want fine julienne vegetables in the salad. Use a mandolin vegetable slicer if you have one for the carrot and cucumber; otherwise, use your sharpest and thinnest knife to cut into thin matchsticks.

Step 1: Caramelised Nuoc Cham Dressing

Make the nuoc cham dipping sauce and reserve.

Place the sugar and water in a heavy-based saucepan on high heat. Watch over the saucepan, stirring ever so slightly so it cooks evenly as it starts to colour. As soon as it reaches a rich darkish caramel, remove from the heat and pour in the nuoc cham. Be mindful that it will bubble up as this is added. Return the pan to the heat and turn down low. Stir until all the caramel has dissolved. Pour into a container, cool and refrigerate until required.

Step 2: Thai-Style Peanut Salad

I like to top and tail the bean sprouts because this gets rid of the slightly bitter top and soft, string-like tail. It's a bit laborious and don't worry if you don't have the time; however, it's the middle of the bean sprout that has all the crunch. Place the bean sprouts in a large mixing bowl with the snow peas. Slice the carrots and cucumber into short, thin strips with a mandolin vegetable slicer if you have one or, with your sharpest and thinnest knife, cut into thin matchsticks. Add to the bowl with the remaining ingredients.

With clean hands, lightly mix all the salad components together, then refrigerate until required.

To get a fine grating of lemongrass, peel off the tough outer leaves and discard. Take up to the first 8cm or so of the inner stalk, roughly chop with a fine knife, then process the pieces in a spice or coffee grinder. It will come out beautifully fine — perfect for this sort of application.

Step 3: To Cook and Serve

Bring the scampi to room temperature, then season with a little sea salt and black pepper. Place a large skillet or sauté pan on high heat. Once hot, add a little cooking oil, then sauté half the scampi at a time for no longer than 30 seconds on each side. They should be just cooked in the centre. Remove and keep warm while you cook the rest.

For the salad, add between a quarter and half of the caramelised nuoc cham dressing. Mix through, then taste. Add more dressing if desired.

To serve, I like to spread the salad out on a platter, then top with the scampi and scatter the chopped nuts over. Serve the lime wedges in a bowl on the side. Of course, you can plate the dish individually if you prefer.

hard of herring

When Less and Sometimes Little, is More . . .

ONE OF THE TERRIFIC THINGS ABOUT COOKING FOR A LIVELIHOOD IS THAT THE LEARNING CURVE REALLY HAS NO END. IT'S NOT OFTEN A DAY PASSES, WHEN I'M NOT LEARNING A NEW TECHNIQUE, A NEW FLAVOUR COMBINATION, OR A DIFFERENT STYLE OR METHOD OF COOKING.

We are bombarded on a daily basis with cooking information. With a proliferation of cookbooks, newspaper articles and magazines, live demonstrations, not to mention the 24-hour Food Channel, which seems to have gained a widespread and slightly addictive cult-like status. I'm not complaining; in fact, I love it all, as, even though I've seen a lot of it thousands of times before, or perhaps a certain dish or recipe makes me cringe, I do still continually pick up bits and pieces to add to my repertoire.

For the past 10 years, we have been buying fresh fruit and vegetables for our restaurant, Logan Brown, from a surprisingly small and somewhat modest produce shop called Cuba Fruit Mart, owned by an extended Indian family since some time in the 1950s. The Dayals have become not only our favourite purveyors, through providing extraordinary service and first-class produce, but also wonderful friends. Every Tuesday and Thursday, I (along with a number of other Cuba Street business owners) have had the pleasure, and may I say the

privilege, to sit out the back of their fruit shop among the banana boxes and enjoy either a pot of Lakhu's chicken curry or Puspa's dhal with fresh homemade roti. I have always regarded it as a precious part of my week — a chance to sit down around a single pot of the most delicious food imaginable, with friends and their family, hearing the latest gossip on the street, as well as sharing stories, while learning wonderful snippets about their lives and culture.

They are a family who love to fish and equally love to cook. Sanjay, who, along with his sister Joshna, has moved through the ranks to run the business now, is as passionate a fisherman as you will ever meet. I doubt there has ever been a day that we have come in contact when the conversation hasn't quickly turned to fishing or gathering of some sort or other. People the length and breadth of Cuba Street hear in an instant if Sanjay has caught a snapper in the harbour (a rarity, I have to say) or a legal-sized blue cod around Scorching Bay. Sanjay and his family don't own a boat or even a dinghy; however, they consume

freshly caught seafood provided by many of the family members week to week. Fresh herring (or more correctly, yellow-eyed mullet), paddle crabs, mackerel and garfish (piper) all regularly make a showing on their dinner table.

When I am lucky enough to hear that Puspa is cooking up her now-famous curried crab and I get the nod, it's not just a bite to eat, it's a treasured experience. Extended family congregate outside around simple tables pulled together. It always feels like a celebration, with bowls of basmati rice, a large saucepan of the curry containing quartered and halved crab frames, various pickles, chutneys, fresh coriander, lemons and limes.

It's a lengthy sit-down, with no stress, no rush, just the simplicity of family and friends spending quality time slowly eating half the afternoon away. What pure pleasure it is, working for each morsel of crab you devour through sucking the cavities, crunching the legs, or smashing the claws. In fact, anything goes in the pursuit of this sweet delicacy. The same goes with garam masala-spiced herrings or smoked mackerel. It's so tactile and, besides the odd fork and spoon to help, it's all about eating with your hands. As mentioned, there is never any hurry and, as I have learned over the years, if it means slowing down and spending more time around the table with friends and loved ones, I'm all for it.

In other parts of the world, many of the above-mentioned species are considered delicacies, while here in New Zealand most Kiwis would describe them as good bait.

I have also been guilty in the past of thinking exactly that, as they always seemed in the too-hard basket — too small, too many bones, takes too long to get a feed and so on.

What puts most New Zealanders off these fish is the dreaded fear of the little bones. Now, sure, there is definitely an issue there, but instead of writing these smaller fish off for that reason alone, keep an open mind, as once you get the hang of extracting the wonderful sweet flesh from these delicious small fish you will soon forget what all the fuss was about.

Any protein cooked with or on the bone will have considerably more flavor than when cooked without. For a simple example, next time you are buying, say,

some boneless groper fillet, ask your fishmonger to add a groper steak as well. Cook both together and taste the difference. Not only will the flavour be more pronounced, but the flesh will be moister. And when eating fish cooked whole or containing bones, be it a large specimen or a couple of dozen herring, the act of sitting down and eating takes longer, which is far more satisfying and civilised.

As luck would have it, through my relationship with the Dayals, I have been introduced to these incredible yet overlooked delicacies that are on our doorstep in abundance, just a local wharf away.

More than One Fish in the Sea?

THERE WILL ALWAYS BE DEBATE ABOUT WHAT'S THE MOST PRIZED FISH TO CATCH OR EAT. IF YOU DIG DEEP ENOUGH, PEOPLE'S FAVOURITES, WHETHER FOR EATING OR CATCHING, ARE MOST OFTEN DIRECTLY RELATED TO WHERE THEY WERE BROUGHT UP OR LIVE TODAY.

In Auckland it's snapper, in Dunedin it's blue cod, and turbot for those on the West Coast and so on. It's brilliant, isn't it? There's no winner. Some fight better, some eat better, but all in all if you fish with the right tackle and learn to cook your variety of fish correctly it's a wonderful marriage. My favourite fish to eat is, of course, fresh Wellington or Wairarapa groper. However, as a fish to catch, well, they fall considerably down the scale. With big gear, in deep water, it's like hauling up a cray pot from a depth of 100 metres. It must have been a blast 60–70 years ago when they were more plentiful and you could catch them in the shallows. Alas, no more!

We are so lucky to be surrounded with such a wonderful resource of fantastic fighting and, just as important, wonderful eating fish. Yes, we are creatures of habit, but isn't it time we started identifying, understanding and, more importantly, enjoying some of the other 200-odd varieties?

I have been lucky enough with my job to travel quite extensively over the past decade. I try to make a point of visiting local fish markets to see what is on offer and also try as much seafood on restaurant menus as possible, for comparison. I was in Spain recently and visited a number of fresh fish markets. The first thing that was glaringly obvious was the size of 'wild caught' fish available. If you were to place a regular-sized legal blue cod in the middle of one of these markets, it would stand out like dog balls! All the species on offer, besides farmed, were extremely small and I found it pretty disconcerting. As seems to happen to me so often these days, the words of one of our lesser known New Zealand philosophers, Professor F. Dagg, came flooding into my head: you don't know how lucky you are, mate! Never was a truer word spoken.

So how do we break this pointless cycle? Actually, I think it's pretty easy and you may find it quite liberating. When you next venture out for a fish, keep a species you have caught that you haven't eaten before or, likewise, next time you're at your local fishmonger, take the time to have a chat with him or her about an interesting species in front of you. Ask whether it would work for the cooking method you have in mind, or how they would suggest cooking it. There are only upsides to this. Not only are you going to learn something about another variety of fish, but it will also be the start of a wonderful new relationship with your fishmonger. In fact, the same goes when buying any fresh produce. Speak up, engage in conversation — it makes shopping and cooking so much more enjoyable when there is a personality behind the product. I believe that, besides the obvious wonderful fresh produce, there lies the success and popularity of farmers' markets the world over — that is, the relationships between consumers and producers.

Part of the problem for Kiwis is that, because we have always had large resources of our most popular species and on the whole they all produce large white fillets with minimal bones, we have never really felt the need to try something new. Well, the news isn't all bad, but those resources are definitely on the decline and if you hadn't noticed, the price of those pearly white boneless fillets is beginning to sky-rocket. All the more reason then, to embrace these equally wonderful and plentiful, not to mention cheaper, fish varieties.

I recall one of the practical exams I sat while completing my culinary arts degree in Vermont in the United States more than 20 years ago. This exam was called the 'magic box'. We seven budding young cooks were all given a closed cardboard box produced from the walk-in chiller. No contents of each box was alike. We had a couple of hours to produce three courses: an entrée, a main and a dessert.

It was nerve-racking enough being in that pressure situation, let alone opening your box to see a small skate sitting on ice as one of your main ingredients. I went into a bit of a decline for the first 10 minutes; for a start I didn't even know you could eat skate, let alone how to fillet one. After getting over my initial shock and slight anger as I saw other students unpacking pre-filleted sea bass, red snapper and, if I recall correctly, the guy next to me had a pound of prawns to deal with, I was a little vexed to say the least. Anyhow, I set to with my sharpest knife and bumbled my way through, not making

a complete hash of removing and skinning the fillets of this unpopular-looking fish.

The two hours shot by at lightning speed and before I knew it, I was plating 'sautéed skate wing on citrus-braised fennel bulb' as my main course. Chef Sam, our tutor, didn't give away much, as with this guy compliments were very few and far between. I can still see him raising the first forkful to his mouth, momentarily closing his eyes while deciphering the flavours and textures, before putting the cutlery down and mumbling, what I was later to learn, his highest flattery: 'It's nearly good'.

I came top in the class for that practical exam and, if I'm true to myself, it was quite a profound moment, not only in my cooking career, but also because I suddenly held a wider respect for fish in general. If skate tasted so good, then what about all the other dozens of species that I had been constantly overlooking in all my years?

So, from that point on, it has been a personal crusade to embrace and understand all the edible fish that come out of the

ocean. There's no question, some do eat better than others. However, there are so many varieties that we seem to overlook.

I've seen people standing in front of a fish counter with shopping lists in hand, completely despairing when they realise there is no tarakihi available. There may be seven or eight other fresh varieties glistening before them, but they only eat tarakihi or that's the variety the recipe calls for. Excuse me if I offend anyone, but this sort of situation is simply ridiculous. All fish have an alternative that exhibits similar qualities. For instance, if there is no tarakihi, then there's a good chance your fishmonger may suggest porae or perhaps gurnard. Both will work equally as well as tarakihi in any recipe.

Until people are prepared to try the other species, we will be stuck in this cycle of eating the same fish time and time again. By choosing another species, you are broadening your culinary horizons and also in a small and meaningful way taking a little pressure off the more overfished popular varieties.

Until people are prepared to try the other species, we will be stuck in this cycle of eating the same fish time and time again.

Shellfish

Shellfish

There are many reasons why I rate shellfish as my hands-down favourite of all the edible treasures given up by our surrounding shores and oceans. As with our fin fish, Aotearoa has had a splendid variety bestowed on it — from our humble pipi and clams to exquisite and world-class delicacies like scallops, oysters, paua and kina. We are most fortunate.

Apart from the obvious pleasure derived from eating our delicious shellfish, for me a huge part of the enjoyment lies in the ritual of gathering these wonderful treats.

So often it's a family or whanau occasion where young and old are side by side at low tide, snorkelling off a reef or doing the 'tuatua twist' between the perpetual breakers.

What I love is the thrill of the anticipation as you head down the beach with onion sack in hand, and the sense of togetherness as all involved are providing for the pot. It's a perfect occasion to educate the young ones about how lucky we are to have these precious resources and how we should only take the legal size and number.

Once again, with all preparation

of shellfish, it is paramount not to overcook these delicacies. Whether raw or put to the heat, the uniqueness of many shellfish lies in their ability to retain the delicious taste or burst of the ocean when devoured.

And let's not forget how remarkably tactile the shells are that house these morsels of good taste, each so beautifully crafted by nature and unique in their individual form. We collect them, we paint them, we make art and jewellery with them and, from year to year, fill our baches and cribs with them.

1. Grip the hood of the squid with your thumb and use your other hand to gently extract the head and the insides.

2. Head, tentacles and tube.

3. Slice off the tough wings at the narrow end of the body. Discard.

4. Remove the plastic-like spine that runs the length of the tube.

5. Split the body lengthwise and, with the back of your knife, scrape out any remaining insides.

6. Trim a 1cm-wide strip off the top of the squid tube where the two small knobs appear. Discard.

7. Remove the outside layer of skin by scraping with the back of your knife.

8. With a sharp knife, score the inside of the tube on the diagonal to form a diamond pattern.

9. Portion into pieces.

10. Cut off the tentacles where they join the head.

11. Cut the suckers off with a knife or scissors, or rub off if the squid is young.

12. Plate of prepared squid.

Step 1: White Bean Skordalia
480g (2 x 240g tins) cooked white beans
⅔ cup ground almonds
¾ tablespoon roughly chopped garlic
3 tablespoons lemon juice
⅓ cup olive oil
salt and freshly ground black pepper

Step 2: Roasted Red Capsicum Vinaigrette
2 roasted red capsicums, peeled, seeded and finely diced
6 (60g) shallots, finely diced
100ml cabernet vinegar
50ml red wine vinegar
1¼ cup olive oil
salt and freshly ground black pepper

Step 3: To Prepare the Squid
3 whole large squid

Step 4: To Cook and Serve
700g chorizo, cut into medium slices on the diagonal
oil for brushing
1 bag mizuna lettuce or similar
1 cup roughly chopped basil
sea salt and freshly ground black pepper

Chargrilled Squid with White Bean Skordalia, Chorizo & Roasted Red Capsicum Vinaigrette

Serves 6–8 as an entrée

This is a full-flavoured dish that we have served in many variations at Logan Brown. Because the squid is textural, with minimal flavour, it takes on the piquancy of the spicy sausage, vinaigrette and garlic in the white bean skordalia. Skordalia is a coarse Greek purée traditionally made with potatoes, olive oil, garlic and lemon juice, with the occasional addition of ground nuts, such as walnuts and almonds. The same components work equally well with white beans, and tinned varieties, such as haricots, work beautifully and can be knocked up in a matter of minutes. It's terrific served just as a dip also.

For tender results cook squid either very quickly or very slowly.

Step 1: White Bean Skordalia
Drain the beans from the brine and give them a quick rinse in a sieve under cold running water. Place in a food processor with the blade attachment fitted. Add the almonds, garlic, lemon juice and olive oil. Purée until smooth.

Taste and if you want the garlic flavour to be a little more pronounced, add a little more (though the garlic flavour will intensify as it sits). Season with salt and pepper to taste.

Transfer to a bowl, cover with plastic wrap and refrigerate until required.

Step 2: Roasted Red Capsicum Vinaigrette
In a mixing bowl, place the red capsicums, shallots and both vinegars. Stir together, then drizzle in the olive oil while whisking continuously. Season with salt and pepper to taste. Refrigerate until required.

Note: This vinaigrette needs a quick whisk to bring it all together just before serving.

Step 3: To Prepare the Squid
Refer to How to Deal to a Fresh Squid on page 79.

Step 4: To Cook and Serve

Put the chargrill on to heat.

Put a dollop of the skordalia in the centre of each plate. Spread it out slightly with the back of a spoon. Roughly cover the skordalia with a few mizuna leaves.

Chargrill the chorizo, then remove and keep warm.

Lightly oil the squid and, making sure your grill is very hot, cook the squid portions for no more than 1–2 minutes to prevent it becoming tough.

Top the skordalia with the squid and chorizo, then sprinkle the basil over. Give the vinaigrette a quick stir or whisk, then spoon some over each serving.

A grind of fresh black pepper and pinch of sea salt to finish. Serve now!

Step 1: Wasabi Mayonnaise
1 cup Al's mayonnaise (see recipe on page 302)
1 tablespoon (or more to your liking) fresh or regular wasabi paste

Step 2: To Prepare the Squid
3 large whole squid (preferably fresh)

Step 3: Crumbing Mix
½ cup fine polenta or cornmeal
½ cup tempura flour or cornflour
½ tablespoon salt
½ tablespoon freshly ground black pepper
1 teaspoon turmeric powder

Step 4: To Cook and Serve
1 litre cooking oil
lemons or limes to serve
sea salt and freshly ground black pepper

Crisp Squid with Wasabi Mayonnaise

Serves 6 as a pass-around

Various versions of deep-fried squid are served throughout the world in any number of cuisines. I haven't met many people who don't like fried squid in some shape or form, and if I see it on a menu I always order it as a plate to share on the table while we decide what we are going to eat. Generally, fried squid, or calamari, is quite neutral to taste, but what appeals to me is its slightly chewy and crunchy texture when coated and deep-fried. It's what is served alongside that gives it the flavour. Use fresh wasabi paste if available, or the powdered Japanese green paste.

Step 1: Wasabi Mayonnaise
In a bowl mix the ingredients thoroughly, then refrigerate until required.

Step 2: To Prepare the Squid
Refer to How to Deal to a Fresh Squid on pages XX.

Step 3: Crumbing Mix
In a bowl mix all the ingredients together until well combined. Keep in an airtight container until required.

Step 4: To Cook and Serve
Pour the oil into a high-sided saucepan and place on medium heat. The oil is ready for frying when you drop a piece of bread in it and it cooks to golden and crisp in a minute or so (about 180°C).

Place about a dozen squid portions in a sieve over a large bowl. Pour some of the crumbing mix over and shake and work through to dust each piece with a thin coating. Place in the hot oil and cook for about a minute until golden. Remove with a slotted spoon and drain on paper towels. Repeat until finished. Strain off the oil and keep for deep frying in the future.

Place the fried squid on a platter with a bowl of the wasabi mayo alongside. Give the squid a good squeeze of lemon or lime, season with salt and pepper and watch it get devoured!

When adding something like wasabi, Tabasco, spice or even salt and pepper to a dish, always add a little at a time and taste as you go. You can always add more, but it's near impossible to remove!

¼–½ cup kina roe
4 eggs
¼ cup cream
salt and freshly ground black
    pepper to taste
fresh tarragon and parsley, finely
    chopped
favourite toast bread

1 tablespoon butter
grated Parmesan
squeeze of lemon

Fresh Kina Scrambled Eggs On Toast

Serves 2

There's something incredibly invigorating about going for a dive at first light. Aside from the pronounced beauty of it all as the sun reveals itself, it also gives me the feeling of having first dibs on what the ocean has on offer after a night of it being left alone.

The one delicacy I will have firmly set my sights on above all will be kina, our New Zealand native sea urchin. The recipe that follows is my favourite breakfast after a morning dive. It's also a great way to introduce people to the flavour of kina if they find it difficult to contemplate the prospect of eating them raw.

Method

The measurements for this dish are relatively random. These quantities would typically feed a couple of people. You can add more or less kina roe as you please. In a bowl, place the fresh kina roe, eggs, cream, and some salt and pepper. Using a wand blender or similar, whisk until smooth. If you have some fresh tarragon add a couple of leaves, along with some parsley.

Start cooking your toast and place a suitable saucepan on medium heat. Add the butter and, once melted, pour in the egg mixture. Constantly stir using a spatula or wooden spoon, to prevent sticking.

Once it's reached your desired doneness (I enjoy mine still slightly wet), spoon onto freshly buttered toast.

A little grated fresh Parmesan works a treat and a healthy squeeze of lemon juice makes this breakfast dish perfect!

Kina are in their prime state for eating from August to January. There are more than 500 species of sea urchins throughout the world, with many considered delicacies in any number of cuisines.

Step 1: Fresh Kina and Crab Pâté
1 cup cream
20 tarragon leaves, finely
chopped
1½ tablespoons lemon zest,
finely chopped
⅓ cup fresh kina roe

2 egg yolks
few drops Tabasco
sea salt and freshly ground black
pepper
⅓–½ cup crab meat

Step 2: To Serve
crostini, bruschetta, crackers or
the like
salsa or sharp pickle of some
sort
lemon for squeezing
sea salt and freshly ground
black pepper

Fresh Kina & Crab Pâté

Makes 1 large or 2 smaller ramekins of pâté

I came up with this delicious, rich combination after diving one day in less than suitable conditions. The visibility was shocking, so I was restricted to the shallows where I fossicked around and managed to pick up a couple of kina and some good-sized red rock crabs. It was through the necessity of having to think about how to stretch my somewhat meagre haul that I decided to make what is basically a savoury custard or brulée. With cream and egg yolks added to the relatively rich kina and crab, you'll see what I mean when I say a little goes a long way. Perfect on crostini, with a squeeze of lemon juice, or try serving a little salsa verde (see recipe on page 317) on top, as they need something with a little sharpness to cut through and balance the richness of the pâté. Alternatively, serve alongside simple crackers.

Step 1: Fresh Kina and Crab Pâté

Preheat the oven to 100°C.

In a small saucepan place the cream, tarragon and lemon zest. Place over low heat and steep for 15 minutes, being careful not to boil.

Meanwhile, purée the kina roe and egg yolks with a wand blender or in a food processor. Pour into a mixing bowl.

Pass the hot cream through a fine sieve, discarding the tarragon and zest.

With a whisk, slowly blend the warm cream into the kina and yolk mix. Whisk in Tabasco to suit your taste and season with a good amount of sea salt and pepper. Stir in the crab meat.

Carefully pour the mixture into 1 large or 2 smaller ramekins, making sure the crab meat is evenly distributed. Place in an ovenproof dish with high sides, then pour in hot water to halfway up the sides of the ramekins. Cover the whole dish with tinfoil and place in the oven.

Check after 20 minutes, then at 5-minute intervals. Remove from the oven when the pâté is mostly set, but still slightly nervous in the centre. Cool on the bench for 30 minutes before refrigerating.

Step 2: To Serve

Serve the pâté spread on crostini or similar, top with a little salsa or sharp pickle of your choice, and add a squeeze of lemon juice, and some sea salt and pepper. Or just serve in the ramekin with a pâté knife alongside for people to help themselves.

Kina is sought after for its delicate, smooth, buttery roe. Kina are both male and female. The male roe is referred to as gonads and is slightly silkier, whereas the female roe is a little more grainy in texture.

Step 1: Mussel and Bacon Fritter Mix
150g rindless bacon
cooking oil for frying
450g cooked mussel meat (from about 2.5kg live in the shell)
⅓ cup finely diced red onion
finely minced zest of 1 lemon
1½ tablespoons lemon juice
¼ cup roughly chopped fresh basil leaves
¼ cup roughly chopped fresh parsley
1 teaspoon sugar
1 cup fritter batter (see recipe on page 314)
sea salt and freshly ground black pepper

Step 2: To Cook and Serve
3 egg whites
cooking oil
lemons to serve

Mussel & Bacon Fritters

Makes 30-odd canapé-size fritters

Lamb, sauvignon blanc and Greenshell mussels would probably be the three most-recognised products to be directly associated with New Zealand by people from other countries. Our Greenshell mussel industry has been built from very humble beginnings into what is now a complete success story as an export earner and a recognised leader in the traditionally fickle world of aquaculture. We are so lucky to have this delicacy fresh, alive and available on a daily basis. I think sometimes that we are guilty of overlooking the modest mussel in favour of other shellfish. And then when I pick some up and cook them in the shell or throw them under the grill with a topping or two, I am constantly blown away by their flavour, texture and juiciness. We do love our fritters in New Zealand and these, with the addition of a little bacon, work a treat.

Step 1: Mussel and Bacon Fritter mix

Fry the bacon in a pan with a little oil until slightly crisp. Remove from the pan, chop into a small dice and place in a mixing bowl.

Place half the mussel meat in a food processor and process until quite finely minced. Add this to the bowl. Roughly chop the rest of the mussel meat into a fine dice. Add to the bowl along with the red onion, lemon zest and juice, basil leaves, parsley and sugar, and season with the sea salt and pepper.

Mix all together, then fold in the cup of fritter batter. Cook a little of the fritter mix to check the consistency and seasoning, as mentioned above. Refrigerate until required.

Step 2: To Cook and Serve

Take the bowl of fritter mix out of the fridge. In a clean bowl, whisk the egg whites until firm. Fold half the egg whites into the fritter mix, then fold in the second half. Heat a skillet or griddle top on the barbecue to medium heat. Add a little cooking oil to the surface, then spoon out small amounts of fritter batter. Cook for a couple of minutes on each side until golden. Place on a platter, give them a good squeeze of lemon juice then serve.

Note: For brunch or breakfast cook larger fritters and serve with hollandaise sauce (see page 313) or a couple of eggs.

When making fritters the key is to get them to hold together without being too doughy. Always add just some of the batter, then cook a small fritter to see how well it stays together. If it's falling apart add a little more batter and cook another one. It's also a good time to check the seasoning of the fritter.

48 medium live Greenshell
 mussels
1 tablespoon finely chopped
 garlic
1½ cups finely chopped leeks
¾ cup finely diced celery

½ cup finely diced shallots
3 tablespoons finely chopped
 fresh tarragon
1 cup sauvignon blanc or similar
2 cups chicken stock (see recipe
 on page 319)

1½ cups cream
¼ cup finely chopped fresh
 parsley
sea salt and freshly ground black
 pepper

Greenshell Mussels with Leeks, Fresh Tarragon & Cream

Serves 6

This is a pretty classic way to prepare fresh mussels. It's super simple to make, producing not only succulent and delicious mussels, but equally wonderful is the soup created from the mussels' natural briny liquid. By all means experiment with different combinations of herbs and spices, and even if all you have is a little white wine, garlic and parsley, the results are always going to be first rate. Hot crusty bread from the oven is a must to serve alongside this, as there's plenty of dipping to be done. Omit the cream if you want to be heart healthy.

Method

Give the mussels a quick scrub and pull out the hairy beard exposed between the closed shells. Place the mussels in a large saucepan and add the garlic, leeks, celery, shallots and tarragon. Pour in the wine and stock, then stir to combine. Cover with a lid and place on high heat.

Cook for 5 minutes then give the saucepan a good shake. Place back on the heat and check after a couple of minutes. The mussels are cooked when they have all opened. Discard any that fail to open.

Using tongs or a slotted spoon, divide the mussels into warm bowls. Place the cooking liquid back on the heat and add the cream and parsley. Bring up to a simmer, taste and season accordingly with sea salt and black pepper. Ladle the soup over the mussels and serve.

New Zealand Greenshell mussels are farmed in three parts of New Zealand: the Marlborough Sounds, Coromandel Peninsula and Stewart Island. The total value of exports in 2008 was NZ$204 million.

Step 1: Arrabiata Sauce
⅓ cup olive oil
2 tablespoons minced fresh
   garlic
½ teaspoon chilli flakes
½ cup port

½ cup red wine
2 x 400g tins whole peeled
   tomatoes, blitzed to a purée
2 tablespoons tomato paste
1 tablespoon sugar
25g butter

sea salt and freshly ground black
   pepper

Step 2: To Cook and Serve
60 live mussels
2 cups white wine or water

400g aged cheddar or similar,
   grated
½ cup roughly chopped fresh
   parsley

Oven-Grilled Greenshell Mussels with Arrabiata Sauce & Aged Cheddar

Makes 60

Grilling mussels is such a wonderful way to eat this iconic New Zealand shellfish. Again, the combinations are pretty much limitless. Garlic, butter and leafy summer herbs always work a treat. Pork products such as bacon, prosciutto and spicy salami all partner up with our humble mussel beautifully.

Arrabiata sauce is a spicy tomato and toasted garlic sauce made with a good amount of red wine and port. It works beautifully matched with good-quality sharp aged cheddar. Cooking mussels this way also works well when entertaining, as everything is set up ahead of time and it's just a case of cooking them under the grill and serving.

Step 1: Arrabiata Sauce

Place the oil in a medium heavy-based saucepan on moderate heat. Add the garlic and chilli flakes, and stir continuously with a wooden spoon, watching the garlic start to change colour. Once the garlic takes on a nice dark-golden colour, immediately add the port and red wine. Be mindful that as you add the alcohol it will spit and bubble for a few seconds.

Simmer the wine for 5 minutes, then add the tomatoes, tomato paste and sugar. Reduce the heat and simmer for another 15–20 minutes until nice and thick. Remove from the heat, whisk in the butter, then taste and season accordingly. Cool to room temperature, then refrigerate until required.

Step 2: To Cook and Serve

Scrub the mussels and pull out the hairy beard exposed between the tightly closed shells. Place the mussels in a large saucepan and add the wine, or water if you prefer. Cover and place on high heat. The mussels are cooked once they all open up. Discard any that fail to open.

Strain the mussels through a colander (reserve the cooking liquor for another use), then spread on a tray to cool. Once cold, remove the top half of each shell and discard. Next, carefully prise away each cooked mussel from the white cartilage, place back in the belly of the shell, then lay them all out on a dish or tray.

Spoon a good amount of the arrabiata sauce over each mussel. Top with liberal amounts of grated cheese. Refrigerate until ready to cook.

To cook and serve, preheat the oven grill. Place the mussels on an oven tray, then place under the grill. Cook for 2–3 minutes until the cheese is melted and slightly golden. Remove the tray from the oven and arrange the mussels on a platter. Sprinkle with parsley and serve to your delighted guests!

When browning the garlic in the method, you will mellow out a lot of the astringent garlic flavour and add a terrific toasted character to any dish.

The 'Bluffie'

CHILLED AND SHUCKED ALIVE, A FRESH BLUFF OYSTER, I CAN CATEGORICALLY STATE, IS MY FAVORITE SEAFOOD!

I consider myself to be one of the lucky ones to have experienced a day out on Foveaux Strait, trawling for 'Bluffies'. It was a year or so ago, but that memory will be etched in my mind forever. It was a 4am start on an old trawler with the crew who worked her, all probably 60-plus. The sight of the sun rising over the strait revealing the snow-capped mountains of Stewart Island in the distance was remarkable.

However, getting to shuck and consume a fresh Bluff oyster moments out of the freezing cold ocean, to taste this 'holy grail' of seafood then and there was, for me, quite an extraordinary moment. As far as oysters go — and believe me I have eaten dozens and dozens of varieties from all around the world — I have yet to experience a variety that packs the punch of a freshly shucked live Bluff oyster.

I say 'live' as it's still hard to fathom that probably 98 per cent get shucked at the source and tossed into plastic pottles before being shipped throughout the country.

They still taste delicious a couple of days after being shucked, but in my opinion start to lose most of their uniqueness from that point on. I am still to get to the bottom of why more aren't shipped live in their shells. It's not as if they need to be air-freighted as oysters are a sturdy shellfish and, looked after and kept in the right conditions, can last easily six or seven days.

If the rest of the world can do it with their oysters, I can't figure out why we can't. I'm picking it's how they have always dealt with them down in that beautiful part of the country and if it 'ain't broke' there's nothing to fix! However, I have a feeling that as more and more farmed oysters start hitting the market live and in their shells, someone will realise the opportunity and the premium position that is just waiting to happen. I have to say a freshly shucked live oyster complete with all its liquor is twice as good as any 'fresh' day-old dead oyster.

HOW TO: | Shuck an Oyster

1. Place the oyster on a non-slip surface, cupped side down.

2. Insert the oyster knife in next to the hinge and twist the blade.

3. Run the knife around the edge of the shell to cut the muscle that holds the two shells together.

4. Remove the top shell.

5. Run the knife under the oyster to release.

Step 1: Oyster and Sherry Soup Base
50g butter
½ cup minced shallots
pinch of dried chilli flakes (or to your taste)
1 tablespoon minced fresh thyme leaves
1½ tablespoons flour

½ cup medium-dry sherry
juice drained from 2 dozen oysters
2 cups cream
2 cups whole milk

Step 2: To Cook and Serve
1 cup 1cm-diced cooked potato
4 cups spinach, washed and cut into thin strips
24 fresh oysters, halved
pinch of sea salt
¼ cup finely chopped chives
freshly ground black pepper
extra sherry (optional)

Fresh Oyster & Sherry Soup

Serves 6

This soup is based on what is typically called 'oyster stew'. It's traditionally served in restaurants up and down the entire eastern seaboard of the United States. A 'must do' in New York City is to visit the legendary Grand Central Oyster Bar that was established in 1913 in Grand Central Station. Here, you can sample a huge array of fresh oysters at one of the many bars in this large restaurant located below sea level. The oyster stew is made to order right in front of your eyes in wonderful old gas kettles. The following recipe is simple to make and ludicrously rich, which is why I only serve it in small portions. It's a delicious way to start a winter meal, with the combination of sherry, cream and fresh oysters being so wonderful and satisfying. I also like to serve it in little espresso cups or similar as a pass-around when entertaining. No 'heart tick' on this one, I'm afraid.

Step 1: Oyster and Sherry Soup Base
In a medium saucepan, place the butter, shallots, chilli flakes and thyme. Place on low heat and sweat for 15 minutes until the shallots are soft but not coloured.

Sprinkle in the flour and stir to combine, followed by the sherry and the oyster juice. Whisk until smooth and cook for 5 minutes, then add the cream and milk. Keep the heat on low and simmer for 10 minutes. Do not boil.

Remove from the heat, cool and refrigerate if not using immediately.

Step 2: To Cook and Serve
Pour the soup base into a large saucepan and place on low heat. Bring to a simmer, then add the potato and spinach. Allow the potato to warm through before adding the oysters. Cook the oysters for no longer than a minute. Taste and add a pinch of salt if required.

Serve in warm bowls, then top each with the chives, a good grind of black pepper, and if you're like me, a small splash of sherry to finish. Serve quick smart!

When cooking shellfish such as clams and mussels in white wine, always freeze any of the briny juices they give up that may be used to make soups, chowders and the like.

Step 1 Chardonnay Vinegar and Chilli Jelly
½ cup chardonnay vinegar
1 teaspoon sugar
1 leaf gelatin
½ tablespoon very finely minced lemon zest
½ tablespoon very finely minced lime zest
½–1 tablespoon very finely minced red chilli (no seeds, and add to your liking)

Step 2: To Serve
crushed ice (from your friendly fishmonger)
24 oysters

Oysters on Ice with Chardonnay Vinegar and Chilli Jelly

Makes 24

Raw oysters are a luxury that should always be served freezing cold and over ice. I do love them in their absolute naked natural state with just a grind of fresh black pepper and a squeeze of lemon juice; however, they are often served with various vinegars that work equally well. The only hassle when serving them with a vinegar is that, more often than not, the oyster slips off the toothpick and into the vinegar. So this recipe is a way of eliminating those occasions and with colourful specks of the other ingredients through the clear jelly, the presentation is pretty cool. Designed to be devoured in one mouthful, you have an explosion of clean sharp flavours incorporating the salty briny oyster, the acidity of the vinegar, the heat of the chilli and the refreshing zest of the citrus.

Step 1: Chardonnay Vinegar and Chilli Jelly

Pour the chardonnay vinegar into a small saucepan along with the sugar. Place on low heat and stir until the sugar dissolves. Remove and let cool slightly for a couple of minutes.

Bloom the gelatin in a small bowl of cold water for 3 minutes, then squeeze out the excess water and stir the gelatin into the vinegar and sugar. Let this sit and cool to room temperature.

Add the lemon and lime zest, and chilli to the cooled vinegar and stir to combine.

Pour the jelly into a small rectangular dish about 10cm x 5cm and place in the fridge to set (about 1 hour).

If for some reason the jelly doesn't seem to be setting, you may need to add more gelatin leaf. No problem. Just warm the jelly until it becomes liquid again, then add another ½ leaf of bloomed gelatin.

Step 2: To Serve

Place the crushed ice on a nice high-sided platter. Arrange the oysters in their half-shells or on Asian soup spoons and push them into the ice so they sit firmly.

Remove the jelly from the container and slice into little squares. Place a square on each oyster. Serve immediately or keep in a very cold fridge for up to an hour before serving.

"As I ate the oysters with their strong taste of the sea and their faint metallic taste that the cold white wine washed away, leaving only the sea taste and the succulent texture, and as I drank their cold liquid from each shell and washed it down with the crisp taste of the wine, I lost the empty feeling and began to be happy and to make plans."
Ernest Hemingway,
A Moveable Feast

Step 1: Rockefeller Topping
¼ cup fresh parsley
¼ cup fresh chives
¼ cup fresh chervil
2 tablespoons fresh tarragon
   leaves
¼ cup yellow inner celery leaves

200g butter, softened
50g Parmesan, grated
1 cup breadcrumbs (preferably
   homemade)
2 tablespoons Pernod (optional)
6–12 drops Tabasco

Step 2: To Set Up, Cook and Serve
2kg rock salt (or similar)
48 oysters (preferably freshly
   shucked and on their shells)

Oysters Rockefeller

Makes 24 (enough topping for 2 dozen oysters)

Oysters Rockefeller is a dish served in restaurants across the length and breadth of the United States. The dish originated in a very famous restaurant in New Orleans called Antoine's, which was founded in 1840. The ingredients for the recipe have been shrouded in mystery since it was first served in 1899. I was lucky enough to eat Oysters Rockefeller at Antoine's in the early 1990s when I was working in New Orleans. They were sensational and lived up to their billing as the restaurant's signature dish. Rockefeller himself was the wealthiest man in the United States at that time, which makes perfect sense when you eat this dish — it is extremely rich! Anyway, here's my version. Good-quality Pacific oysters lend themselves beautifully to this recipe and actually you could use this topping on most shellfish to great effect.

Step 1: Rockefeller Topping

Using your sharpest knife, chop the fresh herbs and celery leaves individually as finely as you possibly can. Place in a bowl. Add the butter, Parmesan, breadcrumbs, Pernod, if using, and Tabasco according to taste. With clean hands, work all the ingredients together until well combined.

Step 2: To Set Up, Cook and Serve

Pour half the rock salt into a shallow-sided baking dish. Take the oysters in the half-shell and gently work into the salt so they stand up by themselves. If the oysters are out of the shell, my suggestion would be to buy some Asian soup spoons and use those as an alternative — and no salt needed as they are freestanding.

Top each oyster with a generous portion of the topping, then place under the grill for 1–2 minutes until the topping starts to become golden and the sides of the oysters begin to slightly curl. Remove and let cool slightly before serving to prevent burnt lips. Serve on the other half of the rock salt that hasn't seen any oven time. Remember, you can use the rock salt over and over again. This is a seriously good way to eat cooked oysters!

It's illegal to open rock and Pacific oysters while they adhere to the object on which they grow.

Paua

WITH THE ABUNDANCE OF SEAFOOD THAT SURROUNDS OUR SHORES, IT'S HARD TO RATE ONE SPECIES ABOVE THE REST. WE ARE WITHOUT QUESTION SPOILT.

Nelson scallops, Bluff oysters, West Coast whitebait — the list goes on and many are only available as seasonal delicacies, which in turn makes them even more appreciated when their season is upon us.

I find it very hard to rate one species above another. However, I'm often asked what my favourite seafood is. Invariably one of the first words to roll off my tongue is paua and not just because of its culinary attributes, as you'll gather.

It is the one shellfish that I have had a special connection with from a very early age. Snorkelling for paua in the rock pools at Matakona — well, actually, in Skellerup sneakers, standing in my Speedos, bent over with a toy mask and snorkel on, and my head half under the water — on the Wairarapa's rugged east coast, is one of my early and fondest memories.

Back then we would all jump onto the back of old utes or get stuffed into dust-covered station wagons. It was the 1970s and without the annoying nuisance of seatbelts you could pack in a dozen or so kids. The drive from the Castlepoint camping ground over the twisted, corrugated gravel hill road was always an adventure and full of expectation. You could hardly hear yourself speak above the deafening sound of the cicadas, as dust dried out your mouth and stung your eyes.

On arrival, parched from the ride, we would pile out and set up camp in the long dry grass. Rugs down, a few low-rider beach chairs and a couple of sun umbrellas hammered into the sand to provide but a skerrick of shade. The green steel Coleman chilly bin, weighed down with large brown bottles of ice-cold beer and more than likely some leftover bacon and egg pie, wrapped in newspaper and stuffed down the side, would complete the scene.

The 'men' would don their wetsuits and head out to the edge of the reef, onion bags over their shoulders, ready to store their expected quarry. We kids would race to the rock pools, squealing with delight at the sight of starfish, kina and crabs, but always keeping an eye out for large oval shells camouflaging that black delicacy hidden beneath.

The mothers, of course, would rub baby oil over their bodies, whip out *New Zealand Woman's Weekly* and slowly bake away under the 29°C sun!

We would gather the shellfish while the fathers were a little further out doing their darnedest to snatch a couple of crays or maybe shoot a moki or butterfish with the Hawaiian sling to go alongside the paua for dinner.

As each dad appeared out of the tide, we would scramble across the rocks to meet them to see what they had gathered but, more importantly, we'd be bursting with enthusiasm to show them the paua we had collected. It was a game of show and tell, but as a young kid there was something profoundly significant about being a part of providing ingredients for the evening meal. It is an emotion that has stuck with me ever since. Whether it's collecting mushrooms, digging for pipi or shooting a rabbit, the pleasure derived from eating something you have hunted, gathered or worked hard for is immensely satisfying.

With all the beer consumed and the tide on its way back in, everyone and everything, along with the wet hessian sack keeping the kaimoana cold, would be packed up.

Stomachs would be beginning to rumble and the realisation of the severity of your sunburnt shoulders would start to take hold. A round of 'Ten Green Bottles Hanging on the Wall' — well, actually, more like 30 — was about the time it took to get back to the camping ground.

With old mincers clamped to the foldaway Formica tables, the paua were dealt to in the same fashion every night: minced with onion, a few beaten eggs, a little flour, then salt and pepper to season. The paua fritters were then cooked on a large, hot steel plate placed over a wood-fired barbecue made from a split 44-gallon drum.

Tasting paua fritters back then was probably my first culinary epiphany. Simply adorned with a squeeze of lemon juice, either on their own or between two slices of white bread, paua fritters are to me as iconic as roast lamb and mint sauce.

These are still very clear memories that evoke in me what is is to live in this country.

Years on and paua still plays a big part in my life. Back in 1996, when Steve Logan and I first opened the doors of Logan Brown Restaurant, I was adamant that I wanted to have paua on the menu. No one else, as far as I could see, was featuring this indigenous delicacy on their menus and it wasn't long before I understood why. At a cost of around $120 per kilo and up to $180 at certain times, especially around Chinese New Year, its pricing prohibited its viability, even on a fine-dining menu. With 99.9 per cent of wild harvested paua being exported, most of it bleached white and stuffed in a can, I did a little research and found a great company in Wellington called Ocean Ranch. Run by the Focas family, the business was involved in every aspect of the paua chain, from quota, harvesting, sustainability, processing and exporting. As with many of our purveyors to the restaurant, we have built up a great relationship with this family, who have allowed us over the years to buy a few kilos at a time every week to sell through the restaurant.

So the biggest problem I faced was how to put paua on the menu in a way that was affordable enough for the diners to order. I worked out that even if I had two 50g fritters on the plate at $120 per kilo, the cost of the paua

alone would be $12, meaning the entrée price would be somewhere between $36 and $40. It was 1996 and it probably would have created a good amount of press, but we would have been laughed all the way down Cuba Street.

Undeterred, I pressed on and created what is probably one of half a dozen or so true original dishes of my cooking career. Paua ravioli was on the first ever Logan Brown menu and, apart from the odd experimental period when we tried to replace it with something new, it still remains today. It's what is described as our signature dish and I shudder to think how many portions we have sold over the past 12 years. Let's say, conservatively, 15 portions a day, that's 105 portions a week, 5460 portions per year and 65,520 portions since opening. No wonder I'm a little over that dish! But the customers love it and in our business that's what matters, so it's there to stay.

I still regularly dive on the south coast of Wellington for paua when the sea is flat and the visibility allows, and it's still one of my favorite pastimes. I am now introducing my two daughters, Alice and Connie, to the wonders of rock pools and the treasures that lie within. The girls never tire of helping me shuck the fresh paua, as a large part of that pleasure is derived from removing each paua and exposing what must be one of the world's most extraordinarily beautiful shells. Each is complete with its own individual work of art.

HOW TO: | Shuck a Paua

1. Run one thumb along the bottom of the shell as the other thumb pulls the paua muscle upwards.

2. Run your thumb under the tissue connecting the paua to the shell.

3. Paua muscle released, with gut still connected.

4. Drop the paua with gut connected back in the shell.

5. Repeat the process from the round end of the shell.

6. Hold the gut in the shell, while releasing the paua.

7. Paua extracted, with gut still attached to the shell.

8. Cut out the two pink and white teeth at the end of the paua.

Step 1: Paua Fritter Mix
1kg paua (shucked weight)
⅓ cup finely diced red onion
1 tablespoon minced garlic
¼ cup roughly chopped fresh
  coriander

¼ cup roughly chopped fresh
  basil
2 tablespoons sweet chilli sauce
1 tablespoon lemon juice
salt and freshly ground black
  pepper

1 cup fritter batter (see recipe on
  page 314, halve the recipe)

Step 2: To Cook and Serve
cooking oil for frying
lemon juice and halves to serve
sea salt to taste

Paua Fritters

Makes 30–50 fritters (depending on size)

It's only a hunch, but of all the paua that gets gathered around our shores, probably 90 per cent ends up being cooked and served in a fritter. It seems everyone has their own favourite recipe handed down through generations of families who have enjoyed the luxurious qualities of this wonderful snail of the sea. As you'll see, there are a number of recipes for paua in this book, which is a fair indication of how highly I rate this shellfish. We live on the southern coast of Wellington, 10 minutes' drive from the CBD, and when the weather permits and visibility is good, it still takes little effort to get a feed of decent-sized paua. With the export quota all heading offshore at well over $100 per kilo, and much of the abalone stocks from the rest of the world decimated through overfishing, we are incredibly lucky to have a recreational resource in relatively good shape. The next time you go for a dive, just take five paua instead of the 10-per-day legal limit. You'll be surprised how far five paua can go when you make them into fritters or any other cooking method, and at the same time you'll be helping to protect this precious resource. It's a very dense and rich shellfish and a little goes a long way.

Step 1: Paua Fritter Mix

Cut each paua into 5 or 6 strips, then wind through a hand mincer or process with the mincer attachment on a Kenwood. Failing this, you could always take the paua down to your local butcher and plead with him or her to run it through their mincer! Put some dry bread through the mincer at the end, just to get every bit of the paua. The next step is optional as I like my fritters to have a combination of smooth and chunky texture. Place half the minced paua in a food processor and blend for 20 seconds or so until smooth, then combine the smooth and minced paua in a mixing bowl.

Add the red onion, garlic, coriander, basil, sweet chilli sauce and lemon juice to the bowl, and season with salt and pepper. Mix all together with a wooden spoon until well combined.

Add ¾ cup of the fritter batter to the paua. Mix again until combined.

Heat a frying pan on medium heat and cook a little fritter. If it needs a bit more binding, add a little more batter. Likewise, check the seasoning and add a little more lemon juice if necessary, or if you would like it hotter, use a little more sweet chilli sauce. Refrigerate until ready to cook.

Step 2: To Cook and Serve

Heat a skillet, frying pan or the griddle top of your barbecue to medium heat. Add a little oil, then spoon out the fritter mix to your desired size. Cook until golden on each side, then place on a platter. Give them a squeeze of lemon juice and a pinch of sea salt. Serve now. Repeat the process until all consumed!

If short on paua and you want to stretch the recipe, grind up some frozen squid tubes and use half paua and half squid.

Step 1: Paua Ravioli

500g paua meat, finely minced
1 teaspoon finely diced garlic
2 tablespoons finely diced
   shallots
¼ cup roughly chopped fresh
   coriander
2 tablespoons sweet chilli sauce
sea salt and freshly ground black
   pepper
1 packet frozen wonton wrappers,
   thawed
3 egg whites, lightly beaten
cornflour for dusting

Step 2: Beurre Blanc

50ml white wine
50ml white wine vinegar
1 shallot, roughly chopped
8 black peppercorns
1 bay leaf
100ml cream
250g butter, cut into 1cm dice
squeeze of lemon juice
sea salt and freshly ground black
   pepper to taste

Step 3: To Cook and Serve

4 tablespoons cooking oil
3 tablespoons roughly chopped
   fresh basil
3 tablespoons roughly chopped
   fresh coriander
flesh of 1–2 limes, finely diced
freshly ground black pepper

Paua Ravioli

Serves 6 as an entrée

I'm a firm believer that all good restaurants should have a signature dish. It makes good business sense, as we are creatures of habit and I'm adamant that people choose restaurants because they feel like eating a certain dish. A signature dish can only become one by being served exactly the same way, in flavour and presentation, time and time again. As with any successful restaurant it's all about consistency. Paua ravioli has been on our restaurant menu since day one and, even though all the chefs and cooks who have passed through our kitchen would readily admit to being sick of the sight of the dish, it's one that our loyal customers continually come back for, with many of them not even reading the other entrées on offer when ordering. It's rich and delicious and has all the components I like in a dish — flavour, balance and texture. It's also a great dish to make if you only have a couple of paua.

If you want to make the beurre blanc sauce a couple of hours ahead, a great way to keep it warm is by putting it in a preheated thermos.

Step 1: Paua Ravioli

Place the paua in a bowl and add the garlic, shallots, coriander and sweet chilli sauce. Season with sea salt and black pepper. Mix thoroughly together. To test the seasoning, take ½ teaspoon of the mixture and microwave for 5 seconds, or drop in boiling water, taste and adjust accordingly. Set aside.

   To make the ravioli, spread 6 wonton wrappers out on a clean work bench. Take a pastry brush and dip it into the egg whites and liberally brush the surface of the wonton wrappers. Place about a teaspoonful of the paua mix in the centre of each of the wonton wrappers. Top with another wonton wrapper and lightly press down over the filling.

   With a cookie cutter that will leave about a 1cm overhang from the edge of the paua mix (around 6cm), depress down through the wrapper. Pick up each one individually and, with your thumbs, pinch the wrappers together, expelling any air.

   Dust a tray with a little cornflour, then place the ravioli on the tray, being careful not to let the ravioli overlap. Repeat until you have 24 ravioli, then refrigerate until required.

Step 2: Beurre Blanc

In a small saucepan place the wine, vinegar, shallot, peppercorns and bay leaf. Place the saucepan on medium heat and reduce the liquid by three-quarters. Add the cream and reduce again by half.

Turn the heat down to as low as you can get it and whisk in the butter chunk by chunk until all incorporated and the sauce is silky smooth. Strain into a suitable jug and discard the solids. Season with a squeeze of lemon juice and sea salt and freshly ground pepper.

The beurre blanc can be made up to a couple of hours ahead, but must be kept in a warm place. You could sit the jug in a container of hot (not boiling) water.

Step 3: To Cook and Serve

Place 2 large saucepans of salted water on high heat and bring to the boil. Add a couple of tablespoons of oil to each to help prevent the ravioli from sticking. Once boiling, divide the ravioli between the 2 saucepans and cook for 2–3 minutes. Pour the beurre blanc into a large warm bowl.

Drain the ravioli and add to the sauce along with the basil, coriander and half the lime flesh. Quickly stir together. Taste the sauce and add the rest of the lime flesh if you think it needs it.

Divide the ravioli into warm bowls, then spoon some of the sauce over. A grind of pepper on each and serve pronto with some crusty bread.

Note: In the restaurant we garnish this dish with a very fine julienne of deep-fried kumara. If you have a mandolin, slice the kumara with the finest blade, then deep-fry in small batches in 180°C oil until golden and crisp. Top the paua ravioli with the crunchy shoestring kumara when serving.

PAUA RAVIOLI

Step 1: Preserved Lemon and Tarragon Butter
250g salted butter (at room temperature)
¼ cup finely chopped preserved lemon peel (see recipe on page 316)
1¼ tablespoons minced garlic
2 tablespoons finely chopped fresh tarragon
3 tablespoons finely chopped fresh parsley
pinch of dried chilli flakes

Step 2: To Prepare the Potatoes
600g small waxy new potatoes
sea salt

Step 3: To Prepare the Paua
3–4 paua (prebashed)
¼ cup canola oil

Step 4: To Cook and Serve
cooking oil for frying
sea salt and freshly ground black pepper
12 thin rounds of preserved lemon and tarragon butter
squeeze of lemon

Sautéed Paua Slivers with Fried New Potatoes & Preserved Lemon & Tarragon Butter

Serves 6 as an entrée

This is my twisted version of 'shellfish and chips'. It's simple and it eats beautifully. It's up to you whether you bash the paua before slicing it into the finest slivers possible. I generally do. However, if I find myself without a meat cleaver or tenderiser, it's no biggie, as the texture may have a little more bite but be no less enjoyable.

Step 1: Preserved Lemon and Tarragon Butter
Place all the ingredients in a small bowl and, with clean hands, work them all together until completely combined.

Cut a piece of plastic wrap and lay out on the bench.

Form the flavoured butter into a sausage shape and place at one end of the plastic wrap. Roll up and twist the ends like a Christmas cracker. Refrigerate until required.

Step 2: To Prepare the Potatoes
In a saucepan place the potatoes, cover with cold salted water and place on the heat. Bring to the boil, then lower to a simmer. Cook until the potatoes are just tender through the centre. Remove from the heat, drain and then cool to room temperature.

When cold, cut into slices about 5mm thick. Refrigerate until required.

Step 3: To Prepare the Paua
Take your sharpest knife and, cutting across the width of the paua, slice into the finest slivers you can manage. Place in a bowl and mix the oil through until well covered. Refrigerate.

Step 4: To Cook and Serve
Heat a cast iron skillet or the griddle top of your barbecue. Add a little oil, then gently add the cooked potato slices and season with salt and pepper. Cook for a few minutes each side until slightly golden and crisp. Remove from the heat and keep warm.

Before sautéing the paua, make sure your skillet, pan or barbecue is as hot as you can get it. Season the paua with salt and pepper. Drizzle a little cooking oil on to your cooking surface, then add half the paua. Spread it out thinly, then leave for about 30 seconds to caramelise before turning and cooking for another 30 seconds.

Just before taking off the heat, add 3 rounds of the preserved lemon butter, toss through, then transfer the paua to a bowl and keep warm while you repeat with the remaining paua.

To serve, distribute the crisp potato rounds onto individual plates or a platter, then top with the sautéed paua. Add the remaining flavoured butter, allow to melt over and give them a good squeeze of lemon. Serve.

Paua have no blood-clotting capabilities and will bleed to death if cut. If possible, measure the paua while it is still stuck to the rock; that way you only disturb and take what is the legal size. If this is not practical, always use a wide, flat, blunt object when removing paua and there is no excuse for not having an official plastic paua measure to make sure you are keeping within the law.

If you have mistakenly taken a paua that is under the legal size of 10cm, don't just toss it back at 20 metres, as paua find it difficult to right themselves and this will make them susceptible to predators and mortality. Instead take it back into the briny and find a nice sheltered ledge or crack in a rock and hold it there for 30 seconds or so until it sticks. With a bit of luck you'll be eating that same legal-size paua in a year's time. Also remember it is illegal to shuck paua below the high tide mark.

SAUTÉED PAUA SLIVERS WITH FRIED NEW POTATOES & PRESERVED LEMON & TARRAGON BUTTER

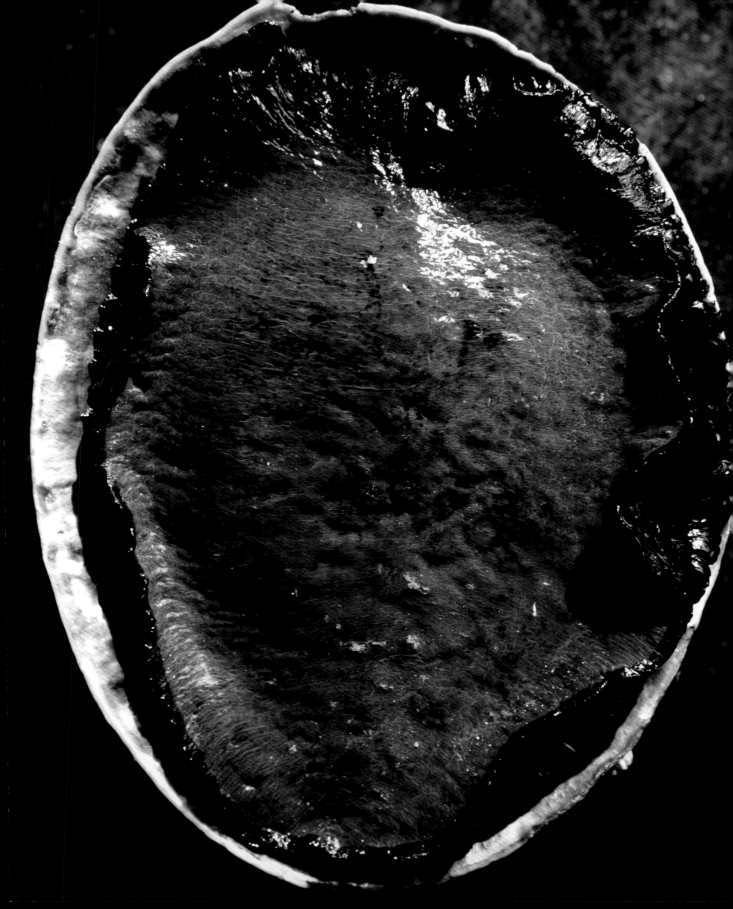

Step 1: Paua Soup

50g butter
2 cups roughly chopped onion
¾ cup roughly chopped celery
3 cloves roughly chopped garlic
grated zest of 1 lemon
pinch of dried chilli flakes
1½ tablespoons chopped fresh
tarragon

5 paua (800g), beaten and
roughly chopped
1½ litres chicken or fish stock
(see recipes on pages 319
and 311)
1 cup cream
squeeze of lemon juice
salt and freshly ground black
pepper to taste

Step 2: To Serve

cream to garnish
lemon-infused olive oil (optional)
lemon wedges to serve

Cream of Paua Soup

Serves 6

This recipe was developed after I was introduced to a wonderful dish of creamed paua made by Kura Broughton of Matakona, near Castlepoint. Deliciously rich, it was served like a dip, with wonderful deep-fried Maori bread alongside. Steve and I were filming an episode of *Hunger for the Wild* and Matai, Kura's husband, who is kaitiaki (caretaker) for that particular piece of Wairarapa coastline, took me over the property and down to a spot where we gathered this delicacy in pretty marginal conditions. After being blown away by Kura's creamed paua, I set about trying to create a paua soup — and here's the result.

Step 1: Paua Soup

Place the butter in a decent-sized saucepan on medium-low heat. Add the onion, celery, garlic, lemon zest, chilli flakes and tarragon, and sweat for 30 minutes, stirring occasionally.

Once the vegetables are soft, add the paua and stock. Bring to the boil then reduce the heat. Simmer for at least 1 hour. Add the cream, stir through and remove from the heat.

Using a blender or liquidiser, purée the soup for 30 seconds or so. The soup should be creamy but still have texture.

Pour the soup back into the saucepan. Taste and season with a squeeze of lemon juice and salt and pepper. Refrigerate if not using immediately.

Step 2: To Serve

Heat up the paua soup slowly, stirring occasionally. Divide into heated bowls. Spoon in a swirl of cream and drizzle a little lemon-infused olive oil over if you have some. Serve right away with wedges of lemon for squeezing and a hunk of crusty bread on the side.

A seemingly insatiable appetite for abalone, or paua, has seen many of the world's wild fisheries collapse over the past few decades due to overfishing, imbalance of ecosystems and pollution. Abalone farming is well established in many countries around the world, including New Zealand, with China leading the charge with over 300 farms producing more than 3500 tons each year.

HOW TO: | Shuck a Scallop

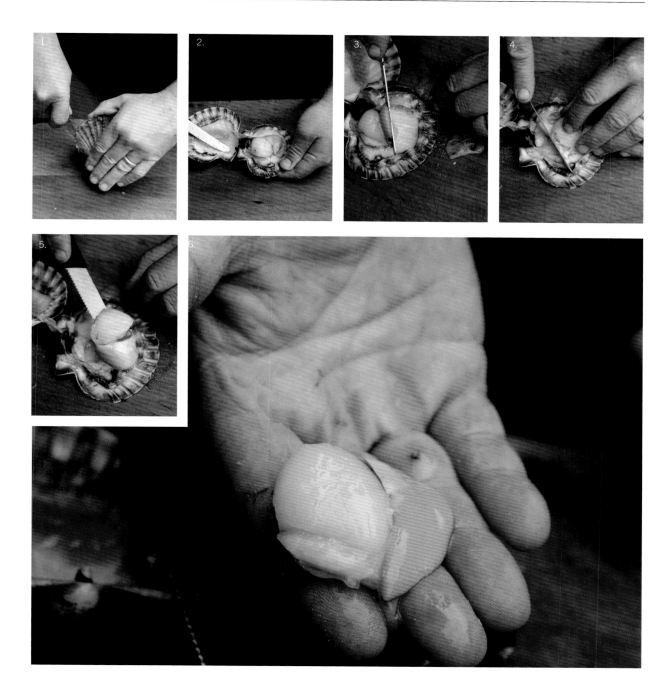

1. With the flat side of the scallop facing up, run a knife, angled slightly down, next to the hinge until the muscle lets go.

2. Open up the scallop.

3. Carefully scrape away the gut and the brown skirt.

4. Run the knife under the scallop.

5. Leave the gut stuck inside the shell.

6. Shucked scallop.

Step 1: Celeriac Purée
1kg celeriac (peeled weight),
    peeled and roughly chopped
2 cups cream
squeeze of lemon juice
sea salt and freshly ground white
    pepper (black pepper is also
    fine)

Step 2: Crisp Prosciutto
8 thin slices prosciutto

Step 3: Cabernet Vinegar Syrup
see recipe on page 304

Step 4: To Cook and Serve
800g fresh scallops
sea salt and freshly ground black
    pepper
cooking oil for frying
mandarin-infused olive oil (or
    similar)
chervil or similar to garnish

Seared Scallops with Celeriac Purée, Crisp Prosciutto & Mandarin Oil

Serves 8 as an entrée

This dish, or variations of it, features on the Logan Brown menu at the start of the scallop season every year. It's a firm favourite of mine and I never tire of it. All the components just seem to harmonise beautifully together, with the scallops still the hero of the dish. It's easy to cook and most of the ingredients can be prepped a day or two beforehand. Another great purée that we serve with the scallops is made with Jerusalem artichoke in exactly the same way as the celeriac purée. The Jerusalem artichoke brings a natural sweetness and nuttiness to the dish. If you don't have a mandarin-infused oil, try lemon- or orange-infused olive oil instead.

Step 1: Celeriac Purée

Place the celeriac in a suitable saucepan and cover with salted cold water. Boil until soft (about 25 minutes).

Drain then add the cream and place back on low heat. Simmer to reduce slightly for 10 minutes, then pour into a liquidiser or use a wand blender to purée until silky smooth.

Pass through a fine sieve into a bowl, then add a small squeeze of lemon juice and season with sea salt and pepper. Keep warm or refrigerate until required.

Step 2: Crisp Prosciutto

Preheat the oven to 180°C.

Place the individual slices of prosciutto on a baking tray lined with baking paper, then top with another sheet of baking paper. Put another baking tray on top to weigh the prosciutto down flat and place in the middle of the oven.

Check after 8 minutes, then at regular intervals thereafter. Keep a close eye as they can burn very quickly. Remove once crisp and golden brown. Cool and store in an airtight container until required. If you find they have lost their crunchiness when it's time to use them, just refresh in a hot oven for a minute or so.

Step 3: Cabernet Vinegar Syrup

See recipe on page 304.

When cooking scallops, always remove them from the fridge and bring them up to room temperature before cooking, as they should always be slightly underdone, and this way they will not be cold in the centre.

Step 4: To Cook and Serve

Reheat the celeriac purée in a saucepan over low heat or for a couple of minutes in the microwave.

Make sure the scallops are dry to touch (or pat dry with paper towels). Season with sea salt and black pepper. Place in a bowl and add a little cooking oil to coat.

Place a skillet or sauté pan on high heat. Once hot, add a little oil then cook the scallops in batches, being mindful not to overcrowd the pan. Cook for no longer than 30 seconds on each side. Remove and keep warm while you finish cooking the rest.

Place a small amount of the celeriac purée in the centre of all the warm plates. Divvy out the scallops, then top each portion with a crisp piece of prosciutto. Drizzle a little mandarin oil around and over, then follow with a little cabernet syrup and chervil to garnish. Serve now!

Step 1: Ratatouille Salsa
olive oil for sautéing
1 cup finely diced red onion
½ tablespoon finely chopped
   garlic
1 cup finely diced zucchini
1 cup finely diced aubergine
2 roasted red capsicum, peeled,
   seeded and finely diced
2 tablespoons olive oil

⅓ cup finely chopped fresh basil
sea salt and freshly ground black
   pepper

Step 2: Creamed Fresh Sweetcorn
50g butter
½ cup roughly chopped shallots
⅓ cup white wine
1 cup cream
3 cups sweetcorn kernels, freshly
   cooked and cut from the cob
sea salt and freshly ground black
   pepper

Step 3: To Cook and Serve
60 scallops (at room temperature)
sea salt and freshly ground black
   pepper
cooking oil for frying
butter for frying

Seared Scallops with Creamed Fresh Sweetcorn & Ratatouille Salsa

Serves 6 as an entrée or light lunch

A fresh scallop opened just moments after being gathered from the sea floor, unadorned or with just a squeeze of fresh lemon juice, is for me one of the most agreeable tastes I can think of. They are truly a special shellfish and a favourite the world over. Scallops are found around the coast in the sand and mud banks of sheltered bays from low tide mark out to about 50 metres. The main areas that produce these delicacies are Tasman Bay, Golden Bay, Marlborough Sounds, Coromandel and Northland coasts.

To gather, they have to be over 10cm in width across the widest part of the shell and the legal limit recreationally is 50 per person. As usual, just because the limit is 50 per person, don't feel you have to take that many. I'm a big believer that, as with so many other shellfish, recreational quotas should be halved. Take enough for a feed and eat them fresh. This dish celebrates all that is good about summer.

Scallops are fast-growing shellfish and, when conditions are ideal, can reach a legal size of 10cm within three years.

Step 1: Ratatouille Salsa

Place a skillet or sauté pan on medium heat. Add a little olive oil, then sauté the red onion and garlic until golden. Remove and place in a bowl. Do the same with the zucchini and then follow with the aubergine.

Add the red capsicum and 2 tablespoons of olive oil. Toss in the fresh basil, then season with sea salt and black pepper. Cover and leave at room temperature for a few hours, or if serving later than that, refrigerate until required.

Step 2: Creamed Fresh Sweetcorn

Place the butter and shallots in a medium saucepan on low heat and sweat without browning for 20 minutes, stirring occasionally.

Add the white wine, turn up the heat a little and simmer to reduce for 5 minutes before adding the cream and corn. Cook for another 5 minutes then remove from the heat.

With a wand blender or in a food processor, pulse the mixture a couple of times to break up some of the corn kernels. You want the creamed corn to still have a slightly chunky texture. Season with sea salt and pepper to taste, then refrigerate until required.

Step 3: To Cook and Serve

Heat the creamed corn gently in a saucepan over low heat or slowly in a microwave.

Place a skillet or sauté pan over high heat. Season and oil the scallops then cook in batches in the hot pan. Cook no more than 30 seconds per side, and after turning, add a couple of knobs of butter, just before removing from the pan. Keep warm while you finish the rest.

To serve, spoon a little creamed corn in the centre of each plate. Top with 10 scallops per serving, then a few spoonfuls of the ratatouille salsa, and add a pinch of sea salt and a grind of black pepper. Serve now!

Step 1: Tuatua with Peking Duck and Fermented Black Beans
⅓ cup cooking oil
2½ tablespoons finely chopped ginger
2 tablespoons finely chopped garlic

7 spring onions (white part and green tops separated), finely chopped
½ Peking duck, skin and meat removed and roughly chopped
5 tablespoons fermented black beans, rinsed and roughly chopped

1 teaspoon sugar
½ cup Shaoxing wine (Chinese cooking wine) or medium sherry
¼ cup soy sauce
1 cup chicken stock
40–60 tuatua (depending on size), purged of any sand

450g dried large rice noodles
1½ tablespoons cornflour
2 tablespoons water

Step 2: To Serve
sesame oil to serve

Tuatua with Peking Duck & Fermented Black Beans over Rice Noodles

Serves 6 as a main course

I ate a dish of clams cooked with fermented black beans years ago in the Chinatown area of Montreal. Ever since, it has been one of my favourite ways of cooking some of the hardier shellfish that take on the bigger flavours with ease, such as mussels, littleneck clams and pipi. Fermented black beans are actually fermented soya beans that have terrific savouriness and saltiness, not too unlike describing the flavour of Marmite or Vegemite to someone. This is a version I have developed only recently, with Peking duck, bought from a Chinese restaurant or takeaway specialist, chopped up and thrown into the mix. It adds a little sweetness and body to the dish, offsetting some of the saltiness of the beans and the tuatua liquor.

Step 1: Tuatua with Peking Duck and Fermented Black Beans

Bring a large saucepan of water up to a rolling boil for the noodles.

Take another large saucepan or wok with a lid and place it on medium-high heat. Once hot, add the cooking oil followed by the ginger, garlic and the white part of the spring onions. Stir for a minute or so before adding the chopped duck, fermented black beans and sugar. Stir together.

Now add the Shaoxing wine, soy sauce and chicken stock, followed by the tuatua. Give them a good stir and place the lid on.

Check after a couple of minutes and, as the shells open, remove immediately and place in a bowl. Continue until you have removed all the open tuatua.

Drop the rice noodles in the boiling water. These will take only about 4 minutes to cook.

While the noodles are cooking, mix the cornflour with 2 tablespoons of water and whisk it into the tuatua cooking liquid to thicken. If too thick add a little more stock or water.

Toss the cooked tuatua back in the thickened sauce along with the reserved green spring onion tops. Mix through, remove from the heat and hold.

Step 2: To Serve

Strain the noodles through a sieve, then run under hot water for 30 seconds. Place the noodles in hot bowls and spoon the tuatua, duck, beans and sauce over. Drizzle a couple of drops of sesame oil over each portion and serve immediately!

You can easily make this recipe without the Peking duck. It's just a luxurious extra that goes very well with the dish. The real flavour here comes from the fermented black beans and ginger.

Step 1: Italian Sausage, Tomato and White Bean Base
¼ cup olive oil
300g good-quality sausage, cut into large dice
2 cups finely diced onion
1 cup finely diced celery

1 cup diced red capsicum
1½ tablespoons finely chopped garlic
1 tablespoon fennel seeds, toasted and roughly ground
pinch of dried chilli flakes
1 cup white wine

400g tinned peeled tomatoes, crushed
2 tablespoons tomato paste
400g tinned cannellini beans, rinsed

Step 2: To Cook and Serve
60–80 tuatua or clams, purged of sand and grit
1 cup white wine
30g butter, cut into chunks
handful fresh parsley, chopped

Tuatua with Italian Sausage, Tomato & White Beans

Serves 6 as a main course

This dish is really more of a big hearty soup than anything else. Always hunt out a good-quality handmade sausage. You could use Spanish chorizo or similar; I like to use an unsmoked sausage that has plenty of fat and good meaty chunks. By adding the sausage and white beans you are actually stretching the catch and using all the tuatua liquor, which really gives this dish a huge depth in flavour. The usual accompaniments like good-quality bread and a salad of some sort will do the trick. A pinot noir would be a ripper with this also!

Step 1: Sausage, Tomato and White Bean Base
Place a large saucepan on high heat. Once hot, add the olive oil followed immediately by the sausage. Brown the sausage, then add the onion, celery, capsicum, garlic, ground fennel seeds and chilli flakes. Reduce the heat and cook for 20 minutes or so, stirring occasionally to prevent sticking.

Deglaze the pan with the white wine and let the liquid reduce for 5 minutes before adding the crushed tomatoes and tomato paste. Cook on low for another 10 minutes, then take off the heat and stir in the cannellini beans. Cool and store in the refrigerator until required, or freeze until needed.

Step 2: To Cook and Serve
Place the tuatua in a large saucepan and pour in the wine. Ladle in the sausage, tomato and white bean base. Place a lid on the saucepan and put on high heat. Shake the saucepan after 5 minutes to mix the sauce through and help open the tuatua. Place back on the heat and check every couple of minutes. Remove the saucepan from the heat as soon as the tuatua have opened. Toss in the butter and parsley, mix through, then divide into bowls, pouring the soupy sauce over the top, then serve.

The most time-consuming aspect of this recipe is the base, which can be made a few days ahead or even frozen at home and then taken along to the bach to whip out on one of those lousy stormy days when all you can gather for the pot is what is offered up at low tide — pipi, clams, mussels and so on.

New Zealand's Commercial Fishery

INNOVATION, INTEGRITY AND SUSTAINABILITY — THESE THREE WORDS ARE ALL OF EQUAL IMPORTANCE WHEN LOOKING AT NEW ZEALAND'S SEAFOOD INDUSTRY. WITH A COVETED REPUTATION, NEW ZEALAND HAS FOR A LONG TIME BEEN RECOGNISED AS A PIONEER IN SUSTAINABLE FISHERIES MANAGEMENT SYSTEMS.

We can be proud as a nation of identifying the importance of understanding, respecting and ultimately looking after our fisheries now and well into the future.

Our industry is small on a world scale, making up less than one per cent of world production and just two per cent of global sales. However, as our fifth largest export earner, employing more than 25,000 people domestically, it is hugely important to us. New Zealand has carved out an international reputation for producing consistently high-quality product, harvested under environmentally sustainable processes.

It can't be underestimated how difficult and complicated the job has been to establish fisheries as well managed as what we have today. (Ever tried counting live fish?) Like all businesses, there have been successes and failures

along the way. What has been critical is the ability to identify where wrong decisions were made in the past, gain knowledge and understanding of those mistakes and adjust accordingly. Orange roughy, scallops, rock lobster, snapper and hoki have all been fisheries that, in the past, we have misunderstood or mismanaged. However, with open minds, progressive attitudes and a dogged will to get it right, we have turned several of those fisheries around. This has been achieved in a number of ways: by scientific investigation, embracing new technology and, most importantly, a willingness by all involved to listen, share and contribute. More significantly, it is equally important to recognise the successes and to celebrate how far we have come, what we have discovered, learned and attained along the way.

Our self-funded industry

contributes up to $35 million annually to fisheries management research. This is generally focused on three areas: fishery stock levels, environmental effects of fishing and ecosystem management. With such a complex industry, I do not envy the jobs of the policy makers, councils, scientists and all those involved in trying to create a positive outcome for all parties involved.

The one common thread that runs through all those with a vested interest, either socially or economically, is a love of the sea and all the creatures that share these unique and precious oceans of ours.

I believe it is now time that we, as individual New Zealanders, started recognising and taking responsibility for the role we all play in keeping not just our fisheries but our oceans, beaches and coastlines in as pristine and as healthy a state as possible.

Fin Fish

Fin Fish

Living in a country with such an astonishing array of fin fish to choose from, it amazes me that so many people still seem so hellbent on catching, buying or cooking the same few varieties of fish all the time. I liken this to restricting oneself to eating just three or four types of fruit or vegetables again and again. We all have our favourites, which is understandable, but eating something new is undoubtedly a lot more interesting and rewarding.

It has always amused me that when we travel overseas we seem far more likely to embrace or try something new. We then invariably extol the virtues of this newly discovered delicacy. So why not here in New Zealand? We have so many terrific varieties of fish to eat. Start breaking some old habits and try a fish species you haven't eaten before. I guarantee you will enjoy the results.

When cooking fish there are just a few basic rules I keep in mind. First, it has to be fresh and looked after from the moment it was landed (see Handling Fresh Fish on page 28). Fresh fish should have no real odour to speak of. If anything at all, it should have a slight, somewhat intoxicating scent of the ocean. Cooking fish well can at times be a delicate process. It pays to have everything else prepared or ready to go before actually starting to cook the fish, so you can give it your undivided attention.

It should never be overcooked. You can always cook it a little longer, but it's impossible to cook it less once you have overcooked it.

By all means use the recipes here, however, never be afraid to cook fish simply in a little butter, seasoned with salt and pepper and served with a squeeze of lemon juice. That's my all-time favourite!

Step 1: Caesar Dressing
3 egg yolks
1 tablespoon minced garlic
1 tablespoon anchovies
½ cup grated Parmesan
⅓ cup lemon juice
1 teaspoon Worcestershire Sauce
½ cup canola oil
⅓ cup olive oil
salt and freshly ground black
   pepper

Step 2: Croûtons
⅓ baguette (or similar)
25g butter
⅓ cup olive oil
sea salt and freshly ground black
   pepper

Step 3: Panko-Crumbed Gurnard
800g boneless gurnard fillets
sea salt and freshly ground black
   pepper
1 cup flour
2 eggs, beaten
3 cups panko crumbs (or regular
   breadcrumbs)

Step 4: To Cook and Serve
¼ cup white wine vinegar
cooking oil for frying
2 cos lettuces, roughly chopped
Parmesan cheese
6 eggs
freshly ground black pepper
3 lemons, halved

Panko-Crumbed Gurnard & Caesar Salad with Poached Egg & Parmesan

Serves 6 as a light lunch

Gurnard is my pick for the coolest looking and most interesting fish inhabiting our waters. Its colours are something to behold. Besides their striking bright orange body, it's their two large pectoral fins in shades of blue and green similar to peacock feathers that always blow me away. These fins act as sensory rays used to locate prey and enable the fish to move sideways across the sandy bottom. They have a very bony head and tiny scales and are a wonderful fish to eat. You catch them year round and they can grow up to a couple of kilograms. For some reason I love gurnard crumbed. Served with a fresh, crisp Caesar salad, a poached egg and a couple of shavings of Parmesan, it makes for a delicious lunch.

Step 1: Caesar Dressing
Using a wand blender or food processor, process the egg yolks, garlic, anchovies, Parmesan, lemon juice and Worcestershire Sauce for 30 seconds until combined.

Slowly drizzle in the 2 oils until incorporated and thick. Taste and season with salt and black pepper. Refrigerate until required.

Step 2: Croûtons
Preheat the oven to 150°C.

Cut the baguette into croûton-sized pieces (about 1cm dice).

Place a skillet or sauté pan on medium heat and add the butter and oil. Once melted together, toss the bread in the pan and cook for a couple of minutes until slightly coloured. Pour into an ovenproof dish, place in the oven and cook for 5–10 minutes until crisp.

Remove and cool. Store in an airtight container until required.

Step 3: Panko-Crumbed Gurnard
Cut the gurnard into 12 manageable strips of about 70g each. Season with sea salt and black pepper.

Take 3 mixing bowls and set up the crumbing station: flour, eggs and breadcrumbs each in a separate bowl.

Dip each piece of fish in the flour, then the egg and finally the breadcrumbs. Place each piece of crumbed fish on a dry plate or tray. Refrigerate if not cooking immediately.

Step 4: To Cook and Serve

Preheat the oven to 100°C and half fill a large saucepan with water. Add the vinegar and bring up to a rolling boil for poaching the eggs. Meanwhile, place a skillet or sauté pan on medium heat. Add a liberal amount of oil, then fry the fillets in batches until golden on each side and just cooked through. Place in an ovenproof dish and keep warm in the preheated oven while you finish cooking the remaining fish.

Place the cos lettuce in a large mixing bowl and add some of the Caesar dressing. Mix through with clean hands. Taste and add more dressing if required. Once dressed, divvy up onto large plates. Toss the croûtons over and grate a liberal amount of Parmesan over each portion of salad.

Now poach the eggs. While they are cooking, place a couple of pieces of the crumbed gurnard on the salads. Once the eggs are poached but still runny in the centre, carefully remove with a slotted spoon and place one on top of each serving. A quick grind of pepper, a half lemon on the side and you're good to go!

I have always prided myself on my rendition of a Caesar dressing. The trick is to get the perfect balance of anchovy, lemon juice and Parmesan.

Panko are coarse Japanese breadcrumbs, available at Asian food markets and some supermarkets. It imparts a wonderful crunchy outer to anything crumbed with it. Homemade or store-bought breadcrumbs will work also.

Step 1: Gurnard Escabeche
600g skinned and boned gurnard
    fillets
sea salt and freshly ground black
    pepper
olive oil for cooking
⅓ cup minced red onion

1 red chilli, minced (seeds
    optional)
1½ tablespoons minced garlic
finely grated zest of ½ orange
pinch of saffron, toasted in a dry
    pan, then crumbled
1–2 star anise

3 tablespoons orange juice
3 tablespoons lemon juice
3 tablespoons sherry vinegar
1 tablespoon honey
⅓ cup olive oil

Step 2: To Serve
20–30 bruschetta (see recipe
    on page 305)
olive oil for drizzling
sea salt and freshly ground black
    pepper

Gurnard Escabeche Bruschetta

Makes 20–30 bruschetta

Escabeche is a form of marinating fish in a spiced dressing immediately after it has been cooked. Various versions are found throughout the Mediterranean and it's also popular in Mexican cuisine. Essentially a form of pickling, it would have been a way of preserving fish in the centuries before refrigeration. I really enjoy cooked fish eaten cold. In the past I have served this style of escabeche with a salad of fresh green beans and a few other bits and pieces. However, I think it's just terrific served on crisp bruschetta, drizzled with a splash of olive oil. Many varieties of fish will work well here. Just bear in mind that thinner fillets will take on more of the marinating flavour.

Step 1: Gurnard Escabeche

Cut each gurnard fillet into 3 pieces. Season with sea salt and black pepper. Cook in a sauté pan with a little oil for 1–2 minutes, then turn and finish cooking on the other side. Remove and place in a ceramic dish or similar in which the fillets all fit snugly.

Place a sauté pan on medium-low heat and add about ¼ cup of olive oil. Add the red onion, chilli, garlic, orange zest, saffron and star anise. Stir over low heat for a couple of minutes to release the flavours into the oil. Pour into a mixing bowl, then add the orange juice, lemon juice, sherry vinegar and honey. Whisk briefly, then continue whisking while drizzling in ⅓ cup of olive oil.

Once combined, pour the mixture over the cooked gurnard fillets, cover and refrigerate for at least 2 hours, but preferably overnight or even a couple of days.

Step 2: To Serve

Remove the escabeche from the fridge at least an hour before serving to bring up to room temperature, or place in a low oven for 5 minutes, just to warm slightly.

Spread the bruschetta out on a flat, clean surface and top each one with a spoonful of escabeche. Spoon some of the marinade over, then drizzle with a little olive oil. A pinch of sea salt and a grind of pepper and you're all set.

There is one other gurnard, much less common, that frequents our New Zealand waters and that is the spotted or Japanese gurnard. With a more pinkish and slightly yellow body, it can be recognised immediately, as it is covered in distinctive black spots. Not quite as large as our regular gurnard, but equally wonderful to eat.

Step 1: Chermoula
¼ cup roughly chopped fresh coriander
¼ cup roughly chopped fresh parsley
1 tablespoon roughly chopped garlic
1 whole chilli, roughly chopped (seeds optional)
finely grated zest of 2 lemons
¼ cup lemon juice
2 teaspoons sweet smoked Spanish paprika

1 teaspoon ground cumin
1 teaspoon ground coriander
1 teaspoon sugar
⅓ cup olive oil
sea salt and freshly ground black pepper

Step 2: Chermoula-Marinated Snapper
1 x 2–3kg whole snapper, scaled and gutted

Step 3: Spiced Israeli Couscous
50g butter
1 cup finely diced onion
1½ tablespoons minced garlic
finely grated zest of 2 lemons
pinch of dried chilli flakes
½ cup currants
pinch of saffron threads, soaked in 1 tablespoon tepid water
juice of 1 orange
1½ teaspoons sweet smoked Spanish paprika

250g Israeli couscous
2½ cups boiling chicken stock or water
1 tablespoon butter
⅓ cup finely chopped parsley
sea salt and freshly ground black pepper

Step 4: To Cook and Serve
sea salt and freshly ground black pepper
lemon halves

Chermoula Roasted Whole Snapper with Spiced Israeli Couscous

Serves 6 as a main course

One of the main points for me in writing this book is to encourage Kiwis to think about how much we waste when we whip the fillets off a fish and toss so much of the good eating away. Cooking a fish whole eliminates this waste and makes one or two fish stretch a lot further. There are plenty of upsides to eating fish this way. A whole cooked fish presents so dramatically and, while on the bone, the whole eating process is slowed down, making it more enjoyable as everyone collectively gathers around a delicious fish and leisurely pulls the moist flesh away from the frame. The fish will always be tastier when cooked on the bone, too. You can marinate practically any fish in this recipe, with delicious results. I also like to serve the slightly sweet spiced Israeli couscous on the side, along with a refreshing green salad.

Step 1: Chermoula
Place all the ingredients except the salt and pepper in a food processor or similar. Process into a roughish purée, taste and season accordingly with the sea salt and black pepper.

Step 2: Chermoula-Marinated Snapper
Make 3 slashes through to the bone on each side of the fish. Place in a large oiled roasting dish. Rub liberal amounts of the chermoula into the scored flesh on both sides as well as inside the gut cavity. Place in the fridge to marinate for at least a couple of hours. Keep the remaining chermoula for later in the recipe.

Step 3: Spiced Israeli Couscous
Place a large saucepan on medium-low heat. Add the butter, onion, garlic, lemon zest, chilli flakes and currants. Sweat for 20 minutes, stirring occasionally, until the onion is soft and golden. Add the saffron and its soaking water, orange juice and paprika. Cook for another 5 minutes.

Add the couscous and stir through, then add the boiling chicken stock or water. Place the lid on the saucepan and cook for 8–10 minutes.

Chermoula is a marinade used in Algerian, Moroccan and Tunisian cooking. There are numerous variations; however, they are usually a mixture of garlic, herbs, spices, citrus and oil.

Once cooked and all the liquid is absorbed, add the butter and parsley. Fluff up the couscous with a fork and season with sea salt and black pepper to taste.

Serve immediately or cool then refrigerate and reheat before serving later.

Step 4: To Cook and Serve

Preheat the oven to 180°C.

Cover the roasting dish containing the marinated snapper with tinfoil and place in the hot oven. Roast for 30 minutes, then remove the tinfoil, brush the snapper with the remaining chermoula and place under the grill to caramelise the presentation side of the fish. Remove from the oven and set aside to rest for 5–10 minutes.

Reheat the couscous in the microwave or in a stainless steel bowl covered with tinfoil and placed over a double boiler. Once hot, check the seasoning before dishing out onto a platter.

Serve the snapper in the roasting dish or carefully transfer onto another platter. Season with a good pinch of sea salt and black pepper. Toss a few lemon halves around the fish and serve immediately with the couscous on the side and plenty of dissecting tools like tongs and spatulas.

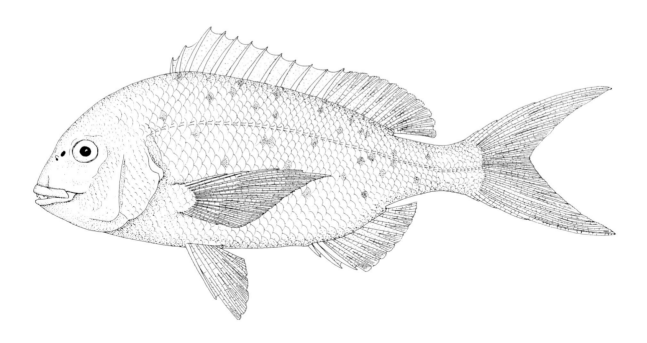

Step 1: Smoked Aubergine Purée
1kg aubergines
sea salt
white sugar
¼ cup olive oil
300g onion, sliced
1 tablespoon finely chopped garlic
pinch of dried chilli flakes
1 teaspoon freshly ground cumin seeds
⅓ cup extra virgin olive oil
sea salt and freshly ground black pepper

Step 2: Capsicums and Artichokes
160g jar of chargrilled globe artichokes in olive oil
1 tablespoon finely chopped garlic
2 roasted red capsicum, peeled, seeded and diced
2 tablespoons roughly chopped capers

Step 3: To Cook and Serve
6 x 150g snapper fillets
sea salt and freshly ground black pepper
cooking oil for frying
¼ cup roughly chopped fresh parsley
¼ cup roughly chopped fresh mint
¼ cup roughly chopped fresh basil
juice of ½ lemon
6 lemon wedges to serve

Sautéed Snapper & Smoked Aubergine Purée with Capsicums & Artichokes

Serves 6 as a main course

It's no secret that I've always loved making smooth silky vegetable purées. It's the combination of the texture and sauce-like qualities that a great purée brings to a dish that have attracted me to experiment with so many over the years. There are plenty included in this book and this smoked aubergine recipe is worth the effort. It's great with this dish, but could easily be served cold as a dip with raw vegetables or on crostini.

Step 1: Smoked Aubergine Purée

Preheat the oven to 150°C.

Cut the aubergines in half lengthwise. With a sharp, thin knife score the flesh at 1cm intervals, creating a diamond pattern. Sprinkle the flesh with liberal amounts of sea salt and white sugar.

Place the aubergines flesh side up on the smoking rack. Sprinkle the bottom of the smoker with wood chips and smoke the aubergine for 15 minutes.

Remove and put in an oiled ovenproof dish, place in the oven and bake for 20 minutes or so until the flesh is soft and cooked.

While the aubergines are smoking, pour the ¼ cup of olive oil into a medium saucepan, place on medium to low heat and add the onion, garlic, chilli flakes and ground cumin seeds. Fry gently for about 30 minutes, stirring occasionally, until the onions are starting to caramelise.

When the aubergines are cooked, take a large spoon and scoop the flesh out from the skin and add it to the onion mix. Cook for a further 10 minutes, then remove from the heat. Add the extra virgin olive oil and purée with a wand blender, or in a liquidiser or food processor, until smooth. If too thick, thin down with a little water. Pass the purée through a fine sieve and discard any lumps. Taste and season with sea salt and pepper. Keep warm or refrigerate until required.

Step 2: Capsicums and Artichokes

Remove the artichokes from the oil and cut into quarters. Pour about ⅓ cup of the artichoke olive oil into a skillet or sauté pan.

Add the garlic and place the pan on medium heat. Stir the garlic with a wooden spoon until it turns golden brown, then quickly add the artichokes, red capsicum and capers. Toss together, remove from the heat and keep warm.

Step 3: To Cook and Serve

Heat the smoked aubergine purée slowly in a double boiler or microwave. Keep warm.

Season the snapper fillets with sea salt and pepper. Place a skillet or sauté pan on medium heat, add a little cooking oil then cook the snapper in batches. Keep the cooked fillets warm while you complete cooking the rest.

Reheat the artichokes and capsicums in a pan then, just before serving, add the parsley, mint, and basil, squeeze in the lemon juice and toss all together.

To serve, place a little of the smoked aubergine purée in the centre of each plate, top with a portion of snapper, then spoon the warm capsicum and artichoke mix over each. A pinch of sea salt, a grind of black pepper, a wedge of lemon and you're good to go. Serve now.

Most root vegetables, such as carrots, kumara and parsnips, work well with the addition of smoke in the cooking process. Oil them, then roast on low heat until soft. Rub a little salt and sugar into them and place in the smoker for 10–15 minutes. Tomatoes, capsicums and pumpkin are other favourites.

SAUTÉED SNAPPER & SMOKED AUBERGINE PURÉE WITH CAPSICUMS & ARTICHOKES

Step 1: Fresh Sweetcorn and Crab Risotto
30g butter
⅓ cup finely diced shallots
⅓ cup white wine
3 tablespoons finely chopped fresh tarragon
2 tablespoons finely grated

lemon zest
2 cups arborio rice
1½–2 litres warm fish or chicken stock (see recipes on pages 311 and 319)
½ cup cream
3 cobs fresh sweetcorn, cooked and kernels cut from the cobs

500g crab meat
1 tablespoon lemon juice
3 handfuls spinach, roughly chopped
sea salt and freshly ground black pepper

Step 2: To Cook and Serve
6 x 150g snapper fillets
sea salt and freshly ground black pepper
cooking oil for frying
2 cups hot fish or chicken stock
lemon-infused olive oil (optional)
6 lemon halves to garnish

Sautéed Snapper with Fresh Sweetcorn & Crab Risotto

Serves 6 as a main course

Without a doubt, snapper would be the most popular fish to catch in New Zealand. It's a terrific fighter, with its distinctive strong nodding action, a stunning-looking fish with its golden-pink tones flecked with blue spots and, last but not least, it's a magnificent fish to eat.

This is a decadent and wonderful way to eat snapper. The fresh sweetcorn and the crab in the risotto make it delicious eating just by itself, but add a piece of perfectly cooked snapper and this dish is something else! Make sure you have all your fillets prepped and ready to cook, as once you start the risotto, it's all on, as you must continually stir the rice while you add the stock a little at a time.

Step 1: Fresh Sweetcorn and Crab Risotto

Place a large saucepan on medium heat and add the butter and shallots. Sweat for 5 minutes, then add the white wine. Simmer to reduce by half, then add the tarragon and lemon zest. Stir to combine, then add the rice and stir to coat the grains.

Add a cup of the stock and, with a wooden spoon, begin the continuous stirring. As the liquid simmers and gets absorbed into the rice, keep adding more stock a little at a time. Continue this process, then after 20 minutes or so, start checking the doneness of the rice. It is very close to being cooked when there is just a very slight resistance in the grains.

Stir in the cream, followed closely by the corn, crab meat, lemon juice and spinach. Taste and season accordingly with sea salt and black pepper.

Step 2: To Cook and Serve

When the risotto is about 10 minutes from being complete, place a skillet or sauté pan on medium heat. Season the snapper with sea salt and black pepper, add a little cooking oil to the pan and cook 3 fillets at a time. Remove from the pan when they are just cooked through.

Serve the risotto in warmed large bowls. Top each serving with a piece of fish. Pour a little of the stock around the risotto and place the rest in a jug to have on the table.

Drizzle a little of the lemon-infused olive oil over the snapper and in the stock. Garnish with a lemon half. Serve now!

I always serve a little extra hot stock around my risotto and put a little jug of it on the side. I do this because as the risotto starts to cool while you are eating it, you can keep working in a little hot stock at a time to prevent it getting stodgy!

'Bragging may not bring happiness, but no man having caught a large fish goes home through an alley.' Anonymous

Step 1: Tartare Sauce
see recipe on page 317

Step 2: Sundowner Batter
2 whole eggs
2 egg yolks (reserve the whites)
2 tablespoons milk
⅓ cup flour
pinch of salt and freshly ground
    black pepper

Step 3: To Cook and Serve
300g snapper fillet offcuts (or
    similar)
oil or butter for frying
lemons for squeezing

Snapper Sundowners with Tartare Sauce

Makes 30–40 canapés

A good friend of mine taught me this simple recipe and it is a fine example of using every inch of the fish. Too often we are all guilty of just whipping off the fillets from our fresh catch and tossing the frames way. There is plenty more good eating to be had from the rest of the fish. It's traditional on Rich's boat that as the fish get filleted, he knocks up the following batter and takes all the snapper bellies, collars, cheeks, throats and so on, removes all the flesh from them and makes these wonderful little morsels that are consumed at the end of the day, as the sun begins to set. Serve with just a squeeze of lemon juice, or smarten them up a bit with a little tartare sauce or similar.

Step 1: Tartare Sauce
See recipe on page 317.

Step 2: Sundowner Batter
Place all the ingredients in a bowl and whisk together to form a smooth, lump-free batter. Refrigerate until required.

Step 3: To Cook and Serve
Slice the snapper offcuts into pieces about 5mm thick and 2cm across.

In a clean bowl, whisk the reserved egg whites together to medium stiffness, then fold into the batter a little at a time until incorporated.

Heat a skillet or flat top on the barbecue to medium hot. Fold the snapper pieces into the batter.

Oil or butter the cooking surface then, using tongs, take out each piece of snapper from the batter and place on the heat. Turn after a minute or so until the snapper inside is cooked.

Continue cooking in batches until finished.

To serve, place a small amount of the tartare sauce on each sundowner, hit them with a squeeze of lemon and serve on a platter.

Step 1: To Roast the Carrots and Aubergine

1kg carrots (peeled weight)
cooking oil for brushing
salt and freshly ground black
   pepper
800g aubergine, sliced in 1cm-
   thick rounds

Step 2: Orange Cumin Vinaigrette

finely grated zest of 1 orange
finely grated zest of 1 lemon
200ml fresh orange juice
2 tablespoons fresh lemon juice
¼ cup finely diced shallots
½ tablespoon finely chopped
   garlic
½ teaspoon Tabasco Chipotle
   Pepper Sauce
½ tablespoon freshly ground
   cumin
1 teaspoon sweet smoked
   Spanish paprika
½ tablespoon sugar
100ml olive oil
sea salt and freshly ground black
   pepper

Step 3: To Cook and Serve

6 x 150g scarpie fillets (have your
   fishmonger fillet the scarpie
   for you)
 sea salt and freshly ground black
   pepper
cooking oil for frying
⅓ cup thinly sliced red onion
4 handfuls fresh rocket (or
   similar), torn or roughly
   chopped

Sautéed Scarpie with Roasted Carrot & Aubergine Salad & Orange Cumin Vinaigrette

Serves 6 as a main course

Also known as scorpionfish and granddaddy hapuku, these guys get a particularly bad rap with most recreational fishermen. Usually caught when targeting other species such as blue cod or tarakihi, 'another bloody scarpie' is the common frustrated cry from anglers as they recognise the distinctive orange and brown markings coming up through the water column. They are a sharp and prickly fish to deal with, but they have good thick, white fillets that eat beautifully. They are great for using in fish stews such as bouillabaisse. Due to their relative unpopularity, they are always a good buy at the market. This dish works well with the underrated scarpie, a fish I now always iki, ice down and keep along with the rest of my catch.

Step 1: To Roast the Carrots and Aubergine

Preheat the oven to 180°C.

   Cut the carrots crosswise into thirds or quarters. Place on an oiled oven tray, season with salt and pepper, and roast in the oven until golden brown (30–40 minutes). Remove and cool, then cut into bite-size pieces.

   Brush each side of the aubergine slices with a little oil then season with salt and pepper. Place a skillet or sauté pan on medium heat. Add a little oil, then when hot, cook a few aubergine slices at a time until a little coloured on both sides. Remove and place on an oven tray and place in the oven to finish cooking (5–10 minutes). Remove and cool, then cut into pieces of similar size to the carrot. Set aside.

Step 2: Orange Cumin Vinaigrette

Place the orange and lemon zest and juices in a small saucepan and place on medium heat. Reduce by half (about 100ml).

   Pour the hot reduced liquid into a bowl. Add the shallots, garlic, Tabasco Chipotle Pepper Sauce, cumin, smoked paprika and sugar. Whisk to combine.

   Continue whisking as you add the olive oil in a steady stream until incorporated. Season with sea salt and black pepper to taste. Refrigerate until required.

Step 3: To Cook and Serve

Heat a skillet or sauté pan on medium heat. Season the scarpie fillets, then add a little oil to the hot pan. Fry the fillets in batches until just cooked through (around 5 minutes). Keep the fish warm while you finish cooking the rest.

For the salad, place the carrot, aubergine, red onion and rocket in a mixing bowl. Toss and dress with about half the vinaigrette.

Divide the salad onto plates, then top each serving with a scarpie fillet. Drizzle some more vinaigrette over the fish, sprinkle with a pinch of sea salt and a grind of black pepper to finish. Good to go!

Be super-careful when removing your hook from a scarpie, as its sharp spikes are poisonous and if you are pricked by one, the wound will swell and be quite painful. When dealing with all hooked fish, always use an old rag or cloth dipped in saltwater to help hold the fish. With a scarpie, place your thumb inside the mouth on the bottom half of the jaw. While you have the scarpie secure, use your other hand to release the hook.

Step 1: Creamed Fennel Purée
700g fennel bulbs
¼ cup olive oil
½ cup finely sliced shallots
½ tablespoon finely chopped
garlic
finely grated zest of 2 lemons

½ cup 1cm-diced potato
1 cup chicken stock
1 cup cream
squeeze of lemon
sea salt and freshly ground black
pepper

Step 2: Witloof and Herb Salad
½ bulb fennel
2 heads witloof (endive), sliced
lengthwise
½ Granny Smith apple
yellow celery heart leaves (from 1
bunch), separated
¼ cup chopped chives
¼ cup fresh Italian parsley leaves

Step 3: To Cook and Serve
6 x 150g tarakihi fillets
sea salt and freshly ground black
pepper
cooking oil for frying
¼ cup walnut oil
1 tablespoon apple syrup or
squeeze of lemon juice

Sautéed Tarakihi with Creamed Fennel Purée & Witloof Herb Salad

Serves 6 as a main course

Found all around New Zealand, but more abundant south of East Cape, around Cook Strait and on both coasts of the South Island, the tarakihi starts growing quickly, reaching 25cm in three to four years, then grows slowly as an adult. Tarakihi can live to up to 50 years old and reach a weight of 6kg. A firm favourite with most New Zealanders, this is a fish suited to nearly all cooking methods. This is an elegant dish with the slight bitterness of the endive salad enhancing the natural sweetness of the fish and the fennel purée.

Step 1: Creamed Fennel Purée

Remove and discard the coarse green stalks from the fennel. Split the fennel lengthwise down the centre and remove the tough inner core. You should have about 500g of tender fennel left. Roughly chop into smallish slices.

Place the olive oil in a medium saucepan and add the fennel, shallots, garlic, lemon zest and potato. Place on medium-low heat and fry slowly for 40 minutes, stirring occasionally, until soft but not coloured.

Add the chicken stock and cream. Simmer for another 15 minutes, then remove from the heat and strain off the liquid. Reserve. With a wand blender, or in a liquidiser, process the fennel mixture, adding just enough of the cooking liquid to create a nice thick, silky-smooth purée. Pass through a fine sieve to remove any coarse fibres. Taste and season with a squeeze of lemon juice, sea salt and freshly ground black pepper. Keep warm or cool and refrigerate until required.

Step 2: Witloof and Herb Salad

Remove and discard the coarse green stalks and the tough inner core from the fennel bulb and cut into long, thin slices. Place in a bowl along with the sliced witloof. Likewise, cut the apple into matchsticks and add to the bowl. Toss in the celery leaves, chives and parsley leaves. Cover and refrigerate until serving.

Tarakihi have little mouths and when targeting these awesome eating fish, I have been taught that the most successful way to catch them is to downsize to small hooks and use minuscule pieces of bait.

Step 3: To Cook and Serve

Slowly heat the fennel purée in a double boiler or microwave. Keep warm.

Season the tarakihi with sea salt and black pepper. Place a skillet or sauté pan on medium heat and, once hot, add a little cooking oil. Pan fry the fillets until golden on each side and just barely cooked in the centre.

Dress the witloof salad with the walnut oil and apple syrup or lemon juice. Season with a little sea salt and black pepper.

To serve, spoon out the fennel purée onto warm plates and top each with a portion of tarakihi. Serve the witloof salad nestled on the side.

HOW TO: | Tunnel Bone Fish

   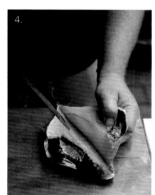

1. Slice each side of the scaled fish on an angle by the head and gills.

2. Cut down and through the back bone of the fish.

3. With the belly facing you, cut along from the excretion tube to the tail.

4. Fillet one side of the fish being careful not to cut through the top.

5. Repeat on the other side.

6. With scissors or kitchen shares, cut out the spine with the bones attached.

7–8. Remove the belly bones from one side. Repeat on the other side.

* The fish can now be stuffed with your fillings of choice. Weave a bamboo skewer through the two bellies to keep the stuffing intact while cooking. Once cooked the last fin bones running along the top of the fish can be extracted with ease, giving you a whole boneless fish.

Step 1: Crab Stuffing
100g butter
½ cup finely diced shallots
½ cup finely diced celery
1½ tablespoons finely chopped
    garlic
finely grated zest of 1 lemon
pinch of dried chilli flakes
1 tablespoon finely chopped
    fresh tarragon

2 tablespoons finely chopped
    fresh oregano
2 tablespoons finely chopped
    fresh basil
200g fresh crab meat
1 cup fish or chicken stock
    (see recipes on pages 311
    and 319)
1 tablespoon lemon juice
3 cups roughly chopped day-old
    bread

sea salt and freshly ground black
    pepper
¼ cup finely chopped fresh
    parsley
¼ cup finely chopped fresh
    chives

Step 2: To Stuff, Cook and Serve
6 whole (about 500g each)
    tarakihi, scaled and tunnel
    boned (see page 161)
sea salt and freshly ground black
    pepper
cooking oil for frying
lemon halves to serve

Whole Boned Tarakihi with Fresh Crab Stuffing

Serves 6 as a main course

The tunnel-boning technique in this recipe can be used for any number of fish. It works well on a small, single-serve whole fish, or when you want to stuff a larger fish for an awesome presentation. It's up to you whether you want to leave the head on. The only bones that remain are fin bones, which run down the back, and these can be easily removed once the fish is cooked. The stuffing is made with a little fresh crab and is another example of using a small amount to good effect. If you don't have crab, by all means use something else, such as crayfish, another fresh fish, scallops, or tuatua.

Step 1: Crab Stuffing

Place a middle-sized saucepan on medium-low heat. Add the butter and, once melted, toss in the shallots, celery, garlic, lemon zest and chilli flakes. Sweat over low heat for 20 minutes until soft.

Stir in the tarragon, oregano and basil. Sweat for 5 minutes, then add the crab meat, stock and lemon juice. Cook for another 5 minutes over low heat before adding the bread. Stir to combine. Once the bread has soaked up all the liquid, remove from the heat, then taste and season with sea salt and black pepper. Once cooled, add the parsley and chives. Refrigerate until required.

Step 2: To Stuff, Cook and Serve

Lay out the tarakihi skin side down on a clean bench. Season the exposed fillets with sea salt and black pepper. Take ½ cup or so of the crab stuffing and form it into an oblong shape. Place this on one side of the fish and fold the other half over to cover.

Using a bamboo skewer or a couple of toothpicks, sew the belly together by weaving the sticks in and out of both sides of the belly until the stuffing is secure. Repeat with the remaining fish.

New Zealand's top 10 seafood export markets in 2008 in order of value: Australia, Hong Kong, the United States, China, Japan, Spain, Korea, Germany, France and Singapore.

Preheat the oven to 160°C.

Place a skillet or saucepan on medium heat. Season the skin of the fish, add a little cooking oil to the pan, then sear the tarakihi in batches on each side for a minute or so until a little golden. Remove and place on oiled oven trays. Once all the fish are seared, place in the oven to finish cooking through. Check after 8 minutes, then at short intervals thereafter.

To serve, place a whole fish on each warm plate and add a lemon half for squeezing. Serve now.

Note: To accompany, try couscous (see recipe on page 306) flavoured with fresh herbs and lemon juice.

WHOLE TUNNEL-BONED TARAKIHI WITH FRESH CRAB STUFFING

Step 1: Flour Tortillas
make 24 x 9cm flour tortillas (see recipe on page 313)

Step 2: Chipotle Mayonnaise
1 cup Al's mayonnaise (see recipe on page 302)
1–2 tablespoons Tabasco Chipotle Pepper Sauce

Step 3: Beer Batter
see recipe on page 311

Step 4: To Cook and Serve
24 x 20g pieces blue cod (long thin portions, like chicken tenderloins)
canola oil
flour for dipping
1 bag rocket
peel of 2 preserved lemons, cut into fine strips

Blue Cod Tortillas with Chipotle Mayonnaise & Preserved Lemon

Makes 24

Fresh blue cod is at the top of the list of eating fish for many Kiwis. This, along with the ease in which they can be caught, has seen many former prolific blue cod fishing grounds decimated from overfishing in the last decade or so. Some of these areas have been closed to fishing for blue cod for a number of years now and the signs are looking positive that these special fisheries are starting to regenerate. Let's hope that when they do open up again, we give them a bit more respect and only take one or two at a time, which is plenty for a feed. This recipe makes a little blue cod go a long way. I encourage you to make the flour tortillas, as they are so much better than store bought and are super simple to make, and kids enjoy the process of rolling them out.

Step 1: Flour Tortillas
See recipe on page 313.

Step 2: Chipotle Mayonnaise
Mix the mayonnaise and chipotle sauce together in a small bowl. Taste and if you prefer it hotter, knock yourself out and add as much as you like!

Step 3: Beer Batter
See recipe on page 311.

Step 4: To Cook and Serve
Preheat the oven to 120°C. Wrap the pile of flour tortillas in tinfoil and place in the oven to heat up.

In a large saucepan add the canola oil. Place on the heat and bring up to 180°C. To test, add a little piece of white bread. It should start to fry immediately and be golden and crisp in about a minute.

Using tongs lightly dust the fish with flour, then dip in the batter, allowing most to drip off, then slowly lower each piece into the hot oil. Remove when golden and cooked through.

To assemble, lay out a few tortillas on a clean surface, place a few rocket leaves in the centre of each and top with a piece of blue cod. Add 2 or 3 strips of preserved lemon, then 1–2 dollops of the chipotle mayonnaise. Fold over and pass to someone to eat as you start on the next round.

New Zealand's 200-mile Exclusive Economic Zone is made up of 4.4 million square kilometres of ocean and includes 15,000 kilometres of coastline!

Step 1: Clam Fritter Mix

5kg live clams (about 100 or
    350g clam meat)
3 cups white wine
3 cloves garlic, roughly chopped
2 bay leaves
10 black peppercorns
100g butter, chopped into cubes
450g potato, diced 5mm cubes
cooking oil for frying
150g rindless bacon, finely diced
1 cup finely diced red onion
½ cup roughly chopped fresh
    basil

½ cup roughly chopped fresh
    coriander
3 tablespoons sweet chilli sauce
juice of ½ lemon
salt and freshly ground black
    pepper to taste

Step 2: Fritter Batter

see recipe on page 314

Step 3: Hollandaise

4 egg yolks (reserve the whites)
2 tablespoons fresh lemon juice
¼ teaspoon sugar
pinch of cayenne pepper
350g butter, melted
salt and freshly ground black
    pepper to taste

Step 4: To Cook and Serve

butter and oil for frying
6 x 120g blue cod fillets
flour seasoned with salt and
    freshly ground black pepper
12 Peppadews, roughly chopped
¼ cup parsely, roughly chopped
3 lemons, halved

Sautéed Blue Cod with Clam Fritters & Hollandaise

Serves 6 for brunch

Blue cod are bottom-dwelling fish, their colour varying depending on the age and sex. Large males tend to have a more prominent blue colouring, with a distinctive golden brown stripe above each eye, while the females are more mottled and have shades of green. Adults are found in depths of up to 150 metres, however, most blue cod reside in the shallower inshore fishery. I do like this comfort-food style of dish where you incorporate fresh fillets of fish with shellfish. I put this dish together for one of our *Hunger for the Wild* television shows where we cooked and ate it with our new-found friends in a boatshed on the Otago Peninsula. This is a terrific brunch dish. By all means substitute other shellfish in the fritters and, of course, you could use another species of fish instead of blue cod.

Step 1: Clam Fritter Mix

Rinse any sand or grit off the clams and place in a large saucepan. Add the wine, garlic, bay leaves, peppercorns and butter. Cover with a lid and place on high heat. Shake the saucepan after 5 minutes, then again after another couple of minutes. Once the clams have opened, remove from the heat and strain off the liquor into another saucepan.

Let the clams cool, then remove the meat and roughly chop. Reserve.

Place the potato in the clam liquor and bring to the boil. Cook for about 5 minutes until the potato is just soft. Strain off the clam liquor and keep for making soup or just to dip crunchy bread into. Reserve the potato.

Place a little cooking oil in a skillet or sauté pan, then add the bacon and red onion. Cook for 10 minutes on medium-low heat until the onion is soft. Strain off any excess fat, then place in a mixing bowl with the clam meat, potato and the remaining ingredients. Reserve.

When fishing for blue cod, always use large wide-gap hooks. This helps to avoid catching the smaller juvenile fish. Barbless hooks are also the way to go, as they make releasing fish a lot easier.

If you don't have barbless hooks, just crimp the barbs flat on the hooks you have. It makes for better sport and better fishermen!

Step 2: Clam Fritter Batter

Make the fritter batter on page 314. Mix 1¼ cups of the batter into the clam and bacon mixture. Heat a sauté pan, add a little cooking oil and cook a tablespoon of the mix. It should just hold together after cooking for 1–2 minutes on both sides. If falling apart a little, add a bit more batter to the mixture and repeat the process until the fritter holds together. Taste and season accordingly. Refrigerate until ready to cook.

Step 3: Hollandaise

With a wand blender or in a food processor, blitz the egg yolks, lemon juice, sugar and cayenne pepper for a few seconds, then add the warm melted butter in a slow, steady stream until all incorporated, creating a rich thick hollandaise. Season with salt and pepper to taste and keep in a warm spot until serving.

Step 4: To Cook and Serve

Preheat the oven to 100°C.

Place the reserved egg whites in a clean bowl and beat until semi-stiff, then fold into the fritter mixture half at a time. This will make the fritters light and airy.

Place a skillet or frying pan on medium heat and fry the fritters in batches in a little butter and oil. Keep warm in the oven.

Wipe out the warm skillet or frying pan and place on medium-high heat. Dip the blue cod fillets in the seasoned flour, then pat off any excess. Add some oil to the pan and a knob of butter. Sauté the fillets in batches until golden on both sides and just cooked on the inner.

Arrange a few fritters per serving on warm plates and top each serving with the blue cod. Add a healthy dollop of hollandaise on each and garnish with chopped Peppadews, parsley and half a lemon on the side. Serve pronto.

Step 1: White Bean Purée

4 x 400g tins cannellini beans
1 cup chicken stock (see recipe on page 319)
grated zest of 2 lemons
1 tablespoon finely chopped garlic
3 tablespoons olive oil
1 tablespoon lemon juice
sea salt and freshly ground black pepper to taste

Step 2: Parmesan Crumbing Mix

1 cup breadcrumbs
100g Parmesan, grated
⅓ cup finely chopped parsley

Step 3: Tomato and Basil Salad

500g fresh tomatoes (use mixed varieties), cut into medium dice
⅓ cup finely diced red onion
½ cup roughly chopped fresh basil
¼ cup extra virgin olive oil
2 tablespoons balsamic syrup (use the same method as for cabernet vinegar syrup on page 304)
sea salt and freshly ground black pepper

Step 4: To Cook and Serve

1 cup flour, seasoned with a pinch of salt and freshly ground black pepper
3 eggs, beaten
12 x 60g portions butterfish
cooking oil for frying
1 bag rocket leaves

Parmesan-Crumbed Butterfish with White Bean Purée, Tomato & Basil Salad

Serves 6 as a main course

Butterfish are also referred to by many as 'greenbone' because of the greenish tinge their frames reveal when filleted. They are also a favourite fish of many spear fishermen as they are not particularly wary and make for fairly easy targets. Butterfish are vegetarians and you find them feeding in rocky areas containing lots of kelp and seaweed.

I've never been a huge fan of this species, but for many nothing eats better. Some love delicate, small-flaked fish like butterfish, blue cod and gurnard, whereas I prefer the larger, firmer-flaked fish such as groper, warehou and kahawai. No winners here — it's whatever you fancy and, to be honest, I love to eat them all.

Step 1: White Bean Purée

Drain the beans in a sieve, then rinse under cold water and place in a large saucepan. Add the stock, lemon zest and garlic.

Place on low heat for 20 minutes to allow the flavours of the zest and garlic to infuse.

Strain the beans, reserving the stock. Using a liquidiser or a wand blender, process the beans with about half the stock to create a smooth and fairly thick purée.

Spoon into a bowl, add the olive oil and lemon juice, mix together, and season with sea salt and black pepper. Refrigerate until required.

Step 2: Parmesan Crumbing Mix

Place all the ingredients in a bowl and mix together. Cover and refrigerate if not using immediately.

Step 3: Tomato and Basil Salad

In a mixing bowl place all the ingredients except the salt and pepper. Stir together then season with a good amount of sea salt and black pepper. Set aside.

Step 4: To Cook and Serve

Place the flour, eggs and Parmesan crumbing mix each in 3 separate bowls.

Take the portions of butterfish and dust with flour, dip into the eggs, then coat in the Parmesan crumbing mix. Place on a tray or plate.

Heat the white bean purée either in a microwave or slowly in a saucepan over low heat while cooking the fish.

Place a skillet or sauté pan with a little cooking oil on medium-low heat. Once hot, add the crumbed portions of butterfish and fry over quite a low heat, as it takes longer to cook crumbed fish and the Parmesan will burn or overcook if the pan is too hot. Cook in batches and keep in a warm oven until finished.

To serve, spoon a portion of the white bean purée onto each warm plate, top each with a few rocket leaves, then 2 portions of butterfish. Spoon the salad and its juices over. Serve now!

Step 1: Gribiche Sauce
1½ cups Al's mayonnaise (see recipe on page 302)
4 hard-boiled eggs, finely chopped
¼ cup finely chopped capers
¼ cup finely chopped red onion
⅓ cup finely chopped gherkins
2 tablespoons finely chopped parsley
2 tablespoons finely chopped chervil
1½ tablespoons finely chopped tarragon
1½ tablespoons wholegrain mustard
sea salt and freshly ground black pepper

Step 2: Red Cod Fish Cakes
600g red cod fillets
1 cup milk
500g peeled floury potatoes (such as Agria), cut into 1cm dice
¼ cup cooking oil
1 cup finely diced celery
2 cups finely diced onion
2 tablespoons finely chopped garlic

¼ cup finely chopped fresh dill
¼ cup finely chopped fresh parsley
4 hard-boiled eggs, roughly chopped
finely grated zest of 2 lemons
1½ tablespoons lemon juice
⅓ cup Al's mayonnaise (see recipe on page 302)
2½ cups breadcrumbs
sea salt and freshly ground black pepper

Step 3: To Cook and Serve
cooking oil for frying
lemon wedges to garnish

Red Cod Fish Cakes with Gribiche Sauce

Serves 6 to 8 as an entrée

Red cod doesn't possess the greatest reputation as an eating fish. It's true that the flesh doesn't have a very pronounced flavour and it flakes very easily. However, I have found that if you catch a few, it's best to remove the heads, scale and gut them, then leave them whole in the fridge for a couple of days before filleting. This makes them firm up nicely and you'll be surprised how well they cook and taste with just a squeeze of citrus on them. For such a humble fish, they also make wonderful fish cakes, which I could eat every day.

Step 1: Gribiche Sauce
In a bowl, mix together all the ingredients. Taste and season accordingly. Keep the gribiche sauce refrigerated until required.

Step 2: Red Cod Fish Cakes
Place the red cod fillets in a medium saucepan and cover with the milk. Place on low heat. Remove from the heat as soon as the fish is cooked through (about 5 minutes). Strain the red cod, reserving half the milk, and place in a bowl.

Place the diced potatoes in a saucepan and cover with cold salted water. Place on high heat and bring to the boil. Reduce to a simmer until just cooked through (check after 12 minutes or so). Once cooked, remove from the heat and strain off the water. Add half the potatoes to the red cod. Mash the other half with the reserved milk and add to bowl.

Place a skillet or sauté pan on medium-low heat. Add the cooking oil, then the celery, onion and garlic. Sweat the vegetables, stirring occasionally, until soft (about 30 minutes). Just before removing from the heat, add the dill and parsley.

Gribiche sauce is basically a fancy tartare sauce with the addition of more fresh herbs and hard-boiled egg.

Stir through then add to the red cod mixture with the eggs, lemon zest and juice, mayo and ½ cup of the breadcrumbs. Gently fold the mixture together until combined. Taste and season with sea salt and black pepper. Refrigerate for an hour so the mixture firms up.

Place the remaining 2 cups of breadcrumbs in a shallow bowl. To make the fish cakes, with your hands mould about ½ cupful into a small cake. Lightly coat with breadcrumbs and place on a tray. Repeat until all the mixture is made into cakes. Refrigerate if you aren't going to cook immediately.

Step 3: To Cook and Serve
Preheat the oven to 120°C.

Place a skillet or sauté pan on medium-low heat. Add some cooking oil then fry the fish cakes in batches. Turn once golden on the first side then repeat on the other. Remove and place on an oven tray. Place the tray in the oven and cook for 8 minutes or so until the fish cakes are hot in the centre.

Divide the fish cakes up onto warm plates or a platter and serve the gribiche sauce on the side or add a dollop onto each cake. Add lemon wedges to finish. Serve now!

Step 1: Roasted Aubergine Sambal

1kg aubergines
2 tablespoons cooking oil
1 teaspoon ground turmeric
1½ teaspoons ground cumin
2 fresh chillies, finely chopped (seeds optional)
⅓ cup finely chopped red onion
1 cup plain natural yoghurt
4 tablespoons fresh lime juice
⅓ cup roughly chopped coriander leaves
sea salt and freshly ground black pepper to taste

Step 2: Yellow Split Pea Dhal

½ cup cooking oil
1 tablespoon black mustard seeds
50 curry leaves
1 cup finely diced onion
2 tablespoons finely chopped fresh ginger
2 tablespoons finely chopped garlic
1 fresh chilli, fine diced (seeds optional)

1 teaspoon sumac
1 tablespoon freshly ground cumin
1 teaspoon ground turmeric
500g yellow split peas, rinsed
1 litre chicken stock (see recipe on page 319)
lemons or limes to season
sea salt and freshly ground black pepper

Step 3: To Cook and Serve

6 x 150g trumpeter fillets
sea salt and freshly ground black pepper
cooking oil for frying
lemon or lime quarters

Trumpeter with Yellow Split Pea Dahl & Roasted Aubergine Sambal

Serves 6 as a main course

Another fine fish I have yet to catch, trumpeter seem to be more prevalent the further south you go. A terrific eating fish, with a firm, medium flake, it's suited to most cooking applications. This is a wintry Indian-style dish, with some good spice and fresh chilli kicking things along. To accompany this rustic meal, I'd be tempted to make a batch of roti (see page 194) to eat alongside. A large fresh green salad on the table would complete the meal.

Step 1: Roasted Aubergine Sambal

Preheat the oven to 200°C.

Cut the aubergines in half lengthwise. Place in a roasting dish, skin side down. Brush the flesh with oil then sprinkle the turmeric and cumin over. Place in the oven for 30 minutes or so until the aubergines are golden brown and very soft. Remove from the oven and let cool completely.

Once cold, use a spoon to scoop the soft flesh from the skin. Roughly chop and place in a bowl. Add the chilli, red onion, yoghurt, lime juice and coriander leaves.

Stir to combine, taste and season with sea salt and black pepper. Refrigerate until required.

Step 2: Yellow Split Pea Dhal

Place a large heavy-based saucepan on medium heat. Once hot, add the oil, mustard seeds and curry leaves. Sauté for 2 minutes before adding the onion, ginger, garlic and chilli. Stir through and reduce the heat to low.

Fry gently for 10 minutes, then add the sumac, cumin and turmeric. Stir through, then add the split peas and chicken stock. Bring to the boil, then lower the heat to a simmer.

Cook for around 40 minutes, stirring occasionally, until the split peas are beginning to break down. If the stock has been absorbed and the split peas are not quite cooked through, add some water a little at a time and continue cooking.

Trumpeter belong to the moki family. They average around 5kg but can grow up to 15kg. They inhabit reefs and rough foul and can be caught in depths of 20–200 metres.

I like my dhal quite wet and slightly sloppy. Remove from the heat and season with a squeeze or two of fresh lemon or lime juice and sea salt and pepper to your taste.

Keep warm or refrigerate until required.

Step 3: To Cook and Serve

Preheat the oven to 180°C.

If the dhal needs reheating, place in a heavy-based saucepan on low heat. You may need to add a little water if it has become too thick. Or microwave the dhal until hot.

Place a skillet or sauté pan on medium-high heat. Season the fish with sea salt and pepper. Add a little oil to the pan, followed by 3 of the trumpeter fillets. Sear on both sides then place in an ovenproof dish, then repeat with the remaining pieces. Place the fish in the oven for a few minutes until just cooked through.

To serve, spoon out some of the dhal into warm shallow bowls, then add a fillet of trumpeter to each serving. Top with a lemon or lime quarter and a dollop of the aubergine sambal and serve immediately.

Step 1: Fennel and Potato Rösti
2 large fennel bulbs
⅓ cup olive oil
1 cup thinly sliced onion
1 tablespoon fennel seeds, dry
   roasted and ground
1kg potatoes (peeled weight)

finely grated zest of 1 lemon
sea salt and freshly ground black
   pepper
cooking oil for frying

**Step 2: Green Olive and Caper
Hollandaise**
hollandaise sauce (see recipe on
   page 313)
⅓ cup roughly chopped pitted
   green olives
¼ cup capers, rinsed and roughly
   chopped

Step 3: To Cook and Serve
6 x 150g porae fillets
sea salt and freshly ground black
   pepper
cooking oil for frying
lemon wedges to garnish

Sautéed Porae with Fennel & Potato Rösti & Green Olive & Caper Hollandaise

Serves 6 for lunch or brunch

We don't get porae down our way in Wellington at all. These good eating fish prefer warmer waters and are more prominent the further north you go. Porae are closely related to and look a lot like tarakihi. However, they are generally larger, growing up to 6kg in weight. You'll catch porae in sandy-bottom areas close to reef habitats in up to 60 metres of water.

A rösti is a Swiss potato cake, or actually more like a hash brown. I've given them a slight twist by adding a bit of fennel, which lightens the cakes a little and gives them a more interesting flavour. Hollandaise is such a rich and wonderful butter sauce and, with the addition of sliced green olives and chopped capers, it's spot on for this sort of brunch-style dish.

Step 1: Fennel and Potato Rösti

Remove any fresh 'herby' tips from the tops of the fennel bulbs and reserve. Remove the tough stalks from the bulbs, split the bulbs in half lengthwise and cut out the tough inner cores. Slice the fennel into thin slivers (you should have around 3 cups).

Place a sauté pan on medium-low heat. Add the olive oil, then the fennel, onion and ground fennel seeds. Fry gently for 30 minutes, stirring occasionally, until soft and tender but not coloured. Remove and cool.

For the potatoes use a mandolin with the small comb attachment fitted and slice the potatoes into shoestrings. If you don't have a mandolin, grate the potatoes on the coarse side of a cheese grater. Squeeze any excess water from the potatoes and place in a mixing bowl. Add the fennel and onion mix, the reserved fennel tips and lemon zest. Mix together and season with sea salt and black pepper.

Place a small saucepan over medium heat and pour in a little cooking oil. Add about half a cupful of the rösti mix to the pan and spread out to the thickness of a pancake. Leave to cook for a couple of minutes until the rösti starts to become golden on the edges. Carefully flip and cook the other side. Remove and place on an oven tray and repeat with the remaining rösti mix. Set aside.

Fish have been on the earth for more than 450 million years and were well established long before the dinosaurs roamed the earth.

Step 2: Green Olive and Caper Hollandaise

Make the hollandaise as directed and pour into a small mixing bowl. Fold in the olives and capers. Keep in a warm spot until required.

Step 3: To Cook and Serve

Preheat the oven to 140°C.

Place the oven tray of cooked rösti in the oven to crisp up.

Meanwhile, place a skillet or sauté pan on medium heat. Season the porae fillets with sea salt and black pepper. Add a little cooking oil to the pan and fry the fillets on both sides in batches until just cooked through.

Place a crisp rösti in the centre of each plate. Top with a fillet of porae, then add a dollop of the green olive and caper hollandaise. Garnish with a lemon wedge and serve.

HOW TO: | Fillet a Skate

1. With the skate on its belly, feel where the fillet runs along and make an incision.

2. Run the knife along that line.

3. Cut through the fillet to the wing bones.

4. Remove the top fillets by running the blade of the knife along the wing bones.

5. Turn the skate over and repeat the process on the under-wings, which give slightly smaller fillets.

6. Skate wing with fillet removed.

7–8. Hold the end of the skin while you slide the knife along to remove the fillet.

Step 1: Grapefruit and Fresh Dill Vinaigrette
⅔ cup freshly squeezed pink grapefruit juice
2 tablespoons chardonnay vinegar (or white wine vinegar)
1 teaspoon Dijon mustard
1 tablespoon sugar
⅔ cup walnut oil
sea salt and freshly ground black pepper
3 tablespoons finely chopped fresh dill

Step 2: To Poach the Skate
1½ cups white wine
juice of 2 lemons
2 shallots, roughly chopped
½ stick celery, roughly chopped
2 bay leaves
600g skate fillets
sea salt to taste

Step 3: To Finish and Serve
2 heads witloof (endive)
½ cup young yellow celery leaves (from the inside of a bunch), roughly chopped
2 handfuls mizuna lettuce, rocket or similar
⅓ cup fresh Italian parsley leaves
⅓ cup fresh chives cut into 5cm lengths
⅓ cup sliced red onion

1½ fresh pink grapefruit
sea salt and freshly ground black pepper

Poached Skate, Witloof & Pink Grapefruit Salad

Serves 6 as a light lunch

Skate has to be eaten fresh, within two or three days of being caught, as after this time it will take on a slight odour of ammonia. Easy to fillet, skate has a similar bone structure to flatfish like flounder or turbot. There is a larger fillet on the top side of each wing, with a slightly smaller one on the underside. (See filleting technique on page 179) Once the fillets have been removed from the wings, there will be no bones, but the inedible skin must be taken off before cooking.

This is a super healthy light salad, with tons of flavour. Keep an eye out for pink grapefruit, as they are less acidic and add just a little sweetness, which helps balance the slight bitterness of the witloof, celery leaves and parsley.

Step 1: Grapefruit and Fresh Dill Vinaigrette
In a small non-reactive saucepan place the grapefruit juice, vinegar, mustard and sugar. Place on medium heat and simmer to reduce by half (about ¼ cup). Pour this hot liquid into a small bowl. Using a wand blender, a whisk or similar, slowly add the walnut oil in a steady stream, whisking until combined. Season with sea salt and black pepper. Add the dill, stir, then refrigerate.

Step 2: To Poach the Skate
Preheat the oven to 140°C.

In an ovenproof dish, place the white wine, lemon juice, shallots, celery and bay leaves. Add enough water so the skate fillets will be just submerged when added. Season the poaching liquid with a good amount of salt. Add the skate fillets, cover with tinfoil and place in the oven.

Check after 15–20 minutes. Once just cooked, remove from the oven. With a slotted spatula or similar, remove the skate from the liquid. Cover with plastic wrap and refrigerate.

Step 3: To Finish and Serve
Cut the witloof lengthwise into quarters. Cut out the inner stalk, then slice into long thin strips. Place in large bowl with the celery leaves, mizuna, parsley, chives and red onion.

Only a quarter of all New Zealanders fished recreationally more than once in the last 12 months.

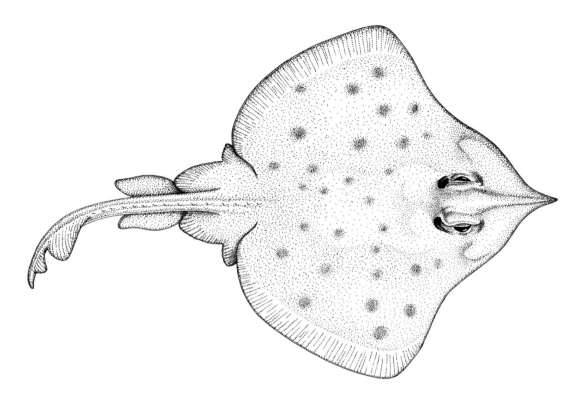

Remove the skin and pith from the grapefruit, then with a sharp knife, carefully cut the segments out of their membrane. Chop the segments into largish pieces and add to the bowl.

For the skate, break up the obvious strands of the fillets into single lengths and add to the salad. Carefully dress the salad with about two-thirds of the vinaigrette. Toss gently together with your hands.

Divide the salad between chilled plates and drizzle the last of the vinaigrette over each serving. A pinch of sea salt and a grind of pepper on each and you're good to go.

Step 1: Ponzu Sauce
½ cup rice wine vinegar
½ cup soy sauce
¼ cup red wine
1½ tablespoons dried bonito
    flakes
2 pickled plums (available at
    Asian stores)
1 lime, quartered

Step 2: To Cook and Serve
6 x 140g boned fresh skate fillets
flour seasoned with salt and
    freshly ground black pepper
clarified butter (or regular butter)
lime wedges to garnish

Pan-Fried Crispy Skate with Ponzu Sauce

Serves 6 as an entrée

This was the signature dish of a restaurant where I worked as a cook in the Tribeca neighbourhood of Manhattan in New York City. On occasions, it was so popular it would out-sell the rest of the entrées on the menu by two to one. Seji, our chef, would procure only small skate wings that, once cooked, presented on the plate like a beautiful outstretched butterfly wing. A dish of ponzu was all that accompanied the skate, now one of my favourite fish. It was here that I truly began to understand and love the whole 'less is more' philosophy of cooking. Ponzu is a classic Japanese dipping sauce that is salty and sour. The skate is lightly floured, which gives it a crisp outer that you dip into the ponzu with each mouthful.

Step 1: Ponzu Sauce

Place all the ingredients in a small saucepan and place on medium-low heat. Bring to a very slight simmer. (Do not boil.) Simmer on very low for 30 minutes to let the flavours infuse.

Remove from the heat and strain through a fine sieve or, better still, a piece of muslin. Cool to room temperature, then refrigerate.

Step 2: To Cook and Serve

Bring a sauté pan up to medium-high heat. Lightly dust the skate fillets in the seasoned flour, patting off any excess.

Once the pan is hot, add a liberal amount of clarified butter. Fry 1–2 skate fillets at a time for a couple of minutes on each side until golden and crisp on the outside. Keep the cooked skate warm by placing on a cake rack in a preheated oven to retain their crispness while you cook the rest.

To serve, place the skate fillets on warm plates with a little dish of dipping sauce and a wedge of fresh lime alongside.

To clarify butter (ghee), place at least 250g of butter in a saucepan and place on medium-low heat. Bring to a simmer for 20–30 minutes to evaporate any water. Remove from the heat, skim off any scum before pouring off the clarified butter and discarding the milk solids at the bottom of the saucepan.

Step 1: Caramelised Fennel Bulb Lentils

2 cups Puy lentils
5 cups water or chicken stock
(see recipe on page 319)
2 bay leaves
pinch of salt
3 medium-large fennel bulbs
⅓ cup olive oil
1½ cups finely diced onion
2 tablespoons finely diced garlic
finely grated zest of 2 lemons
⅓ cup finely chopped fresh
parsley
⅓ cup extra virgin olive oil
1½ tablespoons lemon juice
sea salt and freshly ground black
pepper

Step 2: Mustard Sabayon Butter

4 egg yolks
3 tablespoons white wine vinegar
1 teaspoon sugar
200g butter, cut into 1cm dice
1½ tablespoons wholegrain
mustard
1 tablespoon Dijon mustard
sea salt and freshly ground black
pepper

Step 3: To Cook and Serve

6 x 140g fillets John Dory, skin
on and scored
sea salt and freshly ground black
pepper
cooking oil for frying
extra virgin olive oil for drizzling

Sautéed John Dory with Caramelised Fennel Bulb Lentils & Mustard Sabayon Butter

Serves 6 as a main course

This is a quite gutsy winter-style dish. The caramelised fennel bulb and lemon zest add a lovely subtle flavour to the earthy green Puy lentils. The mustard sabayon butter is very similar to a hollandaise, but a little lighter and works well with the lentils. Keep the skin on the John Dory fillets as they have no scales and it crisps up in the cooking process, adding texture and flavour to the dish.

Step 1: Caramelised Fennel Bulb Lentils

Place the lentils in a medium saucepan and add the cold water or stock, bay leaves and a healthy pinch of salt. Place on high heat, bring to the boil, then reduce to a simmer and cook for 30–40 minutes until the lentils are just soft through the centre but holding their form. Strain, discarding the bay leaves, and reserve.

Meanwhile, with a sharp knife, remove the green fibrous stems from the fennel bulbs, reserving any of the fresh green tips. Halve the fennel bulbs lengthwise down the centre and cut out and discard the tough middle core. Finely dice the rest of the fennel.

In a large skillet or sauté pan, place the olive oil, fennel, onion, garlic and lemon zest. Place the pan on low heat and sweat the vegetables for 40 minutes, stirring occasionally. Once soft, increase the heat and sauté until they start to caramelise.

Stir the fennel mixture into the lentils and add the parsley, reserved fennel tips, olive oil and lemon juice. Mix well and season with sea salt and black pepper. Keep warm.

Step 2: Mustard Sabayon Butter

Place the egg yolks, vinegar and sugar in a small stainless steel bowl and put the bowl over a small saucepan containing 1½ cups of water, creating a double boiler. The bottom of the bowl should not be touching the water in the saucepan. Place the double boiler on medium-low heat.

Whisk the mixture continuously until it becomes thickened and airy (2–4 minutes). Take the bowl off at times if it becomes too hot.

Once thick and airy, add a few chunks of butter at a time, whisking continuously until melted and incorporated.

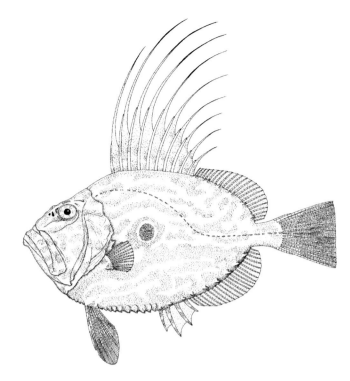

Remove the bowl from the saucepan and mix in the mustards. Taste and season with the sea salt and black pepper.

Step 3: To Cook and Serve
Place a skillet or sauté pan on medium-high heat. Season the fillets. Once the pan is hot, add a little cooking oil then place 3 fillets skin side down in the pan. Fry until golden and crisp on the skin side, then turn and finish on the other. Keep the cooked fillets warm while you repeat with the rest.

To serve, spoon out some of the caramelised fennel bulb lentils on each plate, top with a portion of fish, spoon a liberal amount of the mustard sabayon butter over, then drizzle some olive oil over to finish. Serve now.

Sabayon-style butters work beautifully with all fish and shellfish, not to mention something like a chargrilled steak. If you don't want to serve the sabayon butter warm, pour it into a container and refrigerate it until required. Remove it from the fridge 30 minutes or so before serving and use a warm spoon to make quenelles which will melt over the warm food. Try other combinations such as horseradish, curry or saffron in place of mustard.

Step 1: Horseradish and Cauliflower Purée
600g cauliflower florets, roughly chopped
1¼ cups cream
⅓ cup horseradish sauce
squeeze of lemon juice
salt and white pepper to taste

Step 2: Buttered Lime Zest Savoy Cabbage
40g butter
2 tablespoons very finely grated lime zest
500g Savoy cabbage, thinly sliced
2 tablespoons water
¼ cup thinly sliced fresh mint
squeeze of lime juice
salt and freshly ground black pepper

Step 3: To Cook and Serve
6 x 160gm John Dory fillets, skin on
sea salt and freshly ground black pepper
cooking oil for frying
several knobs butter
lime wedges to garnish

Crisp-Skinned John Dory with Horseradish & Cauliflower Purée & Buttered Lime Zest Savoy Cabbage

Serves 6 as a main course

I have to confess — and it's a bit of a bugbear for me — that I have never caught a John Dory. It's an extraordinary looking and wonderful eating fish. If you happen to be partial to walks along the coast at first light, you can sometimes find the odd John Dory washed up on the beach. With their oval yet quite slender shape, John Dory have a habit of chasing bait fish into the shallows at low tide where their greed for a meal can often be at their peril, as they run out of water and fall on their sides, unable to right themselves again.

I like to cook this dish in winter when cauliflowers and cabbages are at their best. The horseradish and lime zest work wonderfully with the brassicas adding a sharpness to the dish. Cook the cabbage just before or at the same time as the John Dory.

Step 1: Horseradish and Cauliflower Purée

Bring a saucepan of salted water to the boil. Add the cauliflower and cook for 7–10 minutes until just soft.

Remove from the heat and strain off the water. Add the cream and horseradish, then place the saucepan back on medium heat. Cook for another 5 minutes until the cream is slightly reduced. Taste and if you want a stronger horseradish 'kick', add more to suit.

Pour the cauliflower mixture into a liquidiser and purée until smooth. Strain through a fine sieve, discarding any tough pieces of horseradish stem.

Finish with a squeeze of lemon juice and season with salt and white pepper. Refrigerate until required.

Step 2: Buttered Lime Zest Savoy Cabbage

Place a large sauté or frying pan on medium heat. Add the butter and lime zest. When the butter is melted, toss in the cabbage and add the water. Cook over medium heat, stirring regularly, until the cabbage is just cooked, without browning. It should still have a slightly crunchy texture. Add the mint and a squeeze of lime. Season with salt and pepper. Keep warm.

Step 3: To Cook and Serve

Either in a small saucepan over low heat or in the microwave, gently heat the cauliflower purée.

With a sharp knife, score each John Dory fillet a couple of times just through the skin — this will help the fish stay flat in the pan, ensuring even cooking. Heat a skillet over high heat and season the fillets with salt and pepper. Add a little cooking oil to the pan, then add 3 fillets skin side down. Monitor your heat and cook for 2–3 minutes until the skin is golden. Turn the fillets, then add a couple of knobs of butter and finish cooking on the flesh side. Remove and keep warm while you repeat with the remaining fillets.

To serve, spoon some cauliflower purée into the centre of each warm plate. Top with the cabbage, then finish with a portion of John Dory resting on top. Garnish with a wedge of lime.

The large black spot prominently positioned on each side of this fish is thought to act as a deterrent to predators. As it senses danger, the John Dory flashes its large evil-looking 'eye' to scare approaching carnivores. By contrast, the spot is also known to many as representing the thumbprint of St Peter, the keeper of the gates to heaven.

Step 1: Tomato, Fennel and Saffron Ragout
⅓ cup olive oil
3 cups diced onion
1 cup diced celery
6 cloves garlic, roughly chopped
grated zest of 2 lemons
350g fennel bulb, stalks and inner core discarded, (reserving green leafy tips) and quartered
2 bay leaves
1 cup white wine
pinch of saffron threads, soaked in ¼ cup warm water
3 cups fish stock or chicken stock (see recipes on pages 311 and 319)
2 x 400g tins whole peeled tomatoes, crushed
⅓ cup tomato paste
1 tablespoon sugar
400g potatoes, peeled and cut into medium dice
sea salt and freshly ground black pepper

Step 2: To Cook and Serve
6 x 150g blue mackerel fillets
¼ cup roughly chopped reserved fresh fennel tips
couscous (optional, see recipe on page 306)
25g butter, cut into knobs

Baked Blue Mackerel in a Tomato, Fennel Saffron Ragout

Serves 6 as a main course

Blue mackerel are the silver bullets of the sea. Related to and shaped like a streamlined tuna, these fish grow up to 40cm in length and weigh in at up to 1.5 kilos. Their flesh is relatively soft, with high oil content, but it firms up once cooked.

This is a great Mediterranean-style dish, with a rich sauce made from the tomato and fennel. The addition of good-quality saffron gives it a fragrant finish. There are potatoes in the sauce so you can serve it by itself as a hearty stew, however, I love to serve it over plainly cooked couscous with a simple green salad on the side.

Six out of 10 recreational fishers report that they are satisfied with their catch.

Step 1: Tomato, Fennel and Saffron Ragout
Place a large saucepan on medium heat. Add the olive oil, followed by the onion, celery, garlic, lemon zest, fennel and bay leaves. Stir together, reduce the heat to low and sweat for 40 minutes until soft and translucent.

Add the white wine and the saffron and its water. Cook for 5 minutes then add the stock, tomatoes, tomato paste and sugar. Simmer for 10 minutes then add the potatoes. Reduce to a low simmer and cook, stirring occasionally, until the potatoes are just soft. Remove from the heat, cool, then refrigerate until cooking the mackerel.

Step 2: To Cook and Serve
Preheat the oven to 150°C.

Pour the tomato, fennel and saffron ragout into a large ovenproof dish. Nestle the mackerel portions in the ragout. Sprinkle the fennel tips over, cover and place in the oven. Bake for 25 minutes or until the fish is just cooked through.

Meanwhile, prepare the couscous, if using.

Remove the portions of mackerel and place in warmed bowls (or over servings of couscous). Add the butter to the sauce and stir in. Spoon the sauce over the fish and serve immediately.

Step 1: Garam Masala Paste
½ cup canola oil
75g finely diced shallots
1½ tablespoon finely chopped garlic
2½ tablespoons finely chopped ginger
2 tablespoons garam masala
1 tablespoon ground cumin
1 tablespoon ground turmeric
2 tablespoons black mustard seeds

Step 2: To Prepare the Potatoes
800g floury Potatoes (such as Agria), peeled and cut into 2cm dice
20g fresh ginger, peeled and chopped into 5–6 pieces
1 teaspoon ground turmeric

Step 3: Kaffir Lime Sauce
30ml white wine vinegar
120ml white wine
500ml chicken stock (see recipe on page 311)
juice of 1 fresh coconut
250ml cream
300ml coconut cream
½ cup grated fresh coconut
1 tablespoon finely chopped fresh ginger
5 kaffir lime leaves
½ tablespoon brown sugar
½ tablespoon fish sauce
juice and finely grated zest of 1 lime
salt and white pepper

Blue Moki with Garam Masala Potatoes & Kaffir Lime Sauce

Serves 6 as a main course

Blue moki is a terrific fish to catch or spear. A great-looking fish, they're good fighters and a prize catch, particularly when surf-casting. You will only catch them using shellfish or crustaceans as bait. I've always enjoyed the large meaty flake and texture of blue moki, and it's another of those species you really don't want to overcook, as it is prone to drying out.

This is quite a long and slightly drawn-out recipe, but you can do many of the steps over a few days. Then if you are entertaining, all you need to do is heat everything up and just cook the moki. This dish is a real favourite of mine and appears on the menu at Logan Brown from time to time.

New Zealand has 15,134km of coastline, the ninth longest in the world.

Step 1: Garam Masala Paste
Place all the ingredients in a small heavy-based saucepan and place over low heat. Sweat for 20 minutes, stirring occasionally. Remove from the heat, cool, then store in a container in the fridge until required. This paste will last a couple of months and is great with vegetables, poultry and fish.

Step 2: To Prepare the Potatoes
Place the potatoes in a large saucepan with the ginger and turmeric. Cover with the cold salted water, place on the heat and simmer until the potatoes are just cooked through.

Strain off the water and cool to room temperature. Remove and discard the pieces of ginger and refrigerate the potatoes until required.

Step 3: Kaffir Lime Sauce
Pour the white wine vinegar and white wine into a medium saucepan. Place on the heat and simmer to reduce until almost dry. Add the chicken stock and fresh coconut juice and reduce slowly until there is about 1 cup of liquid left.

Add the remaining ingredients except the salt and pepper and, on very low heat, bring up to the slightest simmer. Stir from time to time, but do not allow to boil.

Step 4: To Cook and Serve

½ cup cooking oil, plus extra for frying
4 tomatoes, peeled, seeded and roughly chopped
¼ cup roughly chopped fresh coriander, plus extra leaves to garnish
juice of 1½ lemons
salt and freshly ground black pepper to taste

6 x 150g blue moki fillets
sea salt
fresh coriander leaves
fried shallots to garnish (optional)
fried fresh curry leaves to garnish (optional)
lemons for squeezing

After 20 minutes, remove from the heat and season with salt and white pepper. Leave at room temperature for an hour or so to give more time for the flavours to infuse. Strain and toss out the solids, then refrigerate the sauce until required.

Step 4: To Cook and Serve

Heat a large sauté pan or skillet, add the oil then 3–4 tablespoons of the garam masala paste. Now add the potatoes and toss through so they all have a good covering of the spice paste. Once the potatoes are hot, toss in the tomatoes, coriander and lemon juice. Season with salt and pepper, remove from the heat and keep warm.

In a small saucepan over low heat, warm up the kaffir lime sauce until hot then set aside.

Heat a skillet or similar to medium heat. Add a little cooking oil. Season the blue moki with sea salt and black pepper. Cook 3 fillets at a time, turning once golden, then finishing on the other side until just cooked through. Remove and keep warm while you repeat with the last 3 fillets.

To serve, spoon out the garam masala potatoes into the centre of warm plates, top each serving with a blue moki fillet, then spoon liberal amounts of the kaffir lime sauce over and around. Garnish with a few fresh coriander leaves, and fried shallots and fried curry leaves, if using, and a squeeze of lemon juice. Serve now!

Step 1: Horseradish Celeriac Remoulade
500g celeriac (peeled weight)
juice and finely grated zest of 1 lemon
⅓ cup sliced red onion
¼ cup roughly chopped fresh basil
¼ cup finely chopped fresh chives
1 cup Al's mayonnaise (see recipe on page 302)
3 tablespoons horseradish sauce
sea salt and freshly ground black pepper

Step 2: To Cook and Serve
1 cup flour, seasoned with salt and freshly ground black pepper
3 eggs, beaten
3 cups breadcrumbs
1kg fresh skinned and boned warehou, cut into 12 portions
cooking oil for frying
butter, cut into knobs
lemon wedges to serve

Crumbed Warehou with Horseradish Celeriac Remoulade

Serves 6 as a main course

Warehou fillet enjoys any cooking method that involves a coating, as it helps retain the moisture. I find that when cooking crumbed fillets that are thick and from larger fish, the best approach is to start cooking them in a pan until just golden on each side, then finish them in the oven, as often people end up overcooking the breadcrumb coating while the fish can still be raw in the centre.

A remoulade is similar to a coleslaw, but made with thin matchsticks of celeriac tossed with mayonnaise and, in this case, some horseradish to give a little zing. This dish has great textures and my favourite accompaniment is citrus mash (see recipe on page 306).

Step 1: Horseradish Celeriac Remoulade

Using a very sharp knife or mandolin, cut the celeriac into thin matchsticks. Alternatively, use a large coarse-edged grater. Place in a bowl.

Add the lemon juice and zest, red onion, basil and chives. Mix through with your hands, then fold in the mayonnaise and horseradish. Taste and season accordingly.

Step 2: To Cook and Serve

Place the seasoned flour, eggs and breadcrumbs in individual bowls. Dip the warehou pieces in the flour followed by the eggs then the breadcrumbs. Place on a clean, dry tray.

Heat a skillet or large frying pan on medium-low heat. Add a liberal amount of cooking oil, then cook the crumbed warehou in batches. Turn after a minute or so when golden, add a little knob of butter and, once golden on the other side, remove and place on an oven tray. Place the warehou in the oven to finish cooking through (3–5 minutes).

To serve, place a good amount of the remoulade in the centre of each plate or serve on a platter. Top with the warehou portions and garnish with a wedge of lemon. Serve now!

Forty per cent of all fish species inhabit fresh water, yet less than 0.01 per cent of the earth's water is fresh.

800g warehou fillets
150g tamarind pulp
¾ cup hot water
¾ tablespoon ground turmeric
¾ tablespoon ground cinnamon
1 tablespoon ground cumin
1–2 fresh chillies, seeded and minced
½ cup roughly chopped fresh coriander
¾ cup canola oil (or similar)
salt

Step 2: Carrot and Coriander Relish

3 cups grated carrot
½ cup thinly sliced red onion
½ cup roughly chopped fresh coriander
¼ cup canola oil
1 tablespoon minced fresh ginger
1 tablespoon minced garlic
60 curry leaves
1 tablespoon mustard seeds
pinch of dried chilli flakes
¼ cup fresh lime juice
salt and freshly ground black pepper

Step 3: Puspa's Roti
2 cups wholemeal flour
2 cups white flour
1 teaspoon salt
70g butter
1⅔ cups water
cooking oil for brushing

Step 4: To Cook and Serve
cooking oil for frying
thick natural yoghurt to serve
fresh lime wedges to garnish

Tamarind-Marinated Blue Warehou with Fresh Roti & Carrot & Coriander Relish

Makes 24

Warehou seems to be one of those underrated fish that people turn their noses up at. I'm very partial to its firm flesh and it is one of my favourite species when ordering 'two pieces and a scoop'! Warehou, along with moki and kahawai, can dry out in the cooking process, so it's important to be extra vigilant to avoid overcooking.

My great Indian cook mentor, Puspa, taught me how to make these delicious roti, which my family adore. There's no mucking around with yeast or a heap of kneading — just make the dough, roll it out and cook.

Step 1: Tamarind-Marinated Blue Warehou

Cut the warehou into strips about the size and shape of chicken tenderloins and place in a bowl. Break the tamarind up with your fingers into another bowl then pour the hot water over and let sit for 5 minutes. With a spoon, or again your fingers, work the tamarind paste away from the indeible pips and husk. Work it all through a sieve into a small bowl, discarding the solids. Add the rest of the ingredients. Mix thoroughly. Pour three-quarters of the marinade over the warehou and mix through with your hands. Refrigerate along with the reserved marinade.

Step 2: Carrot and Coriander Relish

Place the carrot, red onion and coriander in a mixing bowl.

Place a sauté pan on medium heat. When hot, add the oil, then the ginger, garlic, curry leaves, mustard seeds and chilli flakes. Sauté for a minute or so before pouring into the carrot mixture.

Add the lime juice, then mix all together until combined. Taste and season with salt and pepper. Cover with plastic wrap and let the fresh relish flavours develop in the fridge for at least an hour.

Step 3: Puspa's Roti

In a large mixing bowl place the flours and salt. Mix together.

Place the butter and water in a saucepan on medium heat and remove once the butter has melted.

Pour the melted butter and water mix into the flour. With your hands, mix the dough together until combined. Tip out onto a lightly floured surface and knead for a minute until you have a smooth dough.

Place a skillet or heavy-based frying pan on low-medium heat. While the pan is heating up, divide the dough into 24 pieces and, on the lightly floured surface, roll each out into a thin round 1mm–2mm thick.

Start cooking the roti as you are still rolling them out. Place in the dry skillet or pan and cook for about 30–60 seconds on each side until slightly golden.

When cooked, brush each on both sides with a little oil to prevent them from drying out. Stack on top of each other.

Continue until all the roti are cooked. Once cooled, cover with plastic wrap and set aside until required.

Step 4: To Cook and Serve

Heat the roti by wrapping them all together in tinfoil and placing in a preheated oven, or just toss them back into a warm skillet or onto the hot griddle top of the barbecue for 30 seconds or so. Keep warm.

For the warehou, heat a skillet or griddle top to medium heat (not too hot as the marinade will burn before the fish is cooked). Add a little oil then the pieces of warehou. Fry for about a minute on each side until cooked through.

Brush the inside of each roti with a little of the reserved tamarind marinade. Add some cooked warehou, then top with some of the carrot and coriander relish. A dollop of yoghurt to finish, then wrap and serve with a wedge of lime. Hand them out as you go and repeat until all are eaten!

Around 85 per cent of New Zealanders think that up to 10 fish per recreational fisher is a reasonable daily allowance and 85 per cent of recreational fishers agree. The current limit is 20 for most fin fish.

TAMARIND-MARINATED BLUE WAREHOU WITH FRESH ROTI & CARROT & CORIANDER RELISH

6 toast slices white bread
6 x 140g fresh trevally fillets
sea salt and freshly ground black
  pepper
cooking oil for frying
½ cup extra virgin olive oil

150g black olives, stones
  removed and sliced into slivers
⅓ cup Peppadews, sliced into
  slivers
3 tablespoons roughly chopped
  capers

½ cup chopped fresh parsley
2 tablespoons lemon juice
lemon wedges

Fresh Trevally with Black Olives, Capers & Sweet Peppadews on Toast

Serves 6 as a main course at lunch

I grew up thinking trevally was only good for bait. I'm sure it had to do with buying those little frozen cardboard boxes that you still get today in most bait freezers at your local gas station. It's now one of my favourite fish to catch today. A good-sized one will give you a great scrap on light tackle and, as far as an eating fish goes, they are way up the list for me. As always, I iki and bleed them immediately, before icing down to keep chilled. They are absolutely amazing to eat raw, along with the usual condiments — good-quality soy and wasabi. I also rate them big time as a cooking species and this dish takes only a couple of minutes to throw together, as most of the components are in a preserved form. It makes a great lunch dish — I'm not exactly sure why I serve it over white toast but I love it.

Peppadews are a brand name for a range of pickled piquante peppers that originated in South Africa. These little red peppers are great for stuffing or just sliced and added to anything to give a little kick. I have a jar in the fridge permanently and reach for them constantly in my cooking.

Method

Start cooking your toast.

Place a skillet or sauté pan on medium heat. Season the trevally fillets with sea salt and pepper. Add some cooking oil to the hot pan and cook the trevally in batches, keeping the cooked fillets warm while you cook the rest.

Once all of the the fish is cooked, place the same hot pan back on the heat. Add the extra virgin olive oil, black olives, Peppadews and capers. Cook for a minute or so before removing from the heat and adding the parsley and lemon juice.

Serve the trevally fillets on the toast and spoon the olive mixture over. A pinch of sea salt, a grind of black pepper to finish, with a wedge of lemon on the side. Serve now!

Trevally grow extremely quickly, reaching maturity in five years, and can live up to the age of 45 years. They feed on krill, plankton and the like, and often cruise in large surface schools.

Step 1: Lemon Chutney
600g lemons (Meyer if possible)
1 cup white wine vinegar
2 cups finely diced onion
2 tablespoons finely chopped
   garlic
1 fresh chilli, finely chopped
   (seeds optional)
2 teaspoons cinnamon
8 whole cloves
2 whole star anise
3 cups brown sugar
sea salt and freshly ground black
   pepper

Step 2: Crisp Falafel
720g cooked chickpeas (3 tins,
   drained of liquid)
3 eggs
¼ cup fresh lemon juice
¼ cup finely diced onion
¾ tablespoon freshly ground
   cumin seeds
¾ tablespoon freshly ground
   coriander seeds
pinch of cayenne pepper
1 teaspoon sugar

1 cup breadcrumbs, plus extra
   for crumbing the falafel
⅓ cup finely chopped parsley
sea salt and freshly ground black
   pepper

Step 3: Saffron Yoghurt
pinch of saffron threads
1½ cups good-quality thick
   natural yoghurt

Step 4: To Cook and Serve
cooking oil for frying
6 x 150g trevally fillets
sea salt and freshly ground black
   pepper

Sautéed Trevally with Crisp Falafel, Saffron Yoghurt & Lemon Chutney

Serves 6 as a main course

This recipe works equally well with fish that have similar attributes to trevally, such as mackerel, kingfish and kahawai. With their large flakes and slightly meaty texture, all stand up well to the big Middle Eastern flavours in this dish. The lemon chutney, with its cinnamon, cloves and star anise, will also work well with any fish cooked on a chargrill.

Step 1: Lemon Chutney

Cut the lemons into thin wedges, slice off the pith at the end of each wedge and remove all the pips. Place in a heavy-based saucepan and just cover with water. Place on high heat and bring to the boil. Lower the heat to a simmer, place a lid on the saucepan and cook on low for 1½ hours. Check from time to time and add a little more water if necessary. There should be about 1 cup of liquid left after 1½ hours.

   Add the remaining ingredients and simmer slowly until the mixture thickens to the consistency of jam or chutney (about 1 hour or so). Remove and store in a couple of jars. You can halve this recipe, but I assure you, you'll find plenty of uses for this interesting condiment (it will keep for at least 4 months, refrigerated).

Step 2: Crisp Falafel

Rinse the chickpeas in a sieve, then place in a food processor. Add the eggs, lemon juice, onion, ground spices, cayenne and sugar. Process to a semi-fine purée, then scrape the mixture into a bowl. Add the breadcrumbs and parsley, and stir to combine. Taste and season with sea salt and black pepper.

   Form the falafel into rounds about 5cm across and 2cm thick. Coat with breadcrumbs and place on a dry tray. Refrigerate until required. You will have about 24 falafel.

Step 3: Saffron Yoghurt

Soak the saffron threads in 1 tablespoon of warm water for 10 minutes, then pour into the yoghurt and mix through. Refrigerate until serving.

Step 4: To Cook and Serve

Preheat the oven to 150°C.

Place a skillet or sauté pan on medium heat and add a little cooking oil. Brown the falafels until golden on each side then place on an oven tray. Place in the oven to cook through (about 10 minutes).

While the falafel are in the oven, season the trevally fillets with sea salt and black pepper, then cook in batches. Be mindful not to overcook.

Place a couple of falafel in the centre of each warm plate, top with a fillet of trevally, then spoon a little of the lemon chutney over and some saffron yoghurt. Serve now! A simple green salad to accompany would be spot on.

When you have brought a trevally to the side of the boat, it pays to use a net to bring it on board as trevally have particularly soft mouths. I have witnessed many a fish dropping back into the briny when someone is attempting to lift them over the side by holding them up by the trace.

When kahawai are schooling and you're keen to nail a couple for the pot, trolling for them can be very effective if you keep in mind a couple of points. First, schooling kahawai are often described as taking on the shape of an iceberg. This means that most of the school are underwater and out of sight. It's imperative that you don't plough through the centre of the school, as this will often drive the fish down and disperse the school completely. Always troll to the side of the school. Personally, I like to get close to the fish, then pull out my old Tongariro 9 weight, complete with a sinking line, and drift while I cast. You won't believe how much fun you can have hooked up to one of these feisty hard-fighting fish!

Step 1: To Prepare the Beetroot
1kg beetroot, skin on
⅓ cup sugar
⅓ cup malt vinegar

Step 2: Black Olive Vinaigrette
2 tablespoons balsamic vinegar
2 tablespoons finely diced
  shallots

1½ tablespoons sugar
150ml olive oil
½ cup good-quality black olives,
  stones removed and cut into
  slivers
¼ cup finely chopped fresh mint
freshly ground black pepper

Step 3: Chargrilled Zucchini
6 small to medium zucchini
olive oil for grilling
salt and freshly ground black
  pepper to taste

Step 4: To Cook and Serve
6 x 150g fresh kahawai fillets
salt and freshly ground black
  pepper

Fresh Kahawai with Chargrilled Zucchini, Beetroot & Black Olive Vinaigrette

Serves 6 as a main course

Fresh kahawai, iki'd and bled immediately upon capture, is perfect for this dish. It has a great taste and the medium-textured flesh works well with the biggish flavours. With the natural sweetness of beetroot, coupled with the saltiness of the black olive vinaigrette, there's plenty going on here. I also love the combination of warm fish served on the cool, slightly sharp salad.

Step 1: To Prepare the Beetroot

In a suitable saucepan, place the beetroot, sugar and vinegar. Cover with cold water and place on high heat. Bring up to the boil, reduce the heat to a simmer and cook until soft through the centre (about 1 hour).

Once cooked, run under cold water for a minute or so, then peel off the skin. Refrigerate until required.

Step 2: Black Olive Vinaigrette

In a medium bowl, place the vinegar, shallots and sugar. Whisk together, then slowly drizzle in the olive oil while whisking until incorporated. Fold in the black olives and mint, and season with a good couple of grinds of black pepper. Refrigerate until serving.

Step 3: Chargrilled Zucchini

Heat the chargrill (or a griddle top or skillet). Slice the zucchini on an angle into rounds about 1cm thick. Place in a bowl and toss with a little olive oil and salt and pepper.

Cook on a hot chargrill for a couple of minutes on each side until golden and slightly charred. Remove and cool to room temperature.

Step 4: To Cook and Serve

Heat the flat top of the barbecue or place a skillet or frying pan on medium-high heat. Season the kahawai and cook until golden on each side and just cooked through.

While the fish is cooking, slice the beetroot into 5mm-thick rounds. Place on a platter if serving family style or put 4–5 rounds on each serving plate.

Carefully place the chargrilled zucchini in a large bowl, then spoon some of the olive vinaigrette over and toss to coat. Place this on the beetroot, then top with the kahawai. Drizzle a little more vinaigrette over the fish and serve pronto.

1 tablespoon butter
2½ cups basmati rice
6 eggs
500g smoked kahawai, flaked
1 cup milk
1 cup cream
100g butter

2 large onions, finely diced
1 tablespoon minced garlic
1 tablespoon minced fresh ginger
1 tablespoon minced fresh chilli
1 tablespoon turmeric
½ tablespoon cumin
½ tablespoon garam masala

⅓ cup finely chopped parsley
salt and freshly ground black
  pepper
4 lemons

Smoked Kahawai Kedgeree

Serves 6 as a brunch or light meal

I was introduced to kedgeree for the first time by well-known Wellington chef Kelda Hains and from the first forkful, it became one of those dishes I have regular cravings for. It's great as a brunch dish, but for some reason I seem to make it a lot on Sunday evenings through the winter months. It rates highly on the 'comfort food' scale and is one of those dishes I really enjoy cooking. There are many versions of kedgeree, with most varieties of smoked fish working well. It's also a recipe that stretches a small amount of fish into a large and satisfying meal.

Method

In a large saucepan place 6 cups of water plus the tablespoon of butter and bring to the boil. Wash the rice under cold water, then stir into the boiling water.

Reduce to a simmer, cover and cook for 20–25 minutes until all the water is absorbed and the rice is soft to the bite. Fluff up the rice with a fork and set aside.

Place the eggs in a saucepan and cover with cold water. Bring to the boil, cook for 4 minutes, then remove from the water. Leave at room temperature to cool, then peel, roughly chop and refrigerate.

Place the flaked kahawai in a small saucepan. Add the milk and cream, place on low heat and steep for 15 minutes just below simmering.

In a large saucepan place the butter, onions, garlic, ginger and fresh chilli. Sauté over medium heat for a couple of minutes, then add the turmeric, cumin and garam masala. Reduce the heat to low and sweat for 20 minutes, stirring occasionally. Add the cooked rice and stir through to coat all the grains.

Now add the steeped kahawai along with the milk and cream. Stir to combine. Fold in the chopped eggs and parsley, then season with salt and pepper. Stir in the juice of 2 of the lemons and cut the other 2 into wedges.

Divide the kedgeree into warm bowls, garnish each with a lemon wedge and serve! Accompany the dish with a simple fresh green salad.

Kedgeree is thought by some to have originated in Scotland, but evolved into an Anglo-Indian dish after it was taken to India by Scottish troops during the British Raj. It's a combination of cooked rice, flaked smoked fish, hard-boiled eggs, curry spices and parsley. It sounds like a slightly odd combination but, believe me, it rocks!

HOW TO: | Smoke a Fish

1. Make an angled cut on either side of the head.

2. Remove head.

3. Cut down 1 side of the back bone.

4. Cut through to just below the skin.

5. Repeat on opposite side.

6. The exposed backbone.

7. With kitchen shears, snip the the backbone out.

8. Butterflied fish ready for seasoning.

9. Apply liberal amounts of sea salt.

10. Apply liberal amounts of sugar.

11. Place in smoker, light the fuel, close the lid.

12. Check after 15-20 minutes. Remove once cooked through.

Step 1: Smoked Kahawai Pie Filling
⅓ cup canola oil
150g rindless bacon
2 cups finely diced onion
1 cup finely diced celery
2 tablespoons minced garlic
2 tablespoons finely chopped fresh thyme leaves
50g butter
50g flour
1¼ litres whole milk

salt and freshly ground black pepper
Tabasco to taste
lemon juice to taste
3 cobs fresh sweetcorn, cooked and kernels cut from the cob
6 hard-boiled eggs, roughly chopped
2 cups peas
1kg smoked kahawai, broken up into bite-sized pieces

Step 2: Kumara Potato Topping
500g floury potatoes (such as Agria), peeled
1kg kumara, peeled
50g butter
1 cup cream
½ cup whole milk
salt and freshly ground black pepper

Step 3: Crunchy Topping
1 baguette
100g butter, melted
½ cup breadcrumbs

Step 4: To Cook and Serve
lemon wedges to serve

Smoked Kahawai & Kumara Pie (Kaimoana Trifle)

Serves 12 as a main course

I doubt there is another dish that so aptly epitomises comfort food as a fish pie. They are just so tasty and satisfying. Fish pie, a green salad, crusty bread and a glass of chardonnay riding shotgun would make it into my all-time top 10 meals. Fish pies also lend themselves perfectly to 'freestyle' cookery where the ingredients can come down to what's available, what's in season, what's in the fridge or, more often, what did Dad catch. The variations on the same theme are limitless. However, when making a fish pie the important points to me are always that the white sauce encasing the ingredients should always be good and runny; the potato top should be no more than a third of the pie; and you should have a good crunchy topping that contrasts beautifully with the slightly sloppy centre.

With the following recipe, I use smoked fish and instead of just a potato topping, I use kumara as well, which introduces a little sweetness to the dish, balancing nicely with the subtle smoky flavour of the fish. I've used a whole smoked kahawai for this recipe and it will easily feed 12 people, or if feeding my close circle of friends, that's 6 plus seconds, with a little left to go on my toast with a couple of poached eggs the next day!

Step 1: Smoked Kahawai Pie Filling
Place a medium saucepan on medium heat. Once hot, add the canola oil and bacon. Fry the bacon on high heat for a minute or so until golden, then add the onion, celery, garlic and thyme. Reduce the heat and cook on low for 20 minutes, stirring occasionally, until the vegetables are soft. Remove and set aside.

For the white sauce, place a heavy-based saucepan on medium heat. Add the butter and, once melted, add the flour. Whisk until combined, then slowly add the milk, whisking as you go to eliminate any lumps. Once all the milk is added, cook on low for 5 minutes. Taste, then season with salt and pepper, Tabasco and lemon juice to your liking. Remove from the heat and pour into a large mixing bowl.

Fold the corn, chopped eggs, peas and kahawai into the white sauce, then pour the mix into a large ovenproof dish or, like me, use a big roasting dish. Cover and set aside while you make the topping.

Step 2: Kumara Potato Topping

Chop the potatoes and kumara into a similar size and place in separate saucepans. Cover both with cold salted water and place on high heat. Bring to the boil, then turn down to a simmer. The kumara should be soft after 10 minutes, while the potato will take closer to 20 minutes.

Remove and strain. Place both in a bowl and add the butter, cream and milk. Mash together until smooth and season with a good amount of salt and black pepper to taste.

While still warm, spoon the mash over the kahawai mixture then, using a spatula, smooth out to cover.

Step 3: Crunchy Topping

Cut the baguette into small croûtons (about 1cm dice). Place in a large mixing bowl and drizzle the melted butter over, mixing as you go so the bread is well covered.

Evenly scatter the fish pie with the soft buttery croutons, then sprinkle the breadcrumbs into any gaps.

Step 4: To Cook and Serve

Preheat the oven to 180°C. If cooking the fish pie straight from the fridge, cover with tinfoil and place in the oven, then check after 30 minutes. When warm through, remove the foil and let the topping get crunchy and golden. If still warm from preparation, just place in the oven uncovered. Bring up to heat and once the topping is golden, remove from the oven and let it sit on the bench for 10 minutes.

Spoon out onto plates with a wedge of lemon alongside. Serve with a simple green salad and crusty bread for mopping up the sauce.

Fish pie is considered a very British dish. Medieval Britons didn't see any need to separate savoury from sweet and fruity. According to Helen Gaffney, writing on the British Food Trust website, mackerel and gooseberry first met under a pie crust; and an English housewife in 1649, Gervase Markham, described cod pie with pears and crystallised lemon peel!

Step 1: Wasabi and Basil Crème Fraîche
250g crème fraîche
3 tablespoons freshly grated
   wasabi paste
2 tablespoons lemon juice
¼ cup finely sliced fresh basil
   leaves
sea salt and freshly ground black
   pepper

Step 2: New Potatoes
600g new potatoes, scrubbed

Step 3: Smoked Mullet
2 x 800g–1kg mullet
1½ tablespoons sea salt
1½ tablespoons white sugar

Step 4: To Serve
lemon or lime wedges to garnish

Warm Smoked Mullet with New Potatoes & Wasabi Basil Crème Fraîche

Serves 6 as a main course

We don't see too many mullet where I live in Wellington. However, when they occasionally turn up at the market, I find it hard not to grab a couple to take home and smoke. They are found in good numbers the further north you go and like to reside in shallow muddy harbours, mangrove swamps and river estuaries. Mullet has great oil content, making it ideal for smoking. I find the flesh slightly sweet, which I believe is probably due to all the small crab they consume.

Step 1: Wasabi and Basil Crème Fraîche
In a bowl mix the crème fraîche, wasabi and lemon juice until well combined. Gently fold in the basil. Season with sea salt and a healthy grind of black pepper. Refrigerate until required.

Step 2: New Potatoes
Place the potatoes in a medium saucepan and cover with cold salted water. Place on the heat and bring to the boil, then lower to a simmer. Cook for 15–20 minutes until cooked through. Remove from the heat, strain off the water and cool to room temperature.

Step 3: Smoked Mullet
See How to Smoke a Fish on page 208.

Step 4: To Serve
Remove the wasabi basil crème fraîche from the fridge and bring to room temperature.

   Cut the cooked potatoes into a small dice. Place in a bowl and add the wasabi basil crème fraîche. Gently mix through to combine.

   Divide the potato mixture between plates and top each serving with the warm freshly smoked mullet. Garnish with a wedge of lemon or lime.

   Serve with a simply dressed green salad. Another great addition to this dish would be a dollop of salsa verde (see recipe on page 317).

There are 130 species commercially fished in New Zealand, 96 of which are in the quota management system.

CHARGRILLED KINGFISH WITH CHICKPEA, TOMATO & CUMIN SALAD & PARSLEY AÏOLI

Step 1: Chickpea, Tomato and Cumin Salad

440g cooked chickpeas (equates to 2 regular tins)

400g vine-ripened tomatoes, quartered and seeded (cut into smaller chunks if large)

¾ cup thinly sliced red onion

½ cup roughly chopped fresh coriander

½ cup roughly chopped fresh mint

minced zest of 2 lemons

⅓ cup lemon juice

1½ tablespoons freshly roasted and ground cumin seeds

2 teaspoons sugar

½ cup olive oil

sea salt and freshly ground black pepper

Tabasco to taste

Step 2: Parsley Aïoli

1 cup Al's mayonnaise (see recipe on page 302)

¾ cup Italian parsley leaves

1 tablespoon finely chopped garlic

Step 3: To Cook and Serve

cooking oil for brushing

6 x 150g kingfish fillets

sea salt and freshly ground black pepper

lemon wedges to serve

Chargrilled Kingfish with Chickpea, Tomato & Cumin Salad & Parsley Aïoli

Serves 6 as a main course

Kingfish is a species held in high regard by all who fish. When you are hooked up with one of these hoodlums of the ocean, many would agree that there is no better fight to be enjoyed while desperately attempting to hold on to your fishing rod. Thousands of kingfish have broken the hearts of numerous anglers who have been fortunate enough to do battle with these extraordinarily powerful and beautiful fish. One of the great things about kingfish is that they are a hardy bunch and if you handle them properly when caught, they have a high survival rate when released back into the sea. This should be considered by anyone who catches a large one. Besides the obvious thrill of watching them glide away to fight another day, the largest kingfish are considered to be the best breeding stock and, like most fish at the large end of the scale, they tend not to make nearly as good eating as their younger siblings. Small to medium-sized kingfish are terrific eating and their large, meaty flake works beautifully with this simple and slightly spicy salad and garlicky aïoli.

Step 1: Chickpea, Tomato and Cumin Salad

If using tinned chickpeas, drain and rinse under cold water in a sieve, then pour into a large mixing bowl.

Add the tomatoes, red onion, coriander, mint, lemon zest and juice, cumin, sugar and olive oil. Carefully mix together, season with sea salt and pepper, and add a few drops of Tabasco to your liking. Cover and refrigerate for at least 1 hour, if possible, to let the flavours mingle and develop.

Step 2: Parsley Aïoli

Once you have made the mayonnaise, pour all but a couple of tablespoons out into a mixing bowl.

Place the parsley in the food processor with the small amount of mayonnaise. Process until the parsley is finely mulched and smooth.

Mix this into the rest of the mayonnaise with the garlic and refrigerate until required.

Step 3: To Cook and Serve

Heat the chargrill, barbecue or skillet to medium-hot. Brush a little oil on the kingfish and season with sea salt and black pepper.

Cook the kingfish on both sides until just cooked though. Divvy up the chickpea salad onto plates, top with a piece of kingfish, then add a dollop of aïoli. A wedge of lemon on the side of each and you're good to go.

Kingfish are regarded as roving carnivores and an open-water species. However, don't be surprised to catch one of these wonderful fish in what may seem an odd location, like a shallow bay or muddy estuary. I would also describe them as a very curious and often quite arrogant fish. Many an angler can relate to the frustration of having these fish seemingly toy with one's offering on a hook, before meandering off.

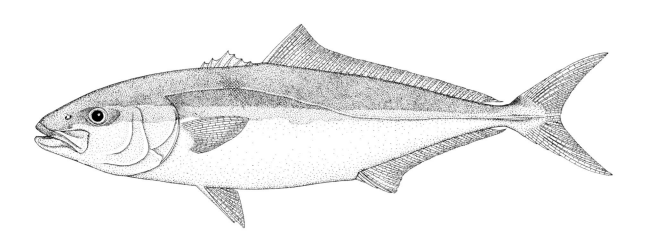

Step 1: Kingfish Belly Confit
1kg fresh kingfish belly
1–2 fresh chillies, finely diced
1 cup roughly chopped fennel
    stalks
finely grated zest of 2 lemons
1½ tablespoons finely diced
    garlic

2 teaspoons sumac
sea salt and freshly ground black
    pepper
1½–2 cups olive oil

**Step 2: Black Olive and Anchovy
Mayonnaise**
1 cup Al's mayonnaise (see recipe
    on page 302)
½ cup good-quality pitted black
    olives
2 tablespoons anchovies

Step 3: Bruschetta
see recipe on page 305

Kingfish Belly Confit with Bruschetta & Black Olive & Anchovy Mayonnaise

Makes 30 or more

This is a terrific way to cook the belly, or 'flap' as some call it, of a kingfish. Confit is a French term meaning to cook slowly submerged in oil or fat. In this case we are using olive oil. You can flavour the belly with practically anything that comes to mind, especially along the lines of fresh herbs, garlic and chilli. In this recipe I've used some fennel stalks I had lying around, as well as a few of the usual suspects. Pippa, my wickedly talented neighbour, came up with the idea of making a black olive and anchovy mayonnaise to top the kingfish with and it's a heavenly combination.

Step 1: Kingfish Belly Confit

Place the kingfish belly skin side down in a relatively tight-fitting ovenproof dish. Rub the chillies, fennel stalks, lemon zest, garlic and sumac all over the fish. Season liberally with sea salt and black pepper and refrigerate overnight.

Preheat the oven to 90°C. Pour the olive oil over the kingfish, cover with tinfoil and place in the oven. Check after 1 hour, then at 20-minute intervals. Remove from the oven when the flesh of the kingfish is soft and cooked through. Leave in the oil and set aside to cool.

Step 2: Black Olive and Anchovy Mayonnaise

Place the mayonnaise in a food processor. Add half the olives and all of the anchovies. Process until smooth, then empty into a small bowl. Slice the remaining olives into slivers and fold through the mayonnaise. Refrigerate until required.

Step 3: Bruschetta

See recipe on page 305.

Step 4: To Plate and Serve

Preheat the oven to 150°C. Place the kingfish belly confit in the oven for 15 minutes to warm through. Strain off most of the olive oil.

To serve, spoon out small amounts of the kingfish onto the bruschetta and top each with a little of the black olive and anchovy mayonnaise.

Alternatively, serve the whole belly on a platter and have the bruschetta on the side along with the mayonnaise for people to help themselves. Serve while warm.

The flesh of kingfish has a relatively low oil content and is prone to drying out, hence this sort of cooking method works well. It pays to bleed kingfish on capture if you intend to eat it.

½ cup cooking oil
⅓ cup capers
800g fresh kingfish fillets
⅓ cup good-quality black olives, sliced into slivers
3 hard-boiled eggs, finely chopped
¼ cup finely diced shallots

¼ cup fresh basil, sliced into thin strips
finely grated zest of 1 lemon
lemon-infused olive oil for drizzling
cabernet vinegar syrup (see recipe on page 304) for drizzling

juice of 1–2 lemons
sea salt and freshly ground black pepper

Kingfish Carpaccio with Crisp Capers

Serves 6 as an entrée or 12 or more as a pass-around

The dilemma facing many anglers when keeping kingfish is what to do with the enormous amount of fillets they produce. A good place to start with a larger fish when freshly caught is to take advantage of its pristine freshness and consume some of it raw. Kiwis are starting to embrace the joys of eating exquisitely fresh raw fish. It's all about texture and the components you pair up with it. It doesn't always have to be about soy sauce and wasabi from a tube. Simply sliced raw fish, with just a squeeze of citrus and a pinch of salt, is delicious. The combinations are pretty much limitless as long as you keep in mind the 'saltiness, acidity, sweetness' rule in mind and use those as the foundations of the dish, then knock yourself out with other ingredients. However, as the saying goes, less is usually more.

Method

Heat the oil in a small saucepan until hot. Squeeze the capers in your hands to extract as much of the brine as possible. Gently place in the oil and reduce the heat to low. Fry for 3–5 minutes until golden and crisp. Strain off the oil and spread the capers out on a paper towel.

With your sharpest knife, slice the kingfish as thinly as possible into bite-size pieces. As you slice the kingfish, lay it out to cover chilled plates or a chilled platter. The pieces should be just slightly overlapping.

Now it's just a case of individually sprinkling the other ingredients over the raw fish. Start with the olives, then the hard-boiled eggs, shallots, basil and lemon zest. Lastly, sprinkle the crisp capers over.

Drizzle liberal amounts of lemon-infused oil over, followed by the cabernet syrup. Squeeze some lemon juice over and sprinkle with sea salt and pepper to finish. Eat now.

When I talk of saltiness, acidity and sweetness, it's all about coaxing the natural flavour out of a dish. If you taste something and it's kind of bland, generally the addition of something salty (salt, capers, olives, for example), something acidic (like lemon juice, vinegar, wine, tomatoes) and something with a little sweetness (sugar or honey) will make a huge difference to the flavour and enjoyment of the dish. The secret is getting the balance right. Remember you can always add a little more of something, but it is near impossible to remove something from a dish once added. Obviously there are a lot of other ingredients that help flavour food — fresh herbs and spices are a good start.

Step 1: Masala Herrings
12 herrings, scaled, heads
    removed and gutted
1½ tablespoons finely diced
    fresh chilli (seeds optional)
¾ tablespoon finely grated ginger
½ tablespoon finely grated garlic
1½ teaspoons salt

1 teaspoon ground cumin
1½ teaspoons ground coriander
½ teaspoon ground turmeric
1½ teaspoons garam masala
pinch of chilli flakes
2 tablespoons cooking oil
⅓ cup finely chopped fresh
    coriander

Step 2: To Cook and Serve
cooking oil for sautéing
lemon or lime halves to garnish

Puspa & Magan's Sautéed Masala Herrings

Serves 6

One of my all-time favourite pastimes and fishing experiences is to go herring fishing with my friend Sanjay, his father, Magan, uncles Lucky and Wal, and more often than not, a handful of their extended family or members of the Indian fraternity. We line up, backs to the wind, vying for the best position as we spread out along the Worser Bay wharf in Wellington. Hand lines, light rods with tiny hooks and sinkers, are the tackle of choice, with a concoction of boiled potatoes and a soggy bread mix for burley. It's a time of chatter, laughter and banter as young and old compete to catch these delicious eating fish. The herrings (or more correctly yellow-eyed mullet) come and go off the bite and, if we are fortunate, at certain times of the year the garfish turn up, too, which is an added bonus. Within a couple of hours it's possible to catch two or three dozen 'fish for tea'! We iki them all immediately and place them in a slurry of ice before divvying them up as we all disperse and wander off. An open invitation is always extended to follow the herrings back to Magan and Puspa Dayal's, where both Mum and Dad cook and clamber over each other in the small domestic kitchen, giving each other tips and advice on such things as the strength of the chilli, the amount of spice, or the heat of the pan. These two have cooked thousands of herrings this way over the years and the results are inevitable — always wickedly delicious.

Step 1: Masala Herrings

With a sharp knife, cut a couple of slashes on both sides of each herring. Place the herrings in a large mixing bowl with the rest of the ingredients.

With clean hands, massage the ingredients over and into the cavities of all the herrings. Set aside for 10 minutes.

Step 2: To Cook and Serve

Place a skillet or sauté pan on medium-low heat. Once hot, add a little oil followed by half the herrings. Sauté on each side for 3 minutes or so. Remove when cooked and keep warm while you cook the remaining herrings.

To serve, place 2 herrings on each plate with half a lemon or lime. Serve while hot.

It's best to eat these delicious fish with your fingers, slowly and deliberately, discarding the bones as you go. The flesh will be moist and sweet. Plenty of handy paper towels and a couple of finger bowls are essential.

There are more than 200 species of herring worldwide. They are high in omega-3 fatty acids and a terrific source of vitamin D. A staple in many cuisines, herrings are eaten raw, cooked, pickled, fermented or cured.

Step 1: Tomato and Thyme
350g vine-ripened tomatoes
2 tablespoons finely diced
   shallots
1½ tablespoons finely chopped
   fresh thyme
1 tablespoon tomato paste

1 tablespoon balsamic syrup
   (use the same method as for
   cabernet vinegar syrup on
   page 304)
3 tablespoons extra virgin olive
   oil
sea salt and freshly ground black
   pepper

Step 2: Bruschetta
½ baguette (or similar)
olive oil for brushing
1 bulb garlic

Step 3: To Cook and Serve
6 whole herrings
salt and freshly ground black
   pepper
¼ cup flour
¼ cup cooking oil
olive oil for drizzling

Sautéed Herring Fillets with Tomato & Thyme Bruschetta

Makes 12 Bruschetta

Herring is definitely near the top of my preferred fish list. Having completely ignored them most of my life — only considering them on occasions as bait for catching something larger — I now look upon herrings as a wonderful and abundant delicacy, right on my back doorstep. Burley of some sort or other is a must. What I love about this sort of fishing is that my daughters, Alice and Connie, get a real kick out of catching fish that end up on the dinner table. If you only catch half a dozen or so, this is a great recipe to stretch the catch and it makes a wonderful pass-around before something more substantial.

Step 1: Tomato and Thyme
Half-fill a saucepan with water, place on the heat and bring to the boil.

Cut out the small core at the top of each tomato and score the skin at the bottom with a small cross. Place a dozen or so ice cubes in a bowl of cold water. Once the water is boiling, carefully drop in the tomatoes, then remove and place in the ice bath as soon as you see the skin starting to peel back (about 10 seconds).

Cool for a minute or so then peel and discard the skin. Cut each tomato into quarters and, with a sharp paring knife, remove the seeds from each segment. Chop the pure tomato flesh into small dice and place in a bowl.

Add the shallots, thyme, tomato paste, balsamic syrup and olive oil. Gently mix together, taste, then season with sea salt and black pepper.

Step 2: Bruschetta
Preheat the oven to 180°C or turn on the grill on the barbecue. Slice the baguette on the diagonal into 1cm-thick slices (you need 12) and brush both sides with olive oil. Slice the top off the garlic bulb and rub both sides of the bread slices with the cut cloves. Place the bread on a baking tray and place in the oven or cook on the barbecue grill. Cook until just crisp and golden on each side. Remove and cool. If you are not using them that day, store in an airtight container until required.

Step 3: To Cook and Serve
Use the back of a knife to scale the herrings. Remove the small fillets from both sides of each fish, then cut away the belly bones and discard. With a sharp knife, lightly score the skin of each fillet with three diagonal slashes.

The British terminology for smoked herrings is as follows: a 'kipper' is a split smoked herring, a 'bloater' is a whole smoked herring and a 'buckling' refers to a hot-smoked herring with the guts removed.

Place a frying pan on medium heat. While it's warming up, spoon the tomato and thyme mix on the bruschetta.

Once the pan is hot, season the herring fillets with salt and pepper, and dust lightly with flour. Add ¼ cup or so of oil to the hot pan then fry the herring fillets in batches for about 30 seconds on each side. Gently remove from the pan and place one on top of each bruschetta. Drizzle a little olive oil over each, place on a platter and serve.

KRISHNA

Step 1: Beetroot Relish
1kg beetroot (peeled weight)
400g onion, cut with the grain
    into thin strips
2 tablespoons fresh thyme leaves
pinch of dried chilli flakes
1 cup sugar
¾ cup balsamic vinegar
½ cup fresh orange juice
¼ cup olive oil
salt and freshly ground black
    pepper

Step 2: Basil Mayonnaise
1½ cups Al's mayonnaise (see
    recipe on page 302)
1 cup tightly packed fresh basil

Step 3: Poached Salmon
1 cup white wine
3 cups water
1 stick celery, finely chopped
4 shallots, roughly chopped
1 lemon, sliced into rounds
2 bay leaves
2 sprigs parsley
1 tablespoon salt
6–8 black peppercorns
8 x 100g salmon portions

Step 4: To Plate and Serve
sea salt and a freshly ground
    black pepper

Chilled Poached Salmon with Beetroot Relish & Basil Mayonnaise

Serves 8 as an entrée

This sounds like a slightly weird combination, but you've got to go with me on this one. It's a terrific dish. Beetroot and basil go well together — and the colours are incredible! All the preparation can be completed at least a couple of days ahead, which makes it a winner when entertaining. You could, of course, serve the salmon hot, directly from the poaching liquid, or if you prefer sautéing the fish that'll work a treat too.

For this dish, you are probably best to buy a whole side of salmon. That way you can use the top half of the fillet and cut the salmon portions to the same size and shape so they all have similar cooking times. The lower belly of the fillet can be served raw as sashimi or tartare. Salmon and potato fish cakes to cook the next day would also be a good idea.

Step 1: Beetroot Relish

Using a mandolin slice the beetroot using a matchstick-size blade or, alternatively, use the coarse side of your grater. Place all the ingredients except the salt and pepper in a large saucepan. Place on medium heat for 10 minutes, then reduce to a low simmer and cook for about 2 hours, stirring occasionally.

The relish is ready when all the liquid has been absorbed and it has a lovely sheen to it. Taste and season accordingly with salt and pepper.

Remove from the heat and cool, then refrigerate.

Step 2: Basil Mayonnaise

Process the mayonnaise and basil using a wand blender, in a food processor, or by the 'old school' method — by chopping the basil super fine with a knife and mixing it with the mayo. Refrigerate until required.

Step 3: Poached Salmon

Preheat the oven to 180˚C.

Place all the ingredients, except the salmon, in a small saucepan and bring to the boil, then simmer for 10 minutes.

Place the salmon portions in an ovenproof dish that holds them fairly snugly, but not overlapping.

If cooking this dish, you are probably best to buy one whole side of salmon. That way you can use the top half of the fillet and cut the salmon portions all the same size and shape, so they all have similar cooking times.

Step 1: Pickled Ginger Jelly
25g pickled ginger (including juice)
juice of 1 lime
1 tablespoon sweet mirin
1 leaf gelatin

Step 2: Soy Jelly
½ cup good-quality soy sauce
3 tablespoons sweet mirin
2 leaves gelatin

Step 3: To Serve
1kg side of fresh salmon
½ just-ripe avocado, diced
⅓ cup wakame seaweed
fresh wasabi paste

King Salmon Sashimi with Pickled Ginger, Soy Jelly, Wakame & Wasabi

Serves 6 as an entrée or 12 or more as a help-yourself platter

We have a well-established salmon farming industry providing fresh salmon to the local market on a daily basis. I do enjoy salmon prepared by most methods, however, raw is my firm favourite. The mouth feel and flavour are what I really love about this fish, and when you eat it cold and raw, it doesn't seem nearly as rich as cooked salmon. Making the pickled ginger and the soy components into a jelly form adds to the presentation, but it also makes the dish a lot easier to eat, without all the messy dipping and dripping.

Step 1: Pickled Ginger Jelly

Process the ginger and its juice in a blender until very fine. Pour into a small saucepan along with the lime juice and mirin. Place on low heat just to warm up.

Take the gelatin and bloom in about 1 cup of cold water for 3 minutes until soft and pliable.

Remove the gelatin, squeeze out the excess water and stir into the pickled ginger mix. Pour into a suitable container and place in the fridge to set.

Step 2: Soy Jelly

Using the same method as the pickled ginger jelly, pour the soy sauce and mirin into a small saucepan. Place on low heat to warm through.

Bloom the gelatin in cold water for 3 minutes until pliable, squeeze out the excess water, then stir into the warm soy. Pour into a suitable container and refrigerate to set.

Step 3: To Serve

Slice the salmon as thinly as possible into bite-size pieces. Spread out on flat plates or a large platter so the pieces just overlap.

Cut the pickled ginger jelly into little pieces and distribute over the sliced salmon, then repeat with the soy jelly. Likewise sprinkle the diced avocado over, then drape strands of the wakame seaweed over it all to finish. Add some fresh wasabi paste on the side and serve.

According to the Food and Agriculture Organization of the United Nations, the average Japanese person consumes approximately 70kg of fish per year. That's nearly 200g per day — a statistic that has remained consistent over the past several decades.

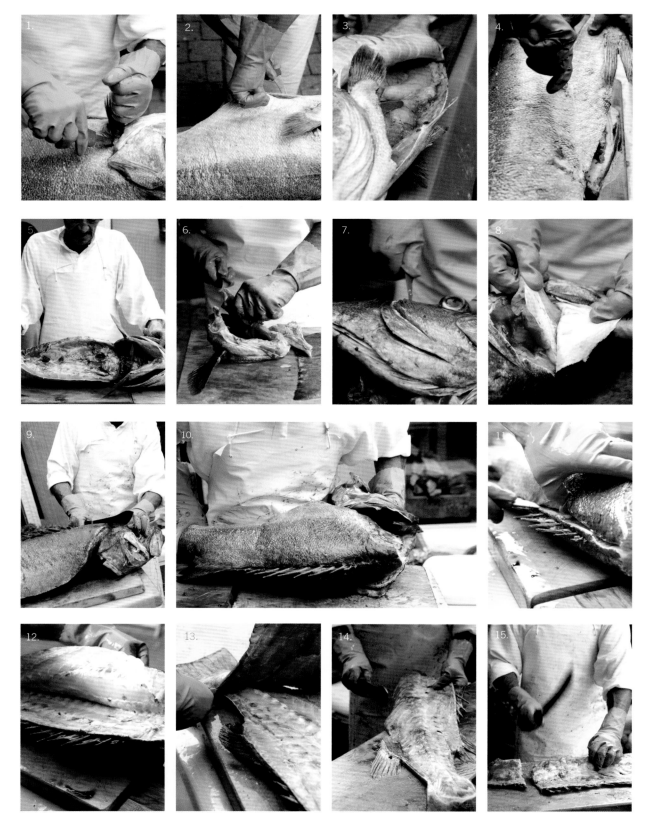

HOW TO: | Break Down a Large Fish (Groper by Billy)

1. Make a cut from the belly up and around the gill plate to the top of the head. Repeat on the other side.

2–3. Slice down and open up the belly and remove the gut.

4. Remove both halves of the belly.

5. Groper with belly and gut removed.

6. Remove the collar wing bones from next to the gills.

7. Cut out the cheeks from the groper head.

8. Remove the skin from the cheek.

9. Chop or slice through to the spine.

10. Snap the spine.

11–13. Remove the large fillets from the frame.

14. Groper frame.

15. Chop up the frame.

Step 1: Gnocchi
1kg large Agria (or other floury variety) potatoes, scrubbed
2 egg yolks, beaten with a fork
50g flour
sea salt and freshly ground black pepper
cooking oil

Step 2: To Cook and Serve
6 x 160g thick groper fillets
sea salt and freshly ground black pepper
cooking oil for frying
flour for dusting
½ cup extra virgin olive oil

pinch of dried chilli flakes (to your liking)
1 tablespoon minced fresh garlic
2 tablespoons finely chopped preserved lemon peel (see recipe on page 316) or lemon zest

¼ cup finely chopped capers
¼ cup finely chopped fresh parsley
¼ cup finely chopped fresh basil
60g butter, cut into cubes
juice of 1 lemon
sea salt and freshly ground black pepper

Pan-Roasted Groper with Sautéed Gnocchi, Fresh Herbs, Capers & Preserved Lemon

Serves 6 as a main course

Groper has been at the top of my list as an eating fish for most of my life. Its large white meaty flakes hold moisture well when cooked and make groper terrific for nearly all methods of cooking. Groper has been our signature fish at Logan Brown since we opened. The waters surrounding Wellington have always held good numbers of these fish, however, they are now caught in much deeper water than in the old days. I have seen old black and white photos of anglers holding groper with their chunky old surf-casting rods in the same picture. Just more evidence of what it was truly like before any real angling or commercial pressure was evident.

Step 1: Gnocchi

Preheat the oven to 180˚C.

Bake the potatoes in their jackets until crisp on the outside and very soft in the centre (about 1 hour). Remove from the oven and let cool for 10 minutes.

Bring a large saucepan of salted water to a rolling boil.

Once the potatoes are cool enough to handle, slice in half lengthwise and carefully scoop out the soft centre into a bowl. Weigh out 400g of the cooked potato.

Working quickly, put the soft potato into a sieve and, with the back of a spoon, push it through the mesh to create a pile of light, lump-free potato. Spread the potato out about 2cm thick on a floured flat surface. Drizzle the egg yolk over, sprinkle the flour over, then season with a little salt and a healthy grind of black pepper. Using your hands, very gently fold the mixture until it just comes together. Do not overwork!

Split the dough into quarters and flour the surface again. With your hands, gently roll the dough into rounded lengths of about 5mm in diameter. With a knife, cut the dough into pieces about 4cm long or smaller if you prefer.

Gently drop a dozen or so at a time into the boiling water. After about 30 seconds the gnocchi will float to the surface. Carefully remove with a slotted spoon or sieve and spread out on an oiled tray to cool. Once the water comes up to the boil again, repeat the process until all the gnocchi is cooked.

Lightly oil the gnocchi, cover and refrigerate until required.

Step 2: To Cook and Serve

Preheat the oven to 180°C.

Place a skillet or frying pan on high heat. Season the groper fillets with sea salt and black pepper. Once the pan is hot, add a little cooking oil and sear both sides of the groper, then remove and place on a lightly oiled ovenproof dish. Set aside. Keep the pan you seared the groper in for the sauce.

For the gnocchi, place a clean skillet or, even better, a non-stick frying pan on medium heat. Lightly dust the gnocchi with flour. Add a small amount of cooking oil to the pan and sauté the gnocchi in batches. Carefully turn with tongs so they are golden on each side. Remove and keep warm while you finish the rest.

Place the groper in the oven.

For the sauce, place the pan you seared the groper in on medium heat. Add the extra virgin olive oil, chilli flakes, garlic, preserved lemon or zest and capers. Fry gently for 1–2 minutes, being careful not to burn the garlic. Remove from the heat and toss in the parsley, basil and cubes of butter. Add the lemon juice and season with a little sea salt and black pepper. Stir to combine.

Check the groper after 5 minutes and remove from the oven when just cooked.

To serve, put a piece of groper in the centre of each plate or put them all on a platter, top with sautéed gnocchi, spoon the sauce over and serve.

For potato gnocchi, always seek out large floury potatoes rather than waxy varieties. Agria, Russet and Idaho all work well as they are high in starch and have a low moisture content.

PAN-ROASTED GROPER WITH SAUTÉED GNOCCHI, FRESH HERBS, CAPERS & PRESERVED LEMON

BILLY (WIREMU KIRK)

Step 1: Tamarind Palm Sugar Vinaigrette
75g tamarind pulp
50g palm sugar, roughly chopped (brown sugar is also fine)
⅔ cup hot water
1 tablespoon lemon juice
1 teaspoon salt
grind of fresh black pepper
¼ cup canola oil

Step 2: Poached Groper Fillet
1 lemon (cut into rounds)
6 x 150g boneless groper fillets (ask your fishmonger for the thickest possible)
½ cup parsley

Step 3: Rustic Croûtons
1 baguette (or similar)
40g butter
¼ cup canola oil
salt and freshly ground black pepper

Step 4: To Serve
1kg ripe summer tomatoes, sliced into rounds
1 cup roughly chopped fresh basil
sea salt and freshly ground black pepper

Chilled Poached Groper with Summer Tomatoes & Tamarind Palm Sugar Vinaigrette

Serves 6 for lunch or brunch

I really enjoy poached fish, especially served chilled on a hot day. The key, I believe, is to use firm-fleshed fish with large, thick flakes. That way you have a lot more control in the cooking process. The other important factor to take into account is that it's paramount not to overcook the fish. Groper works perfectly for this dish. I like to use the plump top half of the fillet, so I can have relatively small but thick, moist fillets. This is such a simple dish, with the combination of tamarind and palm sugar with good-quality ripe summer tomatoes working a treat.

Step 1: Tamarind Palm Sugar Vinaigrette

In a bowl, break up the tamarind with your fingers, then add the palm sugar and hot water. Let this sit for 5 minutes. Rework the mixture with your fingers to make sure the sugar is dissolved, then pass the liquid through a fine sieve and discard the coarse tamarind pulp and seeds.

   Add the lemon juice, salt and black pepper, then whisk in the canola oil. Check the seasoning then refrigerate.

Step 2: Poached Groper Fillet

Preheat the oven to 150°C.

   Place the fillets in an ovenproof dish that holds them snugly in place. Heat up some salted water and pour this over the fillets just to cover, toss in the lemon rounds and parsley. Cover with tinfoil and place in the centre of the oven.

   Check after 5 minutes, then at regular intervals. Remove the fish when it is still slightly translucent in the centre. Once cooked, take the fish out of the poaching liquid and let both the fish and the liquid cool to room temperature. Once cooled, place the fish back in the poaching stock and refrigerate until required.

Step 3: Rustic Croûtons

Carefully remove the crust from the baguette, then tear the bread into small rough pieces.

Place a skillet or sauté pan on medium heat and add the butter and oil. Once hot, toss in the bread. Stir to coat with the butter and oil, season with salt and pepper, then tip onto an oven tray and place in the oven. Cook for around 5 minutes until golden. Remove and cool before storing in an airtight container until needed.

Step 4: To Serve

Layer some tomato rounds in a circle in the centre of each serving plate and drizzle with liberal amounts of the vinaigrette. Top each portion with a fillet of groper.

Place the basil in a bowl with the croutons, toss until combined, then sprinkle evenly over each portion. Finish with salt and a grind of pepper and serve.

Tamarind is a souring agent made from the pods of the tamarind tree, which originated in Africa, but was introduced to India centuries ago where the pulp is used extensively in their cuisine. It is sometimes referred to as Indian date, with the tamarind orchards of India producing more than 275,000 tons annually. Other countries that use tamarind in their respective cuisines include Thailand, Mexico, Africa, Vietnam and the Philippines, as well as Latin American countries. Tamarind is also an ingredient in two popular 'Western' sauces, Worcestershire and HP Sauce.

CHILLED POACHED GROPER WITH SUMMER TOMATOES & TAMARIND PALM SUGAR VINAIGRETTE

Step 1: Salsa Verde
1 green capsicum, seeded and
  finely diced
¼ cup finely diced shallots
½ tablespoon minced garlic
2 tablespoons minced capers
⅓ cup finely diced gherkins

1 tablespoon minced anchovies
  (optional)
⅓ cup finely chopped fresh
  parsley
¼ cup finely chopped fresh mint
¼ cup finely chopped fresh basil
1 tablespoon finely chopped
  fresh tarragon

finely minced zest of 1 lemon
2 tablespoons lemon juice
½ cup lemon-infused olive oil or
  regular olive oil
½ tablespoon sugar
a good grind fresh black pepper

Step 2: To Cook and Serve
whole groper belly or bellies, skin
  and scales on
olive oil for rubbing
sea salt and freshly ground black
  pepper
oil for cooking
lemon halves to serve

Roasted Groper Belly with Salsa Verde

Serves a few or many, depending on the size of the groper

The belly of the fish, referred to in more derogatory terms by many people as the 'flap', is considered one of the least desirable parts. This is ironic, as in many countries this part of the fish is treasured and often has the highest value, such as sashimi-grade tuna belly, which is the part most prized by many Japanese. The belly of the fish contains the most fat and what I can tell you is that fat equals flavour, hence its popularity. I like to remove the belly of a large fish, such as a groper or a good-sized snapper, as a whole section with the skin on, complete with its two 'undercarriage' fins. It cooks beautifully as a whole large piece that I usually serve on a big platter with a pile of forks on the side for everyone to dig into. You won't believe how moist and good it is. It's delicious and rich, so something like this acidic and salty salsa verde, served alongside or over the top, works beautifully.

Step 1: Salsa Verde

Combine all the ingredients in a bowl and refrigerate for half a day, whisking every so often to help the flavours blend and develop. Check the seasoning and add a little more lemon juice if you think it's required. Keep in the refrigerator for up to a week.

Step 2: To Cook and Serve

Preheat the oven to as hot as you can get it.

  Place a roasting dish in the hot oven for 5 minutes to get it super hot.

  Score the flesh side of the belly with a sharp knife, making a couple of criss-cross incisions.

  Rub olive oil into the scored flesh, then season liberally with sea salt and black pepper.

  Remove the hot roasting pan from the oven, add some cooking oil, then place the groper skin side down and put immediately in the oven. Cook for 5 minutes on high, then turn the oven to the grill function and move the pan right under the grill to finish cooking and to create a caramelised and slightly golden appearance.

  Carefully place on a platter and spoon some of the salsa verde over. Lemon halves on the side and you're good to go.

Cuts like the belly, throat and cheeks may not be readily available at your fish market. But if you ask your local fishmonger, it's normally not too big a deal to have it arranged in a couple of days if the weather is good and the boats are out fishing.

Step 1: Chorizo Potatoes
800g new waxy potatoes, scrubbed
cooking oil for frying
300g chorizo, sliced into rounds
¾ cup thinly sliced shallots
2 roasted red capsicums, peeled, seeded and roughly chopped
sea salt and freshly ground black pepper

Step 2: Crayfish Mayonnaise
200g cooked crayfish meat, roughly chopped
½ cup Al's mayonnaise (see recipe on page 302)
¼ teaspoon sweet smoked Spanish paprika
1 teaspoon tomato paste
3 tablespoons finely sliced chives
sea salt and freshly ground black pepper

Step 3: To Cook and Serve
3 tablespoons sweet Spanish sherry vinegar
¼ cup extra virgin olive oil (best quality, please!)
6 x 150g groper portions
sea salt and freshly ground black pepper
cooking oil for frying
½ cup roughly chopped fresh basil

Roasted Groper with Chorizo Potatoes & Crayfish Mayonnaise

Serves 6 as a main course

This is a dish I like to serve for lunch or brunch on a wintry weekend with generous amounts of red wine to wash it all down. A good red wine lends itself perfectly to the gutsy and robust flavours in this dish. It's an easy one to prepare, with steps like the crayfish mayo and boiling the spuds able to be done a day or two ahead. To finish, just cook the groper, finish off the chorizo potatoes and maybe toss a quick green salad together to complete the scene. One crayfish is all that is needed for the mayonnaise, but by all means substitute another large flaky fish for the groper.

Step 1: Chorizo Potatoes

Place the potatoes in a medium saucepan, cover with cold salted water and place on high heat. Once boiling, reduce to a simmer and cook until just tender through the centre. Remove, strain off the water and cool, then slice into 5mm-thick rounds.

Heat a skillet to medium heat, then add a little cooking oil. Add the chorizo and shallots, and fry for 5–10 minutes, tossing occasionally, until all slightly caramelised. Remove from the heat and place in a bowl.

Place the same skillet back on the heat and sauté the potatoes in batches until golden on both sides. Place in an ovenproof dish and spoon the chorizo and shallots over. Distribute the red capsicums evenly over the top. Season with sea salt and black pepper. Cool then cover and refrigerate until required.

Step 2: Crayfish Mayonnaise

Place the crayfish meat in a mixing bowl. Take another small bowl and mix together the mayonnaise, paprika, tomato paste and chives, then add to the crayfish and mix together. Taste and season accordingly.

Step 3: To Cook and Serve

Preheat the oven to 150°C.

Whisk together the vinegar and olive oil. Set aside.

Place the chorizo potatoes uncovered in the oven. Once heated through, remove and keep warm.

New Zealand's top 10 export seafood species in 2008, in order of value at that time, were Greenshell mussels, rock lobster (crayfish), hoki, squid, mackerel, orange roughy, paua, salmon, ling and tuna.

ROASTED WHOLE TURBOT WITH GREEN OLIVE & CAPER TOASTS

Step 1: Green Olive and Caper Tapenade
1 cup green olives, stones removed (I use relatively mild green olives)
3 tablespoons capers
3 tablespoons olive oil
2 tablespoons lemon juice

Step 2: Bruschetta Toasts
1 baguette (or similar)
olive oil for brushing
sea salt to taste

Step 3: Marinated Turbot
1 whole turbot (2–3kg)
2 tablespoons finely chopped fresh oregano
2 tablespoons finely chopped fennel herbs
1½ tablespoons finely chopped garlic
1 tablespoon finely chopped lemon zest
pinch of dried chilli flakes (or more if desired)
⅓ cup olive oil

Step 4: To Cook and Serve
salt and freshly ground black pepper
cooking oil for roasting
lemon juice

Roasted Whole Turbot with Green Olive & Caper Toasts

Serves a bunch of people

I have recently had a wood-fired pizza oven built in my backyard. As soon as it was completed I had a cord of beautiful two-year-old manuka delivered that is now stacked and sorted. I fire the oven up as often as possible, as I have found there is practically nothing that can't be cooked in it.

This dish exhibits a lot of the way that I like to entertain. A whole fish straight from the oven just plonked down on the table for everyone to slowly dissect. A large turbot is an ideal fish to serve this way, as the bone structure allows for easy access to its delicious moist flesh. Once the top fillet has been eaten, it's just a case of removing the main skeletal configuration to reveal the underfillet. I serve it with crisp bruschetta toasts, smeared with a green olive and caper tapenade, which adds a slightly salty and sour flavour to the mix.

Step 1: Green Olive and Caper Tapenade
Place all the ingredients in a food processor and blend until smooth, or just chop the olives and capers as finely as possible, then mix in the olive oil and lemon juice. Cover and store in the refrigerator until required.

Step 2: Bruschetta Toasts
Preheat the oven to 180°C. Slice the bread into pieces about 1cm thick. Brush with olive oil on both sides and sprinkle with a little sea salt. Place on an oven tray and bake until just crisp. Remove, cool and store in an airtight container until serving.

Step 3: Marinated Turbot
See How to Fillet a Flat Fish on page 256.

Lay the turbot down on a board, take a sharp knife and score the flesh of the fillet by making a dozen or so slices in a herringbone pattern about 5mm deep.

Rub the ingredients liberally over the turbot, gently working it into the scored flesh. Marinate in the fridge for a couple of hours, or more if you have the time.

Turbot are the largest flatfish to inhabit our waters. They live on the sandy bottom, feeding on crabs and the like, hence their sweet flesh. Mainly caught on the west coasts of New Zealand, they are a more common catch the further south you go. A large turbot can grow up to 7kg in weight.

Step 4: To Cook and Serve

Preheat the oven to 180°C.

Take the turbot out of the fridge and season with a good amount of salt and pepper. Place a roasting pan that will fit the turbot in the oven to get searing hot. Remove the pan after 5 minutes, add a little cooking oil and place the turbot in belly side down. Quickly cover with tinfoil and put in the oven. Roast for 15 minutes then remove the foil and finish cooking for another 10 minutes or so until the flesh comes away easily from the bone.

While the turbot is cooking, smear the tapenade on the bruschetta toasts.

Remove the turbot from the oven and let it sit for 5 minutes to cool slightly. Carefully remove the turbot from the pan onto a platter, or just leave it in the pan, and serve with the olive and caper bruschetta alongside. Squeeze some lemon over and place a palette knife nearby for the folks to help themselves by topping the bruschetta with the sweet morsels of turbot, while you get on to the next thing!

Step 1: Citrus Mash
1kg peeled floury potatoes (such as Agria), quartered
pinch of salt
300ml cream
finely grated zest of 1 lemon
2 tablespoons lemon juice
sea salt and freshly ground black pepper to taste

Step 2: Fennel Slaw
400g fennel bulbs
½ cup red onion, very thinly sliced
¼ cup finely chopped fresh dill
¼ cup finely chopped fresh parsley
½ cup Al's mayonnaise (see recipe on page 302)
sea salt and freshly ground black pepper

Step 3: Beurre Blanc
see recipe on page 319

Step 4: To Cook and Serve
12 x 70g (or close to) portions turbot
sea salt and freshly ground black pepper
cooking oil for frying
lemon wedges to garnish

Sautéed Turbot with Fennel Slaw & Citrus Mash

Serves 6 as a main course

I was first introduced to turbot only about 10 years ago when I was fortunate enough to be picked to compete for Seafood Chef of the Year (I didn't win!). The cook-off was held in Nelson as part of a weekend that included the New Zealand Seafood Industry Conference and a seafood festival that was held down on the wharf. It was at the festival that I was acquainted for the first time with turbot. I had heard of the species in and around the UK, but had no idea that they were a relatively common catch on the West Coast of the South Island. It's no wonder none of it ever ended up gracing a table up our way, as from the first bite of my sautéed turbot sandwiched between two pieces of buttered white bread, I immediately understood why! Turbot is simply an outstanding eating fish, which I'm sure the 'Coasters' have concealed, along with many other local secrets, from the rest of the country, doing their best to consume all that is caught themselves. I was so taken with the flavour and moistness of the flesh that I managed to organise a field trip for Steve Logan and myself down to Westport to meet the fishermen who caught these large flatfish. From that week on, turbot has regularly featured on the Logan Brown menu. It seems to show up at the fish market more these days, as it has been discovered in other areas and is not just confined to the West Coast. This is a simple dish, but one that I think is terrific. The citrus mash is decadently rich, the fennel slaw crisp and fresh, and with the sautéed, moist turbot, it works a treat.

Step 1: Citrus Mash

In a large saucepan place the potatoes, cover with cold water and add a healthy pinch of salt. Place on high heat then, once boiling, reduce to a simmer and cook until soft.

Pour the cream into a small saucepan and add the lemon zest. Place on low heat to steep.

Once the potatoes are soft, strain off the water completely. Pour in the cream, add the lemon juice and mash until smooth and silky. Season with the sea salt and pepper. Keep in a warm place, or reheat over a water bath or in a microwave when required.

Step 2: Fennel Slaw

With a sharp knife remove and discard the tough green stems from the fennel bulbs. Cut in half lengthwise and remove and discard the tough inner core. Slice the bulbs wafer thin across the grain, with a mandolin vegetable slicer if possible. If not, use the large holes on a grater. You want the fennel to be as thin as possible.

Place the fennel in a bowl and run cold water over it for at least 10 minutes or, even better, place in iced water for up to 1 hour. This makes the fennel super crunchy.

Strain off the water and dry the fennel in a clean tea towel, then place in a mixing bowl. Add the red onion, dill, parsley and mayonnaise. Mix together, then season with sea salt and pepper to taste.

Step 3: Beurre Blanc

See recipe on page 319.

Step 4: To Cook and Serve

Place a skillet or sauté pan on medium-high heat. Season the fish with sea salt and pepper. Add a little cooking oil to the pan and cook the turbot in batches, being careful not to overcrowd the pan, for a couple of minutes on each side until golden and cooked through. Keep the turbot in a warm place while you finish the other portions.

To serve, spoon out a liberal amount of the citrus mash in the centre of each plate, top with the fennel slaw, add 2 pieces of turbot, then pour over a little of the beurre blanc sauce and garnish with a lemon wedge.

Other flatfish of the world include brill, flounder, sole, halibut, megrim, plaice and tonguefish.

CONNIE AND ALICE

SAUTÉED TURBOT WITH FENNEL SLAW & CITRUS MASH

Step 1: Fries
see the recipe on page 305 and fry the chips for the first time, then set aside

Step 2: Chilli and Caper Beurre Noisette
250g butter
½ teaspoon dried chilli flakes
finely grated zest of 1 lemon and juice
2 tablespoons capers
⅓ cup chopped fresh parsley

Step 3: To Cook and Serve
6 whole flounder
1 cup flour, seasoned with salt and pepper
cooking oil for frying
butter for frying

2 litres canola oil
sea salt and freshly ground black pepper
lemon halves to garnish

Whole Flounder with Chilli & Caper Beurre Noisette & Fries

Serves 6 as a main course

Flounder seems to have lost favour over the years and I believe that it's probably due to a lot more recreational fishermen having boats now and access to far more of the fishery than in yesteryear. With what now seems to be an insatiable appetite for pearly white boneless fillets, flounder have been forgotten. I have a real soft spot for flounder and sole, not just for their delicious eating qualities, but because I grew up with the wonderful New Zealand tradition of dragging a net at low tide in river estuaries, lagoons and even straight off beaches when there was an offshore wind with no swell to speak of. Dragging a net for flounder still gives me as much pleasure as any other form of fishing. It's full of laughs, anticipation and an activity that young and old can all get involved in. A whole flounder, lightly dusted in seasoned flour, then sautéed simply in a bit of oil and butter with a squeeze of lemon on the side is pure heaven. It's so wonderfully tactile, extracting the delicate sweet flesh with not much more than fingers and fork, and ending up with a perfectly clean skeleton on your plate.

Beurre noisette is a French term for browned butter sauce, where the milk solids caramelise to create a terrific nutty flavour. I've zhooshed it up a bit with the addition of chilli flakes and chopped capers.

New Zealand imports more than NZ$100 million of seafood products annually.

Step 1: Fries

See the recipe on page 305 and fry the chips for the first time, then set aside.

Step 2: Chilli and Caper Beurre Noisette

It's important to have all your ingredients prepped and ready to go before starting this sauce. It will take about 5 minutes from beginning to end.

Place the butter and chilli flakes in a small saucepan and place on medium heat. Stir continuously with a wooden spoon. The butter will boil away with quite large, continuous bubbles. Keep stirring and, once the milk solids are beginning to brown, the bubbles will start to subside until very fine and the liquid butter will start to turn golden brown. At this exact point, remove from the heat and add the lemon zest and juice, and capers. It will froth up immediately then subside again. Let the sauce cool a bit to just warm before adding the chopped parsley. Keep warm until required.

Step 3: To Cook and Serve

Preheat the oven to 150°C.

Using scissors, cut away the dorsal and anal fins that encircle the flounder. Remove the heads with the scissors as well. To remove the dark skin from the top of the flounder, carefully edge your thumb between the skin and flesh directly where the tail connects to the body. Once started, the skin should separate from the flesh and pull away easily, revealing the top fillet (see diagram page 256). The skin on the underside is finer and delicious to eat (the top skin is also edible, but requires scaling before cooking).

Lightly dust the flounders with seasoned flour.

Place a large skillet or sauté pan on medium heat. Once hot, add a little cooking oil and butter then cook the flounder 1 or 2 at a time. Place the flounder flesh side down in the pan, fry for 1–2 minutes until golden, then turn and repeat on the underside. With a spatula, remove and place on an oiled oven tray, while cooking the others. Set aside.

Place a large saucepan on medium heat, add the canola oil and bring up to approximately 180°C. You can test the temperature by adding a little piece of white bread. It should start to fry immediately and be golden within a minute. Once the oil is the right heat, start cooking the fries in batches.

Place the tray of flounder in the oven to finish cooking (around 5 minutes, depending on the size). Check by pulling away some of the fillet from the flounder with a fork. It should come away from the bone easily.

To serve, place a flounder on each warm plate with a handful of fries. Give the beurre noisette a good stir before spooning over the flounder. A half lemon on the side and you're good to go!

FRESH FLOUNDER FILLETS WITH LEEK & OYSTER CRUST

Step 1: Leek and Oyster Crust
100g butter
3 cups finely diced leeks
½ cup finely diced celery
1½ tablespoons finely chopped garlic
1 tablespoon finely grated lemon zest
1½ tablespoons finely chopped fresh thyme leaves
1 cup cream
liquor from a pottle of 12 oysters

1 tablespoon lemon juice
12 oysters, finely chopped
2 cups day-old bread, roughly chopped into small pieces
¾ cup breadcrumbs
sea salt and freshly ground black pepper
¼ cup finely chopped fresh parsley

Step 2: To Prepare the Flounder
6 flounder
butter for greasing
sea salt and freshly ground black pepper

Step 3: To Cook and Serve
50g butter
12 handfuls spinach, washed
juice of 1 lemon
sea salt and freshly ground black pepper
lemon wedges to garnish

Fresh Flounder Fillets with Leek & Oyster Crust

Serves 6 as a main course

Like all flat bottom-feeding fish, flounder has a terrific sweet and moist flake due to a diet of small crabs and other crustaceans. This is a terrific and rich, rustic style-dish that manages to stretch just a dozen oysters and half a dozen flounder a long way. The leek and oyster crust is simply a moist stuffing that crisps up under the grill, adding a terrific texture to the dish. Normally I'll serve this dish with spinach. It's just a matter of tossing it in a pan with a little butter, lemon juice, sea salt and fresh black pepper until just wilted and no more. By all means use this leek and oyster mixture to stuff other varieties of fish or to serve as an accompaniment.

Step 1: Leek and Oyster Crust

Place a medium saucepan on low heat. Add the butter and, once melted, toss in the leeks, celery, garlic, lemon zest and thyme. Sweat until the vegetables are soft (about 25 minutes).

Add the cream, the liquor from the oysters and lemon juice. Cook for a further 5 minutes, then add the chopped oysters. Stir these in, followed by the stale bread and breadcrumbs. Remove from the heat and mix through. The mix should resemble a moist stuffing. If it's still too wet, add some more breadcrumbs.

Taste and season with sea salt and pepper. Finely fold in the parsley and refrigerate to cool right through.

Step 2: To Prepare the Flounder

To remove the fillets from the flounder, see page 256 or ask your fishmonger if he or she would be so kind as to do so.

Prepare a couple of ovenproof dishes by rubbing a little butter on the base of each to prevent the fish from sticking when cooking.

You will have 2 skinless top fillets and 2 bottom fillets with the skin on from each flounder. From the 4 fillets removed from a flounder, each side has a large fillet and a smaller fillet. Take 2 of the top fillets (one large, one small) and place them overlapping to create one large fillet in the bottom of one of the ovenproof dishes.

There are more than 25,000 identified species of fish on the earth. There are also more species of fish than all the species of amphibians, reptiles, birds and mammals combined.

Do the same with the 2 bottom fillets, overlapping and skin side down. Repeat with the rest. Season the fillets with a little sea salt and pepper.

Now take the chilled leek and oyster mix and, with your hands, form a patty that's the same shape and length as the laid out flounder fillets. Place a patty on top of each overlapped fillet. The crust should be about 1cm thick. Cover and chill the prepared flounder in a refrigerator if not cooking immediately.

Step 3: To Cook and Serve

Preheat the oven to 160°C.

Take the flounder out of the fridge 30 minutes before cooking to bring up to room temperature.

Place the flounder in the oven. Check after 15 minutes. Once cooked, turn the oven onto grill and put each dish under the heat for a minute or two to get a golden crust on top.

While the flounder is cooking, prepare the spinach by melting the butter in a large saucepan. Add the spinach, then the lemon juice. Wilt down just a little, then season with sea salt and black pepper.

To serve, place a pile of wilted spinach in the centre of each warm plate. Using a spatula, top each serving of spinach with 2 of the flounder fillets. Serve with a wedge of lemon.

Note: To make this dish a little more decadent or posh, make a little beurre blanc sauce (see recipe on page 319) to serve alongside.

Step 1: Arrabiata Sauce
see recipe on page 302

Step 2: To Cook and Serve
¼ cup olive oil, plus a little extra
250g dried angel hair pasta
    (spaghetti or linguine fine also)
500g monkfish, cut into bite-size
    pieces

sea salt and freshly ground black
    pepper
cooking oil for frying
2 bags fresh wild rocket (about
    6 cups)
fresh Parmesan for grating

Monkfish with Angel Hair Pasta, Arrabiata Sauce, Rocket & Parmesan

Serves 6 as a main course

Monkfish, or correctly stargazer, is becoming more and more popular in New Zealand as people start to realise that even the ugliest of fish can taste fantastic. Often referred to as 'poor man's lobster' due to its texture and taste — which personally I think is quite a stretch — monkfish is so highly regarded in the northern hemisphere that it fetches a premium price in all markets. The flesh doesn't flake easily, lending itself well to certain types of cooking, such as chargrilling and roasting, that can be difficult with the more flaky types. It's perfect in the following recipe, as the pieces stay together even when tossed with pasta. You'll love the simple but deep-flavoured arrabiata sauce and you'll find you can use it many dishes — and not just with seafood!

Step 1: Arrabiata Sauce

See recipe on page 302.

Step 2: To Cook and Serve

Preheat the oven to 100°C. Fill a large saucepan with salted water, and add about ¼ cup olive oil. Place on high heat and bring to a steady rolling boil.

Place the arrabiata sauce in a saucepan on low heat and stir occasionally as it warms up.

Once the water is boiling, add the pasta and stir for the first minute to make sure the pasta strands are well separated.

While the pasta is cooking, place a skillet or sauté pan on high heat. Season the monkfish with sea salt and black pepper. Add a little oil to the hot pan and cook the monkfish in 2 batches. Remove from the pan when golden on both sides and keep warm in the oven.

Once the pasta is cooked, strain off the water and work through some olive oil to prevent it sticking. Pour the pasta into a couple of warm large bowls to more easily mix the other ingredients through. Add the rocket, half the arrabiata sauce and the pieces of monkfish. Mix all through to combine. Pour the remaining sauce into a bowl to serve alongside.

Portion out the pasta into warm bowls and give each serving a good grating of Parmesan. Serve now!

Accompany with warm buttered crusty bread, a green salad and leave that block of Parmesan nearby for a fresh grate halfway through.

Step 1: Monkfish Prosciutto Skewers

600g monkfish (choose large, thick fillets)
100g prosciutto slices
24 black olives, halved and stones removed
2 zucchini, sliced into 1cm-thick rounds
1 red capsicum, seeded and cut into rough squares
1 red onion, cut into rough squares
160g artichokes in olive oil, quartered (oil reserved)

Step 2: Preserved Lemon and Oregano Marinade

extra olive oil
finely chopped peel of 1 preserved lemon
3 tablespoons finely chopped fresh oregano
2 tablespoons finely chopped garlic
pinch or 2 of dried chilli flakes

Step 3: To Cook and Serve

sea salt and freshly ground black pepper
lemon halves to garnish

Monkfish Prosciutto Skewers, Marinated in Preserved Lemon & Oregano

Makes 24 mini skewers

Monkfish works well with this sort of application. Due to its large meaty flake it can take a bit of the knocking around that comes with wrapping it in prosciutto, threading on skewers and cooking over a chargrill. These little skewers can be made up with any number of ingredients and are an ideal pass-around that can be prepared ahead. The longer the marinating, the tastier the end result — overnight is perfect!

Step 1: Monkfish Prosciutto Skewers

Cut the monkfish into nice thick chunks about 2.5cm square. You should have around 24 pieces.

Soak 24 skewers in water to prevent them from burning when cooking.

Slice the prosciutto into small strips. Wrap the strips around the monkfish pieces. It doesn't matter if the prosciutto only goes around three sides of the monkfish as it will hold in place once you thread the skewer.

To make up the skewers, start with half an olive, followed by a zucchini round, a piece of capsicum, then prosciutto-wrapped monkfish, onion, an artichoke quarter, and finish with another half olive. Repeat until all 24 skewers are prepared. Refrigerate.

Step 2: Preserved Lemon and Oregano Marinade

Take the reserved olive oil from the artichokes and add enough olive oil to make up to ½ cup. Pour into a bowl, then add the remaining ingredients. Whisk together, then pour over the skewers. Massage the marinade loosely over the skewers, then refrigerate.

Step 3: To Cook and Serve

Get your chargrill into good cooking shape, with a solid base of red and white embers.

Season the skewers liberally with sea salt and black pepper.

Chargrill until the monkfish is cooked through and the vegetables are slightly charred. Remove and place on a platter. Chargrill the lemon halves at the same time as the skewers and place these on and around the skewers as a useful garnish.

Around 88 per cent of New Zealanders eat fish once a month, while nearly half of us, 45 per cent, eat it once a week.

Step 1: Fresh Tortilla Chips
1 batch tortilla dough (see recipe on page 313)
1 litre (or more) cooking oil
sea salt

Step 2: Ling and Tequila Ceviche
600g fresh ling fillets, cut into 1cm square pieces
½ cup finely diced Peppadews
1 hot fresh green chilli, finely diced (with or without seeds — up to you!)
1 cup seeded and diced fresh tomato
1 avocado, diced same size as the ling

⅓ cup finely diced red onion
⅓ cup roughly chopped fresh coriander
¼ cup fresh lime juice
¼ cup fresh lemon juice
3 tablespoons tequila
3 tablespoons olive oil
sea salt and freshly ground black pepper

Step 3: To Serve
lime wedges to garnish
the remaining tequila (optional)

Ling and Tequila Ceviche with Fresh Tortilla Chips

Serves 6 as an entrée (or serve in a bowl as a pass-round)

Ceviche is a terrific and healthy way to eat fish. There are many variations and methods of preparation from country to country, however, they all contain a good deal of citrus juice or vinegar. It's the action of the acid that actually 'par-cooks' the raw fish. You can make ceviche with any number of species, but the larger-flaked fish with thick fillets work the best. I love to use ling as it ticks all the aforementioned boxes and is a super-white fillet, which makes the finished dish look so fresh and vibrant.

Step 1: Fresh Tortilla Chips
Divide the tortilla dough into 24 balls, then roll out as thinly as possible into rounds. Cut into smallish triangles.

Place at least 1 litre of cooking oil in a saucepan and place on high heat. Bring up to between 160°C and 180°C. Test by adding a piece of white bread. It should start frying immediately and turn golden and crisp in a minute or so.

Deep fry the tortilla chips in batches, then place on paper towels. Season with salt and, once cool, store in an airtight container until required.

Step 2: Ling and Tequila Ceviche
In a large bowl, mix together all the ingredients. Cover and refrigerate for at least 2 hours, stirring occasionally. The longer you leave the ceviche to marinate, the more tender it will become. I like to serve it when it's still raw in the centre and has a little texture in the bite.

Step 3: To Serve
Serve the ceviche in a bowl surrounded by the fresh tortilla chips, or as individual entrées. Garnish with the lime wedges and chill that tequila down to serve alongside!

Ling is a deep-water fish that is found in depths of 300 to 500 metres. They can grow up to 20kg in weight. They are related to the eel family and are similarly shaped but with distinctive orange and pink markings.

Step 1: Black Turtle Bean and Avocado Salsa
3 tins black turtle beans (or 2½ cups dried beans, soaked overnight and cooked until soft)
1½ large avocados, cut into 1cm dice
⅓ cup finely chopped red onion
⅓ cup finely chopped Peppadews
⅓ cup finely chopped fresh coriander
¼ cup lemon juice
1 teaspoon Tabasco Chipotle Pepper Sauce
⅓ cup olive oil
sea salt and freshly ground black pepper

Step 2: Coriander Aïoli
1 cup Al's mayonnaise (see recipe on page 302)
¾ tablespoon finely chopped garlic
½ cup finely chopped fresh coriander
2 teaspoons freshly ground cumin
2 teaspoons fresh lemon juice
sea salt and freshly ground black pepper

Step 3: To Cook and Serve
cooking oil for brushing
6 x 150g fresh ling fillets
sea salt and freshly ground black pepper
fresh lime wedges to garnish

Chargrilled Ling Fillet with Black Turtle Bean & Avocado Salsa & Coriander Aïoli

Serves 6 as a main course

This is a great summer dish, with 'Tex Mex' flavours. The ling with its large meaty flake works perfectly well here, chargrilled and served up with this delicious salsa and aïoli. It's also a very colourful dish, with the black salsa contrasting with the very white fillet of the ling. For speed and ease, I've used canned black turtle beans, but you will most definitely get a better result by soaking dry beans overnight and then cooking them slowly in seasoned water or stock.

Step 1: Black Turtle Bean and Avocado Salsa
Place all the ingredients except the salt and pepper in a large mixing bowl and, with clean hands, fold gently together. Season with the sea salt and pepper and refrigerate for a couple of hours, stirring occasionally to let the flavours develop.

Step 2 Coriander Aïoli
Place the mayonnaise in a mixing bowl. Fold in the garlic, coriander, cumin and lemon juice. Taste, then add some seasoning if necessary. Refrigerate until required.

Step 3: To Cook and Serve
Heat up the chargrill to good and hot. Lightly oil the ling fillets, then season on both sides. Place the fillets on the grill and don't touch for a couple of minutes. This gives the fish time to set and helps prevent it from sticking. Once half cooked, turn and finish cooking on the other side.

To serve, spoon out the black turtle bean and avocado salsa on serving plates and top each with a ling fillet. Add a dollop of the coriander aïoli and place lime wedges alongside. Serve now with some cold cerveza.

The export of New Zealand ling was worth NZ$41 million in 2008. Ka-ching!

Step 1: Fish Curry Base
⅓ cup canola oil or ghee
40–50 curry leaves
4 cardamom pods, split
1 cinnamon stick
2 teaspoons black mustard seeds
pinch of dried chilli flakes
2 medium onions, roughly
    chopped
1½ tablespoons finely chopped
    ginger
1½ tablespoons finely chopped
    garlic
2 teaspoons ground cumin
2 teaspoons ground coriander

1 teaspoon turmeric
1 teaspoon garam masala
1 tablespoon sea salt
800g whole peeled tomatoes,
    roughly chopped
35g tamarind pulp
1 cup hot water
425ml coconut cream
2 cups fish stock (see recipe on
    page 311) or water
350g potatoes, peeled and cut
    into medium dice
300g peas

Step 2: Basmati Rice
4 cups water
2 cups basmati rice
2 kaffir lime leaves (optional)

Step 3: To Serve
1kg boned conger eel fillets (or
    2cm pieces)
1 teaspoon garam masala
juice of 1 lemon
½ bunch fresh coriander
yoghurt, cucumber, pickles and
    relishes to serve

Conger Eel, Potato and Pea Curry

Serves 6 as a main course

Well down the line in the popularity stakes, the conger eel works perfectly in this fish curry, with its relatively firm flesh holding together well. Like most curries, seafood curries seem to eat so much better the next day when the flavours have had time to develop. I always add the fish or crustaceans at the last moment before serving to prevent overcooking, which makes sense. However, if served a day later, the seafood has had more time to release and disperse much more of its natural flavour.

Step 1: Fish Curry Base

Place a large saucepan on medium heat and add the canola oil or ghee. Once the oil is hot, add the curry leaves, cardamom pods, cinnamon stick, mustard seeds and chilli flakes. Stir for a minute or so with a wooden spoon, then reduce the heat slightly.

Toss in the onion, ginger and garlic. Stir through the oil and spices and fry for 5–10 minutes until the vegetables begin to caramelise.

Now add the cumin, coriander, turmeric, garam masala and sea salt. Stir through, then pour in the tomatoes and stir to combine. Reduce the heat to a simmer.

Break the tamarind up with your fingers into a bowl then pour the hot water over and let sit for 5 minutes. With a spoon or again your fingers, work the tamarind paste away from the inedible pips and husk. Pour it all through a sieve into the curry, discarding the solids.

Add the coconut cream and stock or water. Let the curry slowly simmer for 30 minutes.

Add the diced potato and cook until just soft (about 20 minutes). Add the peas and turn off the heat. Reserve.

Step 2: Basmati Rice

Place the water in a medium saucepan and bring to the boil.

Give the rice a good wash under cold water before cooking.

Once the water has boiled, add the washed rice and the kaffir lime leaves, if using. Place a lid on the saucepan, lower the heat and simmer for 20–25 minutes. Remove from the heat and set aside, covered, for 10 minutes.

Step 3: To Serve

Heat the fish curry base to a simmer and add the conger eel. Cook for 5 minutes until the eel is cooked through.

Sprinkle the garam masala over, add the lemon juice and fold in the coriander.

Divide the rice onto hot plates and spoon the curry over. Serve with an array of condiments such as yoghurt, cucumber, pickles and relishes.

When fishing and you hook a conger eel, be very wary when you bring one on board or when removing the hook. They have very strong jaws and can inflict a pretty painful bite.

Step 1: To Prepare the Chips
2 litres canola oil
1.5kg Agria potatoes, peeled

Step 2: Beer Batter
140g flour
3 tablespoons cooking oil
250ml lager
salt and freshly ground black
  pepper

Step 3: To Cook and Serve
2 litres canola oil
12 x 80g lemonfish fillets
flour for dusting
salt and freshly ground black
  pepper

Lemonfish and Chips

Serves 6 as a main course

Fish and chips are unequivocally our national takeaway. They are known to many as 'shark and taties' and for good reason, as the particular variety of shark, known so eloquently as lemonfish, works beautifully when coated in batter and deep-fried. Lemonfish is also known as rig, spotted dogfish, gummy shark and, my favourite, smoothhound. My potato of choice is Agria, and any decent fish and chip shop worth its salt will be using this variety and making their own chips on the premises. Frozen pre-cut chips are completely inferior.

Step 1: To Prepare the Chips
Pour the oil into a large heavy-based saucepan and place on medium heat.
    Rinse then slice the potatoes into the chip size of choice.
    Once you think the oil is hot, test it by adding a little piece of white bread. It should start to fry immediately and be golden within a minute. If you have a thermometer, the oil should be around 180°C.
    Add the potatoes and, with a wooden spoon, carefully move them around so they don't stick together, then fry for 2–3 minutes, depending on how thick you have cut the chips, until just cooked through. Remove with a slotted spoon or metal sieve and place on paper towels to drain off any excess oil. Cover and keep at room temperature if you are planning to cook them on the same day, or refrigerate until required.
    Note: I like to fry the chips twice, as you get a crisper result.

Step 2: Beer Batter
In a mixing bowl, place the flour, oil and lager. Whisk until you have a lump-free, smooth batter. Season with salt and black pepper. Refrigerate for at least 30 minutes before using.

Step 3: To Cook and Serve
Preheat the oven to 100°C.
    In your largest saucepan, place the oil and bring up to about 180°C.
    Once hot, cook the chips in batches until golden. Remove and place in an ovenproof dish lined with paper towels. Keep warm in the oven while you continue cooking the rest.
    For the fish, lightly dust with flour then dip through the batter, allowing most to drip off, then slowly lower into the hot oil. Remove when golden and cooked through and place on the hot chips while you continue cooking the rest of the portions. Season with salt and freshly ground black pepper.
    To serve, it's up to you: plates, platters, newspaper, Mr Wattie's finest on the side, some cut-up lemons and you're good to go!

Sharks don't have air bladders like most fish to keep afloat, so must swim continually or rest on the bottom.

Step 1: Harissa

1 cup peeled, seeded and roughly chopped roasted red capsicum
2 tablespoons seeded and chopped fresh red chilli
1½ tablespoons chopped garlic
½ cup chopped fresh coriander
⅓ cup chopped fresh mint
⅓ cup chopped fresh parsley
½ tablespoon freshly ground cumin seeds
½ tablespoon sweet smoked paprika
2 tablespoons brown sugar
1 tablespoon tomato paste
2 tablespoons lemon juice
2 tablespoons fresh lime juice
100ml olive oil
sea salt and freshly ground black pepper

Step 2: Green Olive and Currant Couscous

⅓ cup olive oil
2 cups finely diced red onion
1 cup finely diced red capsicum
½ cup good-quality green olives, pitted and sliced
⅓ cup currants, roughly chopped
2 cups water
2 teaspoons salt
2½ cups couscous
¼ cup extra olive oil
1 tablespoon butter, cut into pieces
½ cup finely chopped fresh parsley
sea salt and freshly ground black pepper

Step 3: To Cook and Serve

cooking oil for brushing
sea salt and freshly ground black pepper
6 x 150g broadbill portions
chopped fresh coriander leaves
lime halves to garnish

Chargrilled Broadbill Swordfish with Green Olive & Currant Couscous & Harissa

Serves 6 as a main course

In the rest of the world, broadbill, marlin and tuna have been fished almost to extinction. We still have relatively good numbers around New Zealand and the practice of 'catch, tag and release' is adopted by most fishermen who target these extraordinary and often large fighting fish. The odd one that is kept often gets smoked, prolonging the shelf life, and is shared among the crew, family and friends.

Harissa is a spicy full-flavoured sauce made of roasted capsicum, fresh chillies, garlic, herbs and spices. It partners up very well with the firm, meaty texture of the swordfish served with the moist couscous. The following recipe works a treat — big fish, big flavours!

Step 1: Harissa

Place all the ingredients except the sea salt and fresh black pepper in a blender and process until smooth. Season to taste and refrigerate until required.

Step 2: Green Olive and Currant Couscous

Place a skillet or sauté pan on low heat. Add the ⅓ cup olive oil and, once hot, add the red onion, capsicum, olives and currants. Sweat on low heat for about 30 minutes until soft.

For the couscous, pour the water and salt into a medium saucepan and bring to the boil. Remove from the heat and stir in the couscous and extra olive oil. Cover and let sit for 3–4 minutes. Add the butter and gently fluff up the couscous with a fork to separate the grains. Add the olive and currant mixture. Stir through with the parsley and season with sea salt and pepper to taste. Keep warm.

Step 3: To Cook and Serve

Heat up the chargrill until very hot. Lightly oil and season the broadbill. Place on the grill and cook for a couple of minutes either side. It's best just slightly undercooked.

Spoon out some of the couscous onto serving plates (or a platter). Top each serving with a piece of broadbill and spoon some harissa over. Garnish with coriander and lime halves.

Broadbill swordfish can be huge and have been known to grow to more than 500kg. They are targeted and caught mainly at night, while in the daytime they reside near the bottom of the ocean in depths of up to 800 metres.

Step 1: Tuna and Horseradish Tartare

500g fresh tuna, cut into small dice

¾ cup blanched, peeled, seeded and diced tomato

½ avocado, cut into small dice

1½ teaspoons finely grated lemon zest

¼ cup finely chopped chives

⅓ cup finely chopped fresh basil

3 tablespoons horseradish sauce

2 tablespoons lime juice

⅓ cup lemon-infused olive oil or extra virgin olive oil

sea salt and freshly ground black pepper

Step 2: To Plate and Serve

lemon-infused olive oil or extra virgin olive oil

sea salt and freshly ground black pepper

fresh lime halves to garnish

assorted crackers, toast, bruschetta or similar

Fresh Tuna & Horseradish Tartare

Serves 6 as an entrée or lots as a pass-around

This is a great way to introduce people to the pleasure of eating raw fish. It is a textural delight and the horseradish gives it a little hit of heat at the end of each mouthful. Serve as a pass-around or you can easily mould the tartare for a terrific presentation as a cold plated entrée. What to serve alongside is up to you — little toast squares, water crackers or even homemade flour tortilla chips (see page 313).

Step 1: Tuna and Horseradish Tartare

In a large bowl place all the ingredients except the salt and pepper. With a large spoon or clean hands, gently mix and fold all the ingredients together. Taste, then season the tartare with sea salt and black pepper accordingly. Chill until ready to serve.

Step 2: To Plate and Serve

Place the tartare in the centre of a platter and drizzle a little lemon-infused or extra virgin olive oil over. Sprinkle with a good pinch of sea salt and a healthy grind of black pepper. Garnish with lime halves in a corner of the platter, then arrange the crackers, toast or bruschetta on the side, or serve on individual plates as an entrée.

Tuna are constantly in motion and can cruise the ocean at speeds of well over 50 kilometres an hour. They can eat up to 10 per cent of their body weight daily. The average annual consumption of tuna in the United States is 3.6 pounds (1.6kg) per person, nearly all of which comes from little round cans!

Step 1: Rock Sugar Dressing
200g pale or yellow rock sugar
200ml rice wine vinegar
100ml white wine vinegar
60ml lime or lemon juice
50ml dark soy sauce
10g fresh ginger, peeled and
  sliced into fine matchsticks

**Step 2: Cucumber, Mint and
  Pickled Ginger Salad**
2 telegraph cucumbers, unpeeled
½ cup tightly packed fresh mint,
  thinly sliced
40g pickled ginger, thinly sliced

Step 3: Preparing the Tuna
1kg fresh yellowfin tuna
wasabi paste
10 sheets nori

Step 4: To Cook and Serve
2 litres cooking oil for deep-frying
150g tempura flour
sea salt to taste

Yellowfin Tuna Tempura with Cucumber, Mint & Pickled Ginger Salad

Serves 10 as an entrée

This dish was on our very first menu back when we opened Logan Brown in December 1996 and still features from time to time. It's classic Japanese, using many of the ingredients this cuisine is famous for: wasabi, tempura, pickled ginger, nori and soy sauce. The sharp, clean flavours work perfectly together. The rock sugar dressing is like a sweet and sour syrup, and so versatile you'll find that you will use it on all manner of dishes, especially with raw fish. Once made, it will last indefinitely.

Step 1: Rock Sugar Dressing
Place the rock sugar in a small heavy-based saucepan. With a meat cleaver or clean hammer, smash up the rock sugar into smallish pieces. Add the remaining ingredients and place the saucepan on medium heat. Bring to the boil, then lower the heat so the liquid is just rolling over. Simmer to reduce for 20 minutes, then take a teaspoonful out and place on a small dish in the fridge. When cold, the liquid should resemble a slightly runny syrup. Continue simmering until this consistency is achieved, then pour into a container, cool and refrigerate.

Step 2: Cucumber, Mint and Pickled Ginger Salad
Using the julienne blade on a mandolin, cut the cucumber into long strands resembling spaghetti or matchsticks. If you don't have a mandolin, use a coarse grater or, even better, hone your knife skills and cut by hand in the 'old school' manner. Use only the outside flesh of the cucumber and not the centre where the seeds are. Place the cucumber in a bowl.

Add the mint and pickled ginger to the cucumber and mix together. Refrigerate until serving.

Step 3: Preparing the Tuna
Cut the tuna into 10 even portions of around 80g–100g each.

Using a pastry brush, lightly brush the tuna with a little wasabi paste.

Rinse the brush and place in a small container of clean cold water. Have a pair of scissors handy.

Take each piece of tuna and wrap up in the nori as if wrapping up a gift, brushing the nori with the wet pastry brush to help seal and stick it to the tuna.

Use the scissors to cut off any overhanging pieces of nori. Place the tuna parcels on a tray and refrigerate until ready to cook.

Step 4: To Cook and Serve

Pour the cooking oil into a large heavy-based saucepan. Place on medium heat and slowly bring up to 180°C.

Place the tempura flour in a bowl and whisk in cold water until you have a thin, runny batter.

Dress the cucumber salad with a little of the rock sugar dressing, mixing through well.

Test the heat of the oil with a piece of white bread — it should turn golden and crisp in under a minute. Once the oil is hot, dip 5 of the tuna portions into the batter. Working quickly, remove each one individually, letting the excess batter drip off, and carefully lower into the hot oil. Fry for about 2 minutes, ensuring that the tuna remains rare in the centre. Remove and place on paper towels while you cook the remaining portions.

To serve, divvy out the salad onto cold plates. Cut the tuna portions into 2 pieces and place on the salad. Drizzle a little more of the dressing over and add a pinch of sea salt. Serve now!

DAD

DOUBLE WHITEBAIT WITH TARTARE SAUCE

Step 1: Whitebait Fritters
250g whitebait
1 whole egg
1 egg yolk (reserve the egg white)
1 tablespoon flour
sea salt and freshly ground black
   pepper

**Step 2: To Prepare the Sautéed
   Whitebait**
250g whitebait

Step 3: To Cook and Serve
butter for frying
2 cups flour
cooking oil for frying
sea salt and freshly ground black
   pepper
tartare sauce (see recipe on page
   317)
lemon wedges to serve

Double Whitebait with Tartare Sauce

Serves 6 as an entrée

What a treasure it is for this country to have these wonderful tiny fish that run up many of our rivers every year, giving us a short season to enjoy this unique delicacy. I can't think of another form of fishing that creates so many dreams, such buzz, conflict, smoke and mirrors, anticipation and sheer delight, and all over a minuscule, transparent fish making its way upriver. These particularly delicate fish are loved by one and all, which I'm sure is due to the mystery and folklore surrounding them. I do like a 'feed of bait' every season but, as far as fish go, I rate so many more species ahead of these little critters. I find the flavour incredibly subtle and too often it can be lost or overpowered by other ingredients. This recipe uses the two methods of cooking whitebait that I like. The first is in a fritter form, which helps a little go a bit further. The second is my preferred method: simply dusted in a micro-covering of flour, sautéed in a little oil and butter, and served with just a squeeze of lemon juice.

Step 1: Whitebait Fritters
Drain the whitebait in a sieve.

   In a small bowl whisk the whole egg and the yolk with the flour to a smooth batter. Season with a healthy pinch of sea salt and a liberal grind of black pepper. Stir in the whitebait. Refrigerate until ready to cook.

Step 2: To Prepare the Sautéed Whitebait
Place the whitebait in a sieve to drain, then tip onto a clean tea towel or paper towel. Carefully dry the whitebait, then place half in your largest clean and dry sieve. Have the other half ready in a bowl. Place the sieve over a large mixing bowl.

Step 3: To Cook and Serve
Whisk the reserved egg white until nearly stiff, then gently fold into the whitebait fritter mix (this makes the fritters delicate and light).

   Heat a skillet or non-stick frying pan to medium-low heat. Add a little butter then, using a small ladle, divide the fritter batter into 6 portions. Fry a few fritters at a time, turning when the first side is golden (a minute or so), then the same on the flipped side. Keep warm once cooked.

Increase the heat and get your pan nice and hot. Pour most of the flour over the dried whitebait in the sieve. With clean hands and shaking the sieve at the same time, work the flour over and through the whitebait until each is separated and has a meagre dusting of flour.

Add a little oil to the pan, then sprinkle in the floured whitebait. Season with sea salt and black pepper. Flip the whitebait when starting to turn golden (less than a minute), add a knob of butter and fry for another 30 seconds or so, then remove from the pan and repeat with the second batch of reserved whitebait.

To serve, place a fritter or two in the centre of each plate, add a good dollop of tartare sauce, then top with the sautéed whitebait. A lemon wedge on each plate and you're away!

A snippet from the Taranaki Herald in 1882 tells of Chinese whitebaiters on the West Coast, who, in prolific years, dried large quantities of whitebait to help feed the goldminers in Otago, as well as exporting considerable amounts back to China. (Taranaki Herald, 9 November 1882, page 2)

Step 1: Nuoc Cham
⅓ cup sugar
3 tablespoons water
¼ cup fish sauce
½ cup fresh lime or lemon juice
1 red chilli, finely chopped (seeds optional)
1 tablespoon finely chopped shallots

1 tablespoon finely chopped garlic

Step 2: Fish Dumplings
500g fresh fish, finely chopped
2 teaspoons sesame oil
3 tablespoons sweet chilli sauce
¼ cup finely chopped Chinese chives (or substitute regular)

¼ cup finely chopped fresh coriander
¼ cup finely chopped fresh basil
finely grated zest of 1–2 limes
sea salt and freshly ground black pepper
1 packet round dumpling wrappers
1 egg white, lightly beaten

Step 3: To Cook and Serve
cooking oil for brushing
lime halves to garnish

Asian Fish Dumplings with Nuoc Cham

Makes 30-odd dumplings

Known to many as 'pot stickers', or in some parts 'Peking ravioli', these little dumplings, which are steamed then fried, are very addictive. They are wrapped in what are commonly called chiao-tzu skins or gyoza wrappers which are available at all Asian supermarkets. You can use them in so many applications. However, I use them most often in this recipe, which also uses all the offcuts and scrapings I save from the frames and bones while filleting fresh fish. It's another example of using up every morsel of the whole fish and eliminating any wastage. From half a kilo of fresh fish bits and pieces you can make 30 dumplings! Nuoc cham is a favourite dipping sauce in Vietnamese and Thai cuisine — it's sweet and sour with a hit of chilli and works a treat with these pot stickers.

Step 1: Nuoc Cham
In a bowl, whisk together the sugar, water, fish sauce and juice until the sugar is dissolved. Add the chilli, shallots and garlic. Refrigerate if not using within the day.

Step 2: Fish Dumplings
Place all the ingredients except the salt, pepper, dumpling wrappers and egg white in a mixing bowl. Mix with clean hands to distribute all the ingredients evenly. Season with a liberal amount of sea salt and a grind or two of black pepper.

To make the dumplings, take a dumpling wrapper and lightly brush with egg white. Place about 1 tablespoon of the fish mixture in the centre. Fold the wrapper over to create a half circle, then pinch the edges together with your fingers or crimp with a fork. Place on a lightly floured tray and continue until all the filling is used. Refrigerate covered if you are not cooking immediately.

Step 3: To Cook and Serve
You can either steam the dumplings first or boil them before sautéing. To steam in a bamboo steamer, place the steamer over a saucepan of boiling water. Brush the base of the steamer with a little oil to help prevent the dumplings from sticking. Steam the dumplings in batches for a couple of minutes with the lid on. Remove carefully and brush with a little more oil so they don't stick together. If you don't have a steamer, it's no biggie — just blanch the dumplings in a couple of batches in rolling boiling water, removing after a couple of minutes with a sieve or slotted spoon. Place on a tray and brush with oil to prevent the dumplings sticking together.

Place a skillet or sauté pan on medium heat. Add a small amount of oil. Once hot, cook the dumplings in batches until golden on each side. They colour up quite quickly, so keep an eye on them. Place on a platter with a small bowl of the dipping sauce and serve with a couple of fresh lime halves. Watch 'em disappear!

The famous ingredient fish sauce is made from fermented fish and used in a lot of Southeast Asian cuisines. Whatever you do, don't smell it directly from the bottle as it could put you off it for life. Used, often sparingly, in so many recipes, it has the magical effect of lifting a dish out of the ordinary.

Step 1: Fish Croquettes
600g boned fish, roughly chopped into pieces
1 cup milk
600g potatoes, peeled and cut into 1cm dice
¼ cup cooking oil
¾ cup finely diced celery
1½ cups finely diced onion
1½ tablespoons minced garlic
finely grated zest of 1 lemon
2 tablespoons butter

2 tablespoons flour
sea salt and freshly ground black pepper
2 tablespoons lemon juice
⅓ cup minced parsley

Step 2: To Crumb the Croquettes
2 cups flour
4 eggs, beaten
3 cups breadcrumbs

Step 3: Rouille
1 cup Al's mayonnaise (see recipe on page 302)
1 roasted red capsicum, peeled, seeded and roughly chopped
6 cloves roasted garlic, peeled
1 teaspoon minced fresh garlic
2–4 anchovies
2½ tablespoons tomato paste
½ tablespoon sweet smoked Spanish paprika
¼ cup breadcrumbs

1½ tablespoons lemon juice
Tabasco to taste
pinch of sugar
salt and freshly ground black pepper to taste

Step 4: To Cook and Serve
2 cups cooking oil
lemon wedges to garnish

Fish Croquettes with Rouille

Makes 18–20

Fish croquettes could be described as old-school comfort food. These pan-fried soft and moist cylinders with a thin crisp outer are very addictive. I've poshed them up a bit, serving them with rouille, a classic French mayonnaise-based sauce, that is traditionally served with their famous fish stew, bouillabaisse. It works beautifully with the croquettes, however tartare sauce, aioli and gribiche would also make excellent accompaniments. Again a dish like this makes a little fish go a long way. It's also perfect for using all the bits and pieces from a fish that more than often get thrown out still intact with the fillet-less frame.

Step 1: Fish Croquettes
Place the fish in a small saucepan and add the milk. Place on medium heat and simmer for 5–10 minutes until the fish is flaky and cooked through. Remove from the heat and strain through a sieve into a bowl, reserving the liquid. Put the fish into a large mixing bowl.

Place the potato in a medium saucepan and cover with cold salted water. Place on high heat and bring to the boil, then lower the heat to a simmer. Cook for 8–10 minutes until just soft, then remove from the heat and strain off the water. Place in the bowl with the cooked fish.

In a skillet or large sauté pan, add the cooking oil followed by the celery, onion, garlic and lemon zest. Place on medium-low heat and sweat for 30 minutes, stirring occasionally, until the vegetables are soft. Remove from the heat and add to the fish and potato.

Next place the butter in another small saucepan on medium heat. Once melted, add the flour and whisk to a paste. Continue to whisk as you slowly add the reserved milk from cooking the fish to make a smooth, lump-free white sauce. Season with sea salt and black pepper before pouring over the rest of the ingredients in the bowl. Mix in the lemon juice and parsley.

With clean hands, mix all the ingredients together. Taste and season accordingly before refrigerating for at least a couple of hours to chill the mixture before moulding into shape.

Step 2: To Crumb the Croquettes

Line up three separate bowls, the first with the flour, the second with the eggs and the third with breadcrumbs. Divide the fish mixture into 20 even amounts, then mould each into a cylinder shape. Dust lightly with flour, dip in the egg and roll carefully in the breadcrumbs. Place on a clean, dry tray and repeat until completed. Cover the croquettes with plastic wrap and refrigerate until required.

Step 3: Rouille

Preheat the oven to 150°C.

Place all the ingredients in a food processor and process until smooth. These quantities work well, however, add more anchovy if you like. Likewise, if you prefer it a bit sharper, add more lemon juice. Refrigerate until required.

Step 4: To Cook and Serve

Preheat the oven to 150°.

Place a skillet or sauté pan on medium heat and add the oil. Once hot, carefully add 5 croquettes. Cook for a couple of minutes until golden all over. Remove from the oil and place in an ovenproof dish. Repeat until all the croquettes are golden, then place in the oven for about 10 minutes to finish heating through.

To serve, spoon a couple of tablespoons of the rouille onto the centre of each plate. Top with a couple of crisp fish croquettes and garnish with a wedge of lemon. Serve now!

Only New Zealanders and New Zealand-owned companies can buy quota to catch New Zealand seafood. Around 50 per cent of fishing quota is owned by Maori.

Step 1: Fresh Herb Gremolata
⅓ cup finely chopped lemon peel
2 tablespoons finely chopped
  garlic
⅓ cup finely chopped fresh
  parsley

2 tablespoons finely chopped
  fresh mint
2 tablespoons finely chopped
  fresh basil

**Step 2: To Roast the Heads,
  Wings, Throats, Bellies and
  Bones**
fresh fish heads, wings, throats,
  bellies and bones
olive oil for roasting
sea salt and freshly ground black
  pepper

Step 3: To Serve
extra virgin olive oil for drizzling
sea salt to taste
lemon halves to garnish

Roasted Heads, Wings, Throats, Bellies & Bones with Fresh Herb Gremolata

Serves 6 as a finger-lickin' entrée or snack

Here in New Zealand we have all grown up surrounded by a healthy and plentiful fishery. If the weather is good, it's highly likely that if you put in a couple of hours' graft, your efforts will be rewarded with a feed of fish, even if you are a bit of a novice. Often we hit a hot spot where the fishing is outstanding and the chilly bin fills up at an alarming rate. I am adamant that too often we take more fish than necessary. In the past I've been guilty of getting lost in the thrill of it all — the fish are on the bite and the adrenalin takes over as we remove each fish as quickly as possible to get our hooks back down to catch another and another. We take that big bin of fish home and start the job of filleting the catch. A couple of cuts and incisions here and there, and two beautiful fresh fillets sit gleaming in the plastic bowl or colander. What happens to the rest of the fish? I'm thinking at least 90 per cent of it goes in the garbage. It really is a crime to throw so much of the fish away. What's ironic is that we're tossing out the tastiest parts of the fish. Unlike secondary cuts from butchered animals, these are moist, tender and absolutely full of flavour, without having to cook them for two or three hours! When you roast the heads, wings, throats, bellies and bones, you're cooking the most tasty and luxurious segments of the fish. There are no small bones to contend with and, as we all know, anything cooked on the bone has more flavour.

Gremolata is a condiment traditionally made up of finely chopped parsley, lemon zest and garlic. I've also added a little fresh basil and mint to mix it up a little.

Step 1: Fresh Herb Gremolata

Place the lemon peel (I use a vegetable peeler to remove the lemon peel, then finely chop from there) and garlic in a small mixing bowl.

Place the parsley, chopped as finely as possible, in a clean tea towel or similar, then twist tightly to remove as much liquid as possible. Add to the mixing bowl along with the mint and basil. Mix together with your hands. Cover and refrigerate if not using immediately.

Step 2: To Roast the Heads, Wings, Throats, Bellies and Bones

Preheat the oven to as hot as possible or about 200°C.

Make sure as many of the scales have been removed from the bits and pieces as possible. Give them a quick rinse, then pat dry. Toss in a bowl with some olive oil

In 2008–09 the total allowable commercial catch was 586,000 tonnes, and in 2007–08 the total landed catch was 446,000 tonnes.

and liberal amounts of sea salt and black pepper.

Place a roasting pan in the oven for 5 minutes to get it good and hot. Remove and quickly add all your 'goodies'. Place back in the oven and roast on high for a good 20 minutes. You want all the skin and fins to caramelise and become crunchy. Don't worry about the fish overcooking as it stays beautifully moist when cooked on the bone and with its skin protecting it.

Once cooked remove from the oven.

Step 3: To Serve

Remove all the roasted bits and pieces and place on a platter. Liberally drizzle some extra virgin olive oil over then sprinkle over a generous amount of the gremolata. Put the rest of the gremolata in a bowl on the table for people to help themselves. Scatter the lot with sea salt, put lemon halves on the side and you're good to go. Serve with a stack of paper towels or napkins, sit down — you'll be in heaven!

Go To Recipes

½ cup canola oil or similar
200g carrots, roughly chopped
200g celery, roughly chopped
200g onion, roughly chopped
2 fennel bulbs, roughly chopped

5 cloves garlic, roughly chopped
1kg crayfish bodies
1 cup brandy
¼ cup tomato paste

1 tablespoon sweet smoked
 paprika
pinch of chilli flakes
4 litres cold water

Crayfish Stock

Makes 3 litres

Like all homemade stocks, the preparation time required here is paid back in spades the moment you taste the finished result, as the depth of flavour will always be superior. Look for crayfish bodies (not tails) at your local fishmonger. They are relatively cheap and a great way to add a heap of crayfish flavour to numerous dishes without breaking the budget. I suggest you make a batch or two in winter, then freeze them in 1 litre portions. This way, when a dish calls for stock, the recipe doesn't seem so daunting as one of your major flavour components is already set to go. Beaut for risottos and soups.

Method

Preheat the oven to 200°C. Place a large roasting pan over high heat and add the canola oil. When the oil is hot, add the carrots, celery, onion, fennel and garlic. Stirring every so often, fry the vegetables until caramelised.

   Meanwhile, pull the crayfish bodies apart and remove any visible guts, plus the little feathery things that run up from both sides of the legs in the cavity.

   Once the vegetables have some colour, top with the crayfish bodies and place the pan in the oven. Cook for about 30 minutes until the crayfish bodies are pink and brittle.

   Remove the tray from the oven. With tongs, take out the crayfish bodies and place in a large saucepan. Take a clean hammer, meat tenderiser or similar and smash the cray bodies as much as possible. This exposes the inner flesh, which greatly enhances the extraction of flavour. Top with the roasted vegetables.

   Place the roasting pan back on the heat. Once hot, pour in the brandy to deglaze the pan, watching for a possible flare up, scrape up all the sticky bits and pieces, then tip everything onto the crayfish and vegetables. Stir the tomato paste, paprika and chilli flakes through.

   Pour the water over and place the saucepan back on the heat. Bring to the boil, then lower to a low rolling simmer. Simmer for 3 hours to extract as much flavour as possible.

   Strain through a fine sieve, cool to room temperature, then refrigerate and use within a week or freeze until required.

with the gills. By all means fillet the catch, but keep in mind what you are throwing in the garbage and remember fish will have a longer shelf life if kept on the bone while refrigerated or iced down.

Fishing competitions? I love them as much as the next angler. Boats of all shapes and sizes, serious competitiveness, great camaraderie and the continuous sledging is pretty infectious. However, these days, the more I attend and the more large fish I see being brought to the weigh stations, one after another, many dull, bent and stiff, the more I start to question the whole formula. We all love to win, but isn't it time we gave it a bit more thought? I think there's a relatively simple solution. Make the winning fish of the tournament a 3.27kg fish or similar, or perhaps a different weight each year. Small and big go back; just a perfect example of the species closest or the exact weight wins. How about having the second-largest prize to the best photo of releasing 'big fish'? We all have digital cameras now. Wouldn't that make wicked viewing on the big screen at the prize giving? As mentioned, I believe the real passion is unquestionably the hook-up, then the battle to bring that beautiful fish to the boat. We can recall the fish we have caught and lost decades ago, but we struggle to recall the individual taste of fillets consumed years on.

So to the future . . .

Educate your kids. Take them fishing, take them rockpooling — they all love the beach and the ocean. It's easy to teach things to kids if they are already fascinated by the topic. We are surrounded by the ocean and a field trip each year by each class should be part of all school curricula.

Make a conscious decision before heading out fishing about how much fish you actually need and intend to bring home, then stick to that decision. When you head to your fish market to buy 600g of tarakihi fillet, I doubt you ever end up purchasing another five kilo of fresh fish to bring home and bag up to put in the freezer.

Let's start embracing the other equally wonderful fish that inhabit our oceans. You have a bunch of recipes here that can work, within reason, with all species. I guarantee that once you experiment with other species you will feel liberated. It's as simple as just buying a small portion of another variety when buying your favourite fish and cooking that as well. Or better still, keep a fish you would normally toss back. Make a game of it — see how many different species you can try over a year. My suggestion would be simply to season the fish with a little salt and pepper, sauté it in a little oil and butter, and serve with a squeeze of lemon juice. This way you really get to taste the individual attributes (flavour, texture and moistness). Give whoever is about a taste and see who can guess what species of delicious fish they are eating. They will be blown away.

We need more traceability in the fishing industry. Seek out and support fish markets and fishmongers who are passionate about their product and where it comes from. At Logan Brown, we buy all our fish from reputable suppliers like Rachel Taulelei's Yellow Brick Road. We can now tell our customers where the fish they are eating came from, when and how it was caught, what boat it was landed on, even the skipper's name and how many sugars he likes in his cup of tea. It may cost a little more, but as far as I am concerned anything as precious as properly handled fresh wild seafood is worth every penny.

Make informed choices when buying fish. Every few years Forest and Bird put out a best fish guide, which ranks species of fish from best to worst choice, based on information garnered from scientists, the regulated commercial fishery and what little can be guessed about the impact of recreational fishing. It is tough to be exact when it comes to understanding each species and the current state it is in. The difficulties involved are complex. Many species are migratory and this makes establishing true counts or estimates near impossible. I use the guide more as an awareness and reminder tool. There are certain species I will never eat due to their overfished status, like certain tuna, orange roughy and the like. What's important to me when buying fish is variety and freshness. Yes, I still purchase fish species that are sometimes edging towards the 'worst choice' on the chart, but I have a clear conscience as I enjoy cooking all species and get as much pleasure out of eating a fresh blue mackerel as I do a groper.

I do not buy fish from super-markets, as in my experience it's

nearly always close to its use-by date and it's ridiculously expensive, probably due to the fact they throw so much away. And forget it when it comes to handling the fillets — they get bent over and tied up in a little plastic bag and thrown on the scales. And remember the word 'fresh' can be put in front of any fish as long as it hasn't been frozen.

I'm a supporter of establishing more marine reserves around New Zealand. In my mind this can only enhance our inshore fishery. New Zealand's first marine reserve, Cape Rodney–Okakari Marine Reserve, was established in 1975. As one of the first reserves

in the world, this is another terrific example of foresight that a few brave Kiwis had back then. There are now more than 30 marine reserves in New Zealand waters. This may sound a lot, but more than 90 per cent of actual reserve is located on two of our most isolated offshore island groups, the Auckland and the Kermadec Islands. Of our total marine environment, just three per cent is protected. As a fisherman, by no means do I want to see huge pieces of the New Zealand coastline turned into no-take marine reserves. But having seen how these recover and the benefits they bring to our marine

environment as a whole, it just makes sense.

So I believe the responsibility and future of New Zealand's fishery falls directly on all our shoulders. In world terms, it is still in great shape but I can't help feeling at times that we are in danger of being a little apathetic about what we have.

We must be proactive and keep our oceans and sea environment front of mind. This is not just regarding the state of our fishery, but caring for our beaches, sand dunes, marine mammals, aquatic birds and everything else that affects all aspects of our coastal environment.

Seven Questions

To get a brief overall picture of what our oceans and fishery mean to us all as New Zealanders, I asked the same seven questions of a cross-section of people. All participants have a personal vested interest, be it commercial, recreational or spiritual. Here are their answers . . .

PHIL RICH, RECREATIONAL FISHERMAN

How often do you go fishing?
I go on around 120 trips per year. Twice a day in January plus many full days of fishing activity throughout the year. My most popular types of fishing for the past few years are spearfishing, gathering (crayfish, paua, scallops), snapper fishing, other sea fishing and back-country fly fishing.

What's your favourite fish and why?
Carcharodon carcharias, the great white shark. *Jaws* — one of the great movies of all time, in my opinion — came out when I was 10. It left an impression on me. I read the book, read many accounts of great white encounters and attacks. I have spoken to divers who have had encounters. I have seen two 'in the flesh' — such an awesome fish, the greatest predator in the world today, perhaps. Great to keep you honest, when you are in the water, to think there is a possible threat somewhere out there. The ultimate adrenalin rush to see one — and the ultimate glamour death for the freediver. You'd be immortalised.

What's the most important thing about the New Zealand fishery to you?
To enjoy it for myself — selfish but truthful. I have always loved fishing and being on the coast and on the water, and in and under the water. To catch a feed is secondary — I'll often just go out and dive down and lie on the bottom among schools of fish, enjoying the tranquility and beauty.

But it's important to me to share it with family and friends, too. On many occasions I have taken friends to view a school of large moki at a rock that I have imposed my own reserve over — and what a beautiful sight. I also take my 10-year-old son to a crayfish hole in just two metres of water that no one else has found yet and that I don't plunder.

What has changed since you started fishing?
Better gear, better boats, better electronics — GPS and sounders give greater access. It is more difficult to go out and not see other boats on the water. In some areas the fishing is just as good; some areas the fishery is under pressure — with smaller fish and fewer fish and fewer classic table fish.

What is the significance of New Zealand's surrounding oceans to you?
I am European but Polynesian words best sum up my feelings for the New Zealand coastline. I think of myself as tangata o te moana — a person who's wrapped up in, and dedicated to, the ocean and the coastal environment of Aotearoa. For most people in New Zealand the ocean is the closest natural environment we have access to. I can be in the 'green room'

under the surface in the tranquil underwater world within 25 metres of my house, completely away from the technologies and paraphernalia of our everyday lives. I can be freediving at Toka-a-Papa reef within a two-minute boat ride from the wharf outside my house. It takes 15 minutes from deciding to leave my home (all my gear and the boat is right at my house and we live opposite the Plimmerton Boating Club). From this reef, this year, I have gathered paua, caught large crayfish, speared multiple kingfish and John Dory, caught snapper — all on the doorstep of our capital city. Can't be bad, eh?

On a scale of one to 10, how do you think the future of our fishery looks?
Short term, it will continue to be a great fishery by current world standards. New Zealand still has a small population and this is the key to keeping a viable fishery. Medium term, the fishery will continue to deteriorate. We underestimate the power of a few people — commercial and recreational — to decimate certain fisheries. The recreational sector will continue to grow, and with continuous improvements in technologies/gear and techniques the fishery will deteriorate.

Long term . . . try fishing off the coast of China? It will be the same everywhere if the world continues as it is.

If you could change one thing?
We are blessed to live in an age when we have the toys — the boats, the gear etc — and yet still have a great fishery. Change? Get rid of recreational set-netting and long-lining — that's indiscriminate fish taking. Decrease the fin fish take

— we should not be fishing for the freezer. Take it fresh, eat it fresh. Only take what we can reasonably use.

PHIL HEATLEY, MINISTER OF FISHERIES

How often do you go fishing?
Less and less as I get more responsibility in Wellington. I used to own a little runabout and went fishing quite regularly just outside the Whangarei Harbour, but I've sold the boat to my neighbour, now that I spend much of my time in Wellington. I'm cheeky enough to borrow it during the school holidays, though, just to get a quick fishing 'fix'. I caught 12 with my wife, Jenny, on Easter Saturday and 10 with a mate the following Monday.

What's your favourite fish and why?
John Dory. You can't try or plan to get one; it just happens or it doesn't. Best fish to eat by a country mile, easiest to fillet, saving most of the flesh, and easy to cook. Jenny loves them.

What's the most important thing about the New Zealand fishery to you?
That while it's by no means

perfect, New Zealand leads the world on how to manage a fishery. We're always working to make it better, but from both an environmental and business perspective — especially the latter, as international consumers increase their awareness of where products come from — we are a world leader, and that should make us all very grateful and very proud.

What has changed since you started fishing?

I've really only fished over the past 15 years, discovering it as an adult rather than as a child. The biggest change would be the number of boats on the water, the high-tech electronic search gear and the use of fancy 'string' rigs and baits. The fish don't stand a chance.

What is the significance of New Zealand's surrounding oceans to you?

Huge. We live by the sea, I fish and water ski, the family camp at Ohiwa in the Bay of Plenty over Christmas, and the wider family has a 50-foot trimaran and a large launch among them. The sea is our playground, just like for a million other Kiwis. I love the fact New Zealand is isolated and we oversee the fourth largest marine area in the world.

On a scale of one to 10, how do you think the future of our fishery looks?

8/10. We are miles ahead of the rest. Our biggest challenge is divvying our sea space up — recreationalists, commercial operators, marine farmers, boaties, reserves, energy generation and mineral exploration. We are rich with choice.

If you could change one thing?

I'd fish more than I talked about it.

ALASTAIR MACFARLANE, GENERAL MANAGER OF TRADE AND INFORMATION, NEW ZEALAND SEAFOOD INDUSTRY COUNCIL

How often do you go fishing?

In the summer, during the holidays.

What's your favourite fish and why?

Turbot and John Dory. I like the flavour of turbot and the delicacy of John Dory together with the fact that John Dory is one of the few with their fish fillets sold skin on.

What's the most important thing about the New Zealand fishery to you?

That it is sustainably managed and provides for all users.

What has changed since you started fishing?

The state of inshore fisheries has improved significantly — especially in the north of New Zealand where they come under most pressure from all user groups.

What is the significance of New Zealand's surrounding oceans to you?

Enormous. I've worked for the seafood industry for the best part of the past 20 years and the oceans have indirectly provided my livelihood and the livelihood of my family.

On a scale of one to 10, how do you think the future of our fishery looks?

I would rate the future 8/10. In order for that outlook to improve, we need to find better ways to make recreational fishing as responsible as commercial fishing is under the QMS (quota management system).

If you could change one thing?

I'd seek public support for an explicit recreational fishing right. We already have something like it with trout fishing in lakes and rivers.

JOHN INKSTER, COMMERCIAL FISHERMAN

How often do you go fishing?

We average around 135 days at sea annually, but we are often chased back to port without getting the trawl wet because of the weather.

What's your favourite fish and why?

Groper. I find it is both sweet and juicy, but the cheeks, throats and liver are to die for!

What's the most important thing about the New Zealand fishery to you?

It has been my way of life for more than 35 years and is by far the most sustainable fishery that I have seen worldwide.

What has changed since you started fishing?

When I started, fishing was what you made it. A lot of people never made it! The advent of the QMS saw many fishers able to cash in — they would have gone by the wayside without it. Three companies now control 75 per cent of our entire fisheries. Then you have the bureaucratic MOF (Ministry of Fisheries) that resembles a mushroom on steroids, which has overregulated the industry and grown totally out of proportion to it. To give you an example, when the hoki TAC (total allowable catch) was cut by 90,000 tonnes, the MOF simply spread their charges over remaining fish stocks, while the industry cut costs, laid off staff and had to adjust to a huge downturn in revenue. Given this, small operators ponder why they still fish and are commonly called the last of the Mohicans!

What is the significance of New Zealand's surrounding oceans to you?

I feel very much in tune with the ocean and could never be far from it. There is something quite unique about the oceans at this end of the world — mostly that they are pristine and unpolluted. Long may it be that way.

On a scale of one to 10, how do you think the future of our fishery looks?

Without some changes, I would give sustainability an eight and the rest of the industry a five.

MIKE BRITTON, GENERAL MANAGER, ROYAL FOREST & BIRD PROTECTION SOCIETY OF NEW ZEALAND

How often do you go fishing?
In my mind, every calm Wellington day, but these (boatless) days, in reality, when I am on holiday and when a friend invites me out with him to fish on the south coast of Wellington.

What's your favourite fish and why?
Kingfish. It is a great sports fish and is my favourite shiromi sushi. John Dory is my favourite pan-fried fish.

What's the most important thing about the New Zealand fishery to you?
The heritage of Kiwis being able to go and catch a feed. And the diversity of life — fish, sea birds, mammals, nudibranchs — in our seas. It's important that our amazing marine environment is restored to good health — only that way will it support our fisheries.

What has changed since you started fishing?
Most fisheries like the Marlborough Sounds are decimated. Whole sounds used to erupt with herring, kahawai and kingis, fat cod fighting to get on to your hook. Now you are lucky to catch a kahawai in a day's fishing and the cod are more like freshwater bullies!

What is the significance of New Zealand's surrounding oceans to you?
It is a magic, ever-changing environment. A place to repair the soul. A challenge. A responsibility to protect for the future.

On a scale of one to 10, how do you think the future of our fishery looks?
3/10. Internationally over half the world's fisheries are being exploited well beyond their (known) sustainable level. In New Zealand, we have very limited information on the sustainability of our fishing, with some stocks doing okay, some heavily overfished to the point of collapse, but most we simply don't know. Much of our fishing is done using environmentally damaging trawl gear. As a result, the impact on habitats and the wider food webs does not bode well for the future of our fish and marine biodiversity. Climate change is now also demonstrably affecting our fisheries, with predictions of ocean warming and acidification of our seas set to make fisheries management an increasing challenge. Currently, no species in New Zealand is being managed on a truly sustainable basis, according to Forest & Bird's Best Fish Guide, although some are pretty close.

If you could change one thing?
Give the oceans a chance through marine protection — 30 per cent of our coastal and EEZ (exclusive economic zone) marine environment is protected, leaving 70 per cent available for exploitation; and destructive non-target fishing methods banned (like set nets and bottom trawling).

BRAD DANNEFAERD, FISHERY OFFICER

How often do you go fishing?
Pretty much as often as possible!

What's your favourite fish and why?
I would have to say, overall, striped marlin because they are such an exciting, visually stunning fish. It is especially cool that New Plymouth is one of the few places in the world you can catch marlin with a snow-capped mountain (Mt Taranaki) as a backdrop. Smoked marlin is also pretty damn good to eat. For 'bottom fish' my favourite to eat would be John Dory, but in terms of catching bottom fish, it's pretty hard to beat the 'thump, thump' of a good snapper.

What's the most important thing about the New Zealand fishery to you?
It provides me with sport, food and a career — it is a huge part of my life!

What has changed since you started fishing?
The change in many (but unfortunately not all) people's attitude towards the importance of our fishery to New Zealand as a whole.

What is the significance of New Zealand's surrounding oceans to you?
Huge! They make us the island state we are, they provide us with food, recreation, income and a measure of national security (helping to prevent illegal immigration etc). Our oceans are an integral part of what makes

New Zealand such an incredible place.

On a scale of one to 10, how do you think the future of our fishery looks?
7/10.

If you could change one thing?
It would be the attitude of that section of society that continues to abuse our natural resources for their own selfish reasons, with scant disregard for the sustainability of those resources.

RICK POLLOCK, GAME FISHING CHARTER OPERATOR

How often do you go fishing?
I'm at sea approximately 250 days each year.

What's your favourite fish and why?
Blue marlin, due to their incredible aerial displays and dogged endurance at the end of the line.

What's the most important thing about the New Zealand fishery to you?
Its ongoing ability to provide such wonderful experiences due to the bountiful fish stocks available. Looking after and enhancing this situation is paramount.

What has changed since you started fishing?
Technology. Vastly improved electronics, rods, reels, lines, terminal tackle, boats, engines etc all add up to increasing pressure on the fishery. So far most species are holding up well in the face of this effort.

Thanks...

Writing *Go Fish* has been a hugely challenging and gratifying experience. I feel indebted to the people that follow.

To my family, Lizzie, Alice and Connie, thanks for being so supportive and letting me indulge in this terrific project. Your encouragement and patience were invaluable. Apologies for all those 5am starts. Who knew that so much noise could be created by the simple task of making instant coffee at that hour? I love you all.

A huge thank you to Cath Cordwell. For all the tireless work (at $2.50 an hour) of running my business, being my 'Special Agent', Mentor and Life Coach and picking up the kids! Thanks for gently pushing me and constantly making me believe in myself. You're a special friend Cath!

To Gary Stewart of Ocean Design. Your conceptual and creative genius never fails to amaze me. Thanks also for all the Pinot-driven late nights and weekends you (and Ronnie) gave up for this little adventure. With wit as dry as Weet-Bix and your infectious sense of humour, it's been a blast! Thanks 'G'!

I have known and worked with Kieran Scott for a dozen years or more. Kieran's extraordinary talent with a camera in hand is boarding on freakish. The photography was exactly what I had envisaged — no lights, no food stylist, no painstaking dots on the plate, just delicious natural food shot as is, where is! Thanks, mate, for being so incredibly patient, and for that wonderful habit of always over-delivering.

To Jenny Hellen and the team at Random House New Zealand. Thanks for the constant support and guidance and belief that I would get there in the end.

Thanks to Toni Mason of *Cuisine* magazine, for interpreting and making sense out of much of my scribble. It's always a pleasure working with you, Toni, you're one hell of an editor!

Also a big thanks to Sarah Crysell and all the others who helped so much at the Seafood Industry Council. I admire your determination, guts and resolve in the unfailing vision to create the best example of a sustainable fishery in the world. God knows it isn't easy!

To Tamarapa and Ngahiwi, of Te Ohu Kaimoana, thank you for your words and insight. It's been a pleasure working with you on this, and understanding the significance and importance of our seas and oceans to Maori.

To Pippa Lee, my brilliant Sous Chef from across the road. Your energy and passion throughout the process of this book, from trialling recipes to setting the table, was invaluable. You have a natural affinity with food and cooking, and I dream of being able to bake like you one day!

A special thanks to the wonderful artist Katherine Smyth for letting me use so many of her beautiful plates, platters and bowls! (www.katherinesmyth.co.nz)

A big thank you to George Clement for the outstanding fish illustrations used throughout.

Thanks also to all the people who contributed their time and thoughtful answers for Seven Questions.

Finally, to all our wonderful friends and neighbours in Lyall and Island bays on Wellington's south coast. Thanks for all the kaimoana, the pots, platters and pans and for being the crash test dummies for many of the dishes coming off our humble electric Atlas range!

Again thanks to you all!

The Final Word

Before I reach the end of the book I'd like to return to the beginning and the story of Maui fishing up the North Island of New Zealand. Unlike Maui's brothers we must co-operate with each other to ensure that this wonderful resource is here in pristine condition for future generations to enjoy. Maui's brothers were more interested in how much fish they could hack away — our respect for the ocean can't be based on how much we can pull out of it but rather on how it could sustain us in 1000 years if we treat it with the respect and dignity that it deserves.

Kia hora te marino
Kia whakapapa pounamu te moana
Kia tere te kārohirohi
I mua i tō huarahi

May peace be widespread
May the sea glisten like greenstone
May the shimmer of light
Guide you on your way